Face-to-Face with 365 people from Bible times

A daily devotional

Published in 2018 by Autumn House Publications (Europe) Ltd., Alma Park, Grantham, Lincolnshire, UK.

British Library Cataloguing in Publication Data. A catalogue record for this book is available from the British Library.

All emphases are the author's.

ISBN 978-1-78665-049-8

Designed by David Bell.

Printed in India.

Preface

A few years ago I wrote a devotional that was well received. This inspired me to write another one. For this devotional book I have selected 365 men and women from the Bible and written a short message about each of them. In each case I have tried to discover something in their story that has a spiritual application for today. This approach may seem somewhat moralistic, but I do not apologise for this, for the Bible itself points us in that direction. The apostle Paul stated: 'For everything that was written in the past was written to teach us, so that through endurance and the encouragement of the Scriptures we might have hope' (Romans 15:4). In 1 Corinthians 10:11 we find words that point us in the same direction: 'These things happened to them as examples and were written down as warnings for us, on whom the fulfilment of the ages has come.'

Among the 365 names, which will appear in alphabetical order, we find quite a few that most readers are well acquainted with. I have, however, also included names that may be unknown to most of us. But I hope that the encounters with well-known persons as well as with those you know little or nothing about will be meaningful. Many biblical characters evoke our admiration and may serve as true role models. Some leave us with many questions. Others leave us with a sense of disgust and provide serious warnings against a way of life that only leads to disaster. In other words: we meet the same sort of people that we encounter in our daily lives in the twenty-first century. Nonetheless, the overall picture is encouraging. God continues to reach out to a world filled with all kinds of people - good and bad. He did so in Bible times and He still does so today.

The format of the daily meditations is quite simple:

1. You find a **date** at the top of every page. This does not, of course, mean that you must start with 1 January, or may never skip a day.
2. The **name** of the person for that day is always given at the top. I have used the spelling of the names that is most common in recent Bible translations. In most cases I have added (in brackets behind the name) the meaning of the name. For this I have used a number of sources.[1]
3. **Who and when?** Here is a short identification of the person and, in many cases, the approximate date when he/she lived or was active.
4. **Want to know more?** A reference to texts and passages in the Bible that tell you more about that particular person.
5. **Thoughts for today.** This section suggests one or more themes or thoughts that may serve as further meditation during the day.

6. **My prayer.** Hopefully, these few words of prayer will give you inspiration in your own personal prayer.

I hope it will be a refreshing experience for you to meet so many men and women from Bible times. And I present this book with the prayer that, as you read about the many lives that God has touched in ages past, this will stimulate you to allow Him also to touch you on a daily basis.

Reinder Bruinsma,
Zeewolde, summer 2017

[1]For example, Jurriaan Wijchers and Simon Kart, *Het Bijbels Namenboek* (the Hague, the Netherlands: Boekencentrum BV, 1982; W. H. Gispen, et al., eds., *Bijbelse Encyclopedia* (Kampen: J. H. Kok, 1975); Siegfried H. Horn, *Seventh-day Adventist Bible Dictionary* (Washington, DC, USA: Review and Herald Publishing Association, 1960); and Herbert Lockyer, *All the Men of the Bible* and *All the Women of the Bible* (Grand Rapids, MI, USA: Zondervan, 1967).

1 January

Aaron (enlightened)

Who and when? Aaron was the brother of Moses and was of the tribe of Levi. He and his male descendants were set apart by God to serve as priests in the sanctuary. He was an able leader. Nonetheless, he committed some grave mistakes.

Want to know more? Read: Exodus 4:29; 32:1-35.

Thoughts for today

Aaron plays a key role in the story of Israel's exodus from Egypt and its sojourns in the wilderness. He became the spokesman for his brother Moses, who was not as eloquent as he was. He accompanied Moses when he confronted the pharaoh. But God also chose him for another, very special, task. He was to be the first high priest, once the tabernacle had been constructed in accordance with detailed divine instructions.

Aaron's greatest privilege was that he, in his high priestly role, was allowed to enter the most holy apartment of the sanctuary, once a year on the Day of Atonement. This was an essential element in the ritual that symbolised the atonement that later would be realised by Jesus Christ. Thus, in a certain sense, Aaron was a 'shadow' of Jesus, the great High Priest. However, Aaron could not be more than only a symbol of Jesus. He himself also needed Jesus' sacrifice – just as we all do.

At a certain point in time Aaron rebelled against Moses. Even worse was that he gave in to the demands of the people who wanted an idol. Yet, when Aaron saw his mistake, God did not distance Himself from him. That is how God is. This thought should continue to give us hope for every day of the year that has begun today.

My prayer

Thank You, Lord, for reminding me that even when I make serious mistakes, there is the great High Priest, who puts things in order for me.

2 January

Abednego

(servant of the god Nabu)

Who and when? Abednego was the Babylonian name of Azariah, one of the friends of Daniel who were deported to Babylon with him.

Want to know more? Read: Daniel 1:6, 7; 2; 3.

Thoughts for today

In the second chapter of the Book of Daniel, the prophet Daniel is the big star. He outranks all the wise men and occult experts of Babylon, and is the only one who is able to tell King Nebuchadnezzar what he had dreamed and what its meaning was. But we should not forget that Abednego and Daniel's two other friends, Shadrach and Meshach (as the Babylonians renamed them), also played an important role: for not only Daniel's, but their lives too, were at stake.

The king was extremely angry when his so-called 'wise' men were incapable of answering his question. He lost his temper and ordered 'the execution of all the wise men of Babylon'. This also implied the death penalty for Abednego. Daniel, however, used all his contacts at the court to urge postponement of the execution. 'Then Daniel returned to his house and explained the matter to his friends . . .' and 'urged them to plead for mercy from the God of heaven concerning this mystery, so that he and his friends might not be executed with the rest of the wise men of Babylon' (Daniel 2:17, 18).

Like his friends, Abednego believed in the power of collective prayer. Daniel could have prayed alone, but he wanted to involve his friends. Nebuchadnezzar also was aware of the role of Abednego, Shadrach and Meshach, for, when the situation had been defused, they were 'appointed . . . administrators over the province of Babylon' (vs. 49).

My prayer

We thank You, Lord, for the power of prayer. And thank You for Your willingness to listen to us.

3 January

Abel

(breath, transitoriness)

Who and when? The second son of Adam and Eve; he chose to be a shepherd. Abel met a tragic death when his brother Cain killed him.

Want to know more? Read: Genesis 4:1-16.

Thoughts for today

As a small child I had already heard the horrendous story of the murder of Abel by his brother. Cain was jealous of his brother when he realised that God appreciated Abel's sacrifice, but 'did not look with favour' on his offering. I remember that we were told how the smoke of Abel's offering went straight up in the sky, while this did not happen with the smoke of Cain's offering.

Later we received another, more satisfying, explanation. Cain sacrificed 'some fruits of the soil', while Abel 'brought fat portions from some of the firstborn of his flock'. This indicates that Abel understood the meaning of what he did. Only the offering of an animal, and the flow of blood, could be an adequate symbol of the Sacrifice that would be brought by the Saviour of the world.

It would seem that, after their first sin, God gave instructions to the first humans about sacrifices. Much is said in the Old Testament on this topic. Reading this leaves us with the clear impression that God is mostly interested in the motives that lead us to bring our offerings. This was the problem in Cain's case. He was jealous of the close relationship his brother enjoyed with God. Seeing the close bond of others with God should lead us also to fully dedicate ourselves to God, so that we will receive that same blessing. God wants nothing more dearly than also to be our God.

My prayer

Lord, give me the insight that You are not interested in pious gestures, but that You first of all look at my heart.

Abiathar (father ofabundance)

Who and when? He was the son of Ahimelech, a priest in the sanctuary in Nob; he escaped the massacre that Saul instigated and fled to David. Later he sided with Adonijah, a rival of Solomon.

Want to know more? Read: 1 Samuel 21:1-7; 22:9-23; 23:6-9; 30:7, 8; 1 Kings 1:7; 2:13-27.

Thoughts for today

David's plea to Ahimelech, the priest in the sanctuary of Nob, to provide some food for his men, had dramatic consequences. Under these special circumstances Ahimelech was willing to give some food to David and his men in the form of the consecrated bread. But when King Saul heard about this he ordered a massacre. Only Abiathar, one of the sons of Ahimelech, was able to escape and stayed alive. He joined the group of men around David, and, later, when David had established himself as the king, he became one of David's regular advisors. Abiathar had taken the ephod with him (the 'breastplate' that was adorned with precious stones and the Urim and the Thummim), which he used to give advice to the king (see Numbers 27:21).

Abiathar had every reason to remain loyal to David, and also to show his loyalty towards Solomon. Being so close to David, he must have known that Solomon had been elected by God to succeed David on the throne. Unfortunately, Abiathar proved himself to be an egocentric opportunist. At a given moment he switched his allegiance to Adonijah, who tried to steal the throne from Solomon. The Bible tells us about his miserable end.

God remains loyal to us, and He expects that we stay loyal not only to Him, but also to the people to whom we owe our loyalty.

My prayer

My faithful God, help me to remain loyal to You and to my friends who deserve my loyalty. May this always be my priority.

5 January

Abigail

(my father rejoices)

Who and when? Abigail was married to Nabal. She manifested her gift for diplomacy when her husband had to deal with David. At a later stage she become a wife of David.

Want to know more? Read: 1 Samuel 25.

Thoughts for today

This story plays out in the period when David was constantly being harassed by King Saul. A few hundred people had teamed up with David. This band of men made itself useful by protecting the herds of a certain Nabal – a fabulously rich man, who owned thousands of goats and sheep. But when David asked Nabal to show his appreciation in a concrete way, the demand fell on deaf ears. This enraged David and he decided to take revenge.

Nabal is pictured as a fool, as someone without a conscience and as 'surly and mean'. It also seems that he was rather intemperate in his alcohol consumption. His wife Abigail, on the other hand, was not only a beautiful woman but also intelligent. She quickly came up with a plan to persuade David not to pursue his angry intentions. She succeeded. David accepted Abigail's gifts as well her apologies. At the close of the story we find Nabal in a drunken stupor. He died shortly afterwards, and David was quick to propose marriage to Abigail.

Abigail possessed a range of positive character traits. She was what we would call 'a strong woman'. Small wonder that the Bible writer devotes an entire chapter to her. Too often the courage of such strong women remains underexposed. But even today it is not an exception that women must rectify the foolish decisions of their husbands.

My prayer

O God, give me the courage to do all I can to bring peace, even if it is clear that the conflict has resulted from pure stupidity.

6 January

Abihu (my father is he)

Who and when? Abihu was one of the sons of Aaron. With his brother Nadab he served as priest in the tabernacle. God punished him because he failed to heed the divine instructions.

Want to know more? Read: Leviticus 10:1-5.

Thoughts for today

Nadab and Abihu knew exactly which rules to follow when serving at the altar. There were strict rules about how to make fire. However, they totally ignored these instructions and brought 'unauthorised fire before the LORD'. God did not wait long to punish them. 'Fire came out from the presence of the LORD and consumed them' (Leviticus 10:1, 2).

Was this not a bit too drastic? Could God not have warned Nadab and Abihu a few times? We tend to think along these lines: a loving God certainly does not act in such a way! Let us, however, not forget that an important principle was at stake. The priests had a vital role. They were mediators between God and the people. They were in continuous contact with the holy God. That put them in a special class: they were also supposed to be 'holy'. They used holy objects in their ministry. Even the fire was special: it was 'holy' fire. Every aspect of the sanctuary service emphasised the infinite difference between God and humankind. Everything pointed to God's absolute majesty. And God wanted to make sure that His people would never forget this.

In a sense all of us are priests. The followers of Christ constitute 'a royal priesthood' (1 Peter 2:5, 9). We have the privilege of coming into God's presence. But we must never forget that God is 'holy', and this also sets us apart as a special class of people. If we ever forget this, we must face the tragic consequences.

My prayer

Heavenly Father, help me realise that You are a holy God, and that You expect me also to be 'holy', so that the people around me can see that I am close to You.

7 January

Abijah

(the Lord is my father)

Who and when? He was the second son of Samuel; appointed as judge by his father. Unfortunately, Abijah was corrupt.

Want to know more? Read: 1 Samuel 8:1-9.

Thoughts for today

Samuel lived and worked in the period of transition from the time of the judges to the beginning of the monarchy. Samuel himself is also often classified among the judges. He was a good man, but he could not resist the temptation to use his position to secure a prominent job for his sons. Through the years such practices have caused innumerable problems. The mere fact that someone is 'a son of . . .' or 'a daughter of . . .' does not automatically mean that this person qualifies as a worthy successor or has the competencies for a particular job.

Samuel's two sons, Joel and Abijah, became 'judges for Israel'. They may have served reasonably well in some respects. If so, the Bible story does not inform us about this. We only hear that 'they turned aside after dishonest gain and accepted bribes.' And thus they entered the annals of history as 'perverters of justice'.

How do you want to be remembered? As someone who did not worry too much about speaking the truth? As a man or a woman who was willing to ignore what was wrong when this brought profit? Or as someone who was totally honest and could always be trusted? This is not a matter of genes or of coincidence, or the result of circumstances. It is a matter of choice. Abijah and his brother chose to give priority to their own interests. What is your choice?

My prayer

Lord, in this world, in which dishonesty and corruption are rampant, I want to be and remain an honest person. Please help me with this.

8 January

Abimelech

(my father is king)

Who and when? A Philistine king at the time of Abraham.

Want to know more? Read: Genesis 20.

Thoughts for today

Many of the Bible stories are about controversies between good and bad people. However, in the story of Abraham and Abimelech things are a bit more complicated. Abraham is not good in every respect. He lies about the marital status of his wife, when he claims that Sarah is his sister. When Abimelech, as Abraham had foreseen, was impressed by Sarah's beauty, Abraham could remain outside the danger zone.

Abimelech is a Philistine and the Bible tends to be quite negative about the Philistines. However, this Abimelech is not a cruel, unscrupulous dictator. He even listens to the God of Israel, when this God warns him that something very serious will happen if he indeed makes Sarah his wife. Abimelech takes the divine threat, that all women in his palace would then become infertile, very seriously.

Abimelech is keen to do everything in his power to rectify the situation. Sarah is returned unharmed to Abraham, who, surprisingly, receives numerous gifts. Then Abraham also shows his good side. He prays for Abimelech. God hears this prayer and then withdraws the punishment that made all women in Abimelech's household infertile.

The story of Abimelech and Abraham teaches us that believers and unbelievers have their good and their dubious sides. This means that every human being desperately needs God's grace and forgiveness.

My prayer

Almighty God, help me to be completely honest and let me constantly realise that I am always in need of Your forgiveness.

9 January

Abinadab (my father is generous)

Who and when? The ark of the covenant was repatriated after this holy object had been with the Philistines for seven months. It was brought to the house of Abinadab, and his son Eleazar was 'consecrated' as the guardian of the ark.

Want to know more? Read: 1 Samuel 6; 7:1.

Thoughts for today

We meet several Abinadabs in the Bible. We know precious little about the Abinadad who is mentioned in 1 Samuel 7:1. He lived in Kiriath Jearim, in the border region between Judah and Benjamin. We are not told why his house was chosen as the temporary abode for the ark. It is hard to believe that it had been Abinadab's own suggestion. In all probability he was a Levite and therefore a suitable candidate. We know that among other things the two stone tablets with the Ten Commandments were kept in this wooden chest that was covered with gold, and that this object would remain for twenty long years in the house of Abinadab. Eleazar, one of his sons, was charged with guarding the ark and ensuring that nothing would happen to it. Twenty years later Uzzah, another son of Abinadab, would lose his life when, during the transport of the ark to Jerusalem, he touched the ark in a way that was considered inappropriate.

We have no idea whether Abinadab was happy with his role as the custodian of the holy ark. It carried a huge responsibility, and he may well have wondered what consequences he could face if something would happen to the ark. Sometimes, however, a responsibility that we cannot refuse comes our way. And, fortunately, there are always people who are prepared to accept an awkward or difficult assignment. Looking at Abinadab's name, we may wonder whether in his case it ran in the family. What about you?

My prayer

Lord, make me willing to accept, if need be, an awkward assignment, especially when You are the One who asks me to do so.

10 January

Abishag

(meaning is uncertain)

Who and when? The young girl charged with caring for the elderly King David.

Want to know more? Read: 1 Kings 1:1-4; 2:13-25.

Thoughts for today

Abishag appears on the scene when King David is old. The people around the king observe that his physical strength is gradually diminishing. They cover him with blankets, but the old monarch does not get warm. It is then decided – as was quite common in these times – to find a young girl as David's personal caregiver. Much care is invested in the search for a young girl, who must not only be pretty but must also be a virgin. The vitality that such a girl would bring along would enhance, it was thought, the well-being of the patient. The search ends when they find Abishag. 'She took care of the king and waited on him' (1 Kings 1:4). The writer explicitly mentions that David did not have sexual relations with her.

In 1 Kings 2 we discover that the bond between Abishag and David also had an official aspect. Upon David's death Adonijah – one of David's sons – tried to outdo his half-brother Solomon. He tried to arrange a marriage with Abishag, who apparently was held in high esteem. Adonijah believed that this move would strengthen his chances to become the successor to the throne. However, the events took another turn.

When we look at the story of Abishag through our twenty-first-century eyes, we see some elements that we find hard to understand. Reading about the background of the Bible stories remains very important.

My prayer

Lord, I want to ask You, the One who has inspired the Bible, to assist me through Your Spirit in my reading of Your Word, so that I may understand its message.

11 January

Abishai

(meaning is uncertain)

Who and when? One of the trusted men in David's circle before he became king.

Want to know more? Read: 1 Chronicles 11:15-21; 2 Samuel 23:8-39.

Thoughts for today

David had assembled a sizeable group of men who had sworn allegiance to him and who supported him in his struggle against Saul and others who wanted to take his life. Among the bravest and most famous of these loyal followers was Abishai, the brother of Joab, who had single-handedly defeated 300 of David's opponents in a single engagement (2 Samuel 23:18-19). In another incident, during which David was pelted with both verbal abuse and stones by Shimei (a member of the house of Saul), Abishai stood ready to leap to his leader's defence if ordered to (2 Samuel 16:9).

In the story of this brave man we see the value of unconditional loyalty clearly illustrated. Both he and the men he commanded were ready to give their lives to defend Israel's king. No task was too great for them, no sacrifice too demanding.

It is great when people demonstrate true loyalty and deep friendship towards us and those who are special to us. It's even more impressive when such qualities are revealed through acts of sacrifice and deeds that are not without risk. For this very reason, we should never take such loyalty for granted. It needs to be reciprocated by expressions of sincere appreciation and deep gratitude.

Hopefully, you will be blessed by having people like Abishai among your friends.

My prayer

Lord, help me in remaining loyal to my friends and to be truly grateful when others are loyal to me.

12 January

Abner

(the father is a lamp)

Who and when? He was chief in Saul's army; and later he supported David.

Want to know more? Read: 1 Samuel 14:50; 17:55-58; 2 Samuel 3:6-39; 1 Kings 2:32.

Thoughts for today

When the people of Israel wanted to have a 'traditional' earthly king, God chose Saul for this task. Later His choice fell on David, who received the promise that he would be the first in a long dynasty – on the condition that he and his posterity would remain obedient to the divine instructions. Regrettably, many of God's intentions were not realised: not because God failed to do His part, but because David's descendants and the people around them were unfaithful. They claimed often enough that they wanted to serve God and that they were going to give priority to the interests of the people, but when analysing the reality we soon discover that, as a rule, their own interests – honour, status and material gain – were their prime motivations.

Abner is a sad example of this tendency. His star rose quickly, and he became one of the most important men in the king's army. But, when Saul died, he supported Ish-Bosheth as Saul's successor, while he knew very well that God had chosen David rather than Ish-Bosheth. However, an incident occurred that disappointed him, and he switched his support to David. Joab, David's chief of staff, saw this as a treacherous move and, without informing David, decided to kill Abner.

It happens all too often – in our own lives and the lives of all those around us – that we push God's plans aside in preference of our own designs. This occurs in all aspects of our lives. Abner's career illustrates the chaos that can easily result when we ignore God's intentions for us.

My prayer

Show me, Lord, the plans You have for me, and help me accept Your intentions for me as the pattern for my life.

13 January

Abraham

(the father is exalted; the father of a multitude)

Who and when? Abraham was a direct descendant of Seth; he is usually referred to as a 'patriarch'. Ca. 1900 BC.

Want to know more? Read: Genesis 11:26-25:11.

Thoughts for today

Who is the most important person in the Bible (apart from Jesus Christ, who cannot be compared to anyone else)? It would seem to me that Abraham certainly is a good candidate for that title. Christianity, Islam and Judaism are often referred to as the three Abrahamic religions, since Abraham plays a key role in all three of these world religions.

The story of Abraham gathers pace in Genesis 12:1: 'Leave your country, your people and your father's household and go to the land I will show you.' Just imagine what Abraham is asked to do! When Abraham left Haran he was 75 years old. He had to leave everything and everyone, and embark on a journey to an unknown destination. He had to be satisfied with the promise that God would show him where to go. If ever there was a journey of faith, this was it!

Are we, as children of Abraham (Galatians 3:29), like the patriarch of old, prepared to follow God's voice – in whatever way He may speak to us? Are we willing to start on the pilgrimage that God has in mind for us? Are we ready to begin the journey of faith, without knowing where it will take us? And are we prepared – if that is what God asks us to do – even to leave the people who are dear to us? And do we then faithfully ask God, every new day, for instructions for the route of that day, without unduly worrying about what will come next?

My prayer

God of Abraham, you are also my God, for by faith I am also a child of Abraham. Help me to show the same kind of faith that Abraham had.

14 January

Absalom

(my father is peace)

Who and when? He was the third son of David; rebelled against his father and planned a coup. Ca. 1000 BC.

Want to know more? Read: 2 Samuel 3:3; 13:1–19:10.

Thoughts for today

It seemed as if life had been very kind to Absalom. As the third son of David and the grandson (on his mother's side) of the king of Geshur (2 Samuel 3:3), he had a dual claim to royal blood. And, apparently, he was a very handsome man: 'In all Israel there was not a man so highly praised for his handsome appearance as Absalom.' His hair, in particular, was exceptional (2 Samuel 14:25, 26).

Yet things went badly for Absalom. He turned against his father David, and, when he was confronted by a group of David's soldiers, the donkey on which he sat broke into a gallop. Unfortunately, the animal passed under a big tree with low-hanging branches, in which Absalom's hair became entangled. He was left hanging in the air, while the donkey continued on at considerable speed. When Absalom was found by David's general Joab and the soldiers that were with him, they beat him to death and then threw his body in a deep hole (2 Samuel 18:8-17).

How could Absalom have come to this ignominious end? The story makes clear that Absalom was driven by a relentless ambition. He saw himself as the best, and could not wait for others to discover this. He realised that he was not the first in line to succeed his father. Therefore, he decided to stage a coup - but this reckless adventure had a tragic ending. Ironically enough, it was his beautiful hair that caused his death. Ambition, fed by unrestrained self-love, always proves to be a dead-end street!

My prayer

Almighty God, protect me against the kind of ambition that became fatal for Absalom.

15 January

Achan

(meaning is uncertain; perhaps: the unhappy one)

Who and when? A man from the tribe of Judah, who, at the time of the victory over Jericho, took from the things that God had claimed for Himself.

Want to know more? Read: Joshua 7; 1 Chronicles 2:7.

Thoughts for today

The story of Achan's disobedience and its consequences is described in some detail in Joshua 7. He is also mentioned briefly in 1 Chronicles. Achan brought disaster upon Israel by taking for himself some of the things that God explicitly had declared to be His alone.

We can decide to voluntarily commit part of our time to God. And we can choose to do certain things for the good of our fellow men, because we know God looks upon this with favour, and we actually serve Him if we assist others. We can reserve part of our time for work in the local food bank, or to work as a volunteer in a care centre for the elderly, et cetera. But some things God has unequivocally declared to be His, and we have no right to them. This, for instance, concerns the giving of a specific part of our income (the tithe) and the setting apart of a specific part of our time (every seventh day). Surely, we do these things out of our own free will, but we really have no option to ignore them, since we know that God demands this from us unconditionally.

When Achan took what had been unconditionally set apart by and for God, it had far-reaching consequences for himself, his family and all the people. God does not always mete out his punishment in such severe ways as He did in this case. Here a clear statement had to be made. But, in any case, we will miss out on much happiness when we ignore the directives that God has given for our benefit.

My prayer

I realise, O Lord, that I owe all I have to You. Help me to be content with what is mine and to gladly dedicate to You what You have claimed as Your part.

16 January

Adam (man)

Who and when? Adam was the first human being. He was created by God, and, together with Eve, he was commissioned to care for God's creation and to populate the earth.

Want to know more? Read: Genesis 1-3; Romans 5:12-21.

Thoughts for today

Do you know how it feels to be the first? What emotions did those explorers experience in past centuries when they became the first persons to set foot on unknown territory? What does it mean for a mountaineer to be the first person to reach a difficult mountain top? When he was still alive, Neil Armstrong was frequently asked what he felt when, in 1969, he was the first person to walk on the surface of the moon. He described it as a small step for a man, but a giant leap for mankind!

You will not remember how it was to take your first step as a toddler; but perhaps you remember how it was when you took your first step on your way towards God: or are you one of those people who have not yet taken that first step? If that is the case, I hope this book will help you to remove your hesitation to do so. And for all who have already embarked on their journey with God new steps must continually be taken, resulting in new faith adventures with Him.

Today we will once again take a new step. We do not know how many more we will still be able to take. In many ways we differ from Adam. He and Eve started alone. Today we live on this planet together with some seven billion people. But, like Adam, we have a God-given task. What was true for him is also true for us today.

My prayer

Lord, be close to me, with every step that I take, every day, and help me always to discern the task that You have given me.

17 January

Adonijah

(my God is Lord)

Who and when? The fourth son of David (with his wife Haggith); born in Hebron; ca. 1000 BC.

Want to know more? Read: 2 Samuel 3:4; 1 Kings 1:5–2:25.

Thoughts for today

Reading about the history of the kings of Israel – from David until the last rulers on the throne of the divided empire – we soon discover that royal successions tended to be eventful moments that were usually accompanied by a lot of violence. Often one intrigue followed another. When David was about to die, Adonijah was determined to succeed him. He knew that his younger brother Solomon had been chosen by God as the one who was to succeed his father, but Adonijah wanted to do all he could to avoid this. He devised a shrewd plan with the intention of confronting the people with a *fait accompli* by presenting himself as the new king. When David and Bathsheba, the mother of Solomon, heard about this, the plan was foiled just in time. After Solomon had become the new king, Adonijah made a second attempt to seize the throne. This time he decided to enlist the help of Solomon's mother, Bathsheba, to usurp the throne. Earlier, Solomon had pardoned Adonijah after his attempt to become king, but this time enough was enough, and he had Adonijah executed.

Fortunately, we do not very often see such scenes today, but they were all too common in ancient Israel. However, there are still many people who are not content with their place in life and who do all they can – often using very dubious means – to take someone else's position. Sometimes their dirty games succeed, but very often things do not work out as planned. Perhaps today things are less dramatic than in the case of Adonijah, but they are just as contemptible.

My prayer

Heavenly Father, help me to be content with my place in life, and never to try to take someone else's position by dishonest means.

18 January

Aeneas (name of Trojan hero)

Who and when? A paralytic who was healed by Peter.

Want to know more? Read: Acts 9:32-35.

Thoughts for today

The apostles had received the promise that they would be able to perform miracles in the name of the Lord. They would place their hands on sick people, and they would get well (Mark 16:18). Peter saw how these words were fulfilled in his ministry. He was with 'the saints' in Lydda (in Old Testament times known as Lod) on the Mediterranean coast, just south of Jaffa, where the international airport of the modern state of Israel is located today.

In just a few words we are told that in Lydda Peter healed a certain Aeneas, who had been bedridden for eight years. Peter made it clear that the healing power that was manifested was not his: 'Jesus Christ heals you.' Peter had no doubt that the man would be healed and therefore he added: 'Get up and tidy up your mat.'

This was the best day of his life! For eight years Aeneas had been dependent on others, but now, suddenly, he could walk again and participate in normal, everyday life. It was a foretaste of the new world in which 'the lame [will] leap like a deer' (Isaiah 35:6). No doubt, God also used this miracle to give extra power to the preaching of the Gospel message in Lydda. There was already a Christian church in Lydda - most likely still very small. This miracle ensured that the entire town would hear about the message Peter had come to preach: 'All those who lived in Lydda and Sharon saw him [the healed paralytic] and turned to the Lord.' That was, of course, the greatest miracle!

My prayer

Loving, heavenly Father, we pray that today somehow You will show Your power, especially as we endeavour to reach people around us with Your message.

19 January

Agabus (locust)

Who and when? A prophet in the first-century church in Jerusalem.

Want to know more? Read: Acts 11:27-29; 21:10, 11.

Thoughts for today

The gift of prophecy was one of the spiritual gifts Christ gave to His church. The New Testament informs us about several people who had this gift, as for instance in Acts 11. A group of prophets came from Jerusalem to Antioch (11:27). This is just a side remark, so, apparently, this was not something out of the ordinary. One of them is mentioned by name: Agabus. He predicted 'through the Spirit' that there would soon be a major food shortage. Therefore, the apostles were to organise, without delay, a fund-raising campaign in order to support the believers in Judah.

The famine came in the reign of Emperor Claudius (AD 41 to AD 54). Clearly, Agabus was a true prophet. We meet him again in Acts 21, after Paul had arrived in Caesarea following his third missionary journey. He was staying with a certain Philip, who had four unmarried daughters: four young women who also had the prophetic gift. Agabus joined them there from Judea and predicted that Paul would be arrested in Jerusalem and handed over to the Gentiles (Acts 21:10, 11).

God communicates with His children in a number of different ways. Since we now have the New Testament, we have the record of who and what Jesus is, and today God speaks to us primarily through His written Word. 'In the past God spoke to our forefathers through the prophets at many times and in various ways, but in these last days he has spoken to us by his Son' (Hebrews 1:1, 2). Our Bible gives us a detailed record of God's deeds in history and, in particular, of the ministry of Jesus on our behalf.

My prayer

We thank You, Lord, that You have not abandoned us, but continue to communicate with us.

20 January

Agag

(meaning is unknown)

Who and when? King of the Amalekites at the time of Saul's reign (ca. 1050 BC).

Want to know more? Read: 1 Samuel 15:1-35.

Thoughts for today

Why does the Bible inform us about Agag in so much detail? He was the king of the Amalekites, one of the main enemies of Israel. The Amalekites lived in the area between the Sinai and the South of Palestine. Their location alone would not have been enough of a reason to pay much attention to Agag. He became important because of his role in the history of Saul and Samuel. Samuel had given clear instructions from God to King Saul on how he was to deal with the Amalekites and their king. Amalek was to be wiped from the map. Saul decided, however, that Agag should be spared, together with 'the best of the sheep and cattle, the fat calves and lambs – everything that was good' (1 Samuel 15:9).

King Saul did not act in a sudden sense of pity for his rival from Amalek. He was simply determined to look after his own interests rather than to listen to God. Samuel himself then arranged for the execution of Agag.

This incident resulted in a complete rupture in the relationship between Samuel and Saul. 'Until the day Samuel died, he did not go to see Saul again, though Samuel mourned for him' (vs. 35). Saul had begun so well. But, as the years went by, he succeeded in estranging himself from all who had been close to him. Thus the story of Agag ends with these tragic words: 'And the LORD was grieved that he had made Saul king over Israel' (vs. 35).

My prayer

Almighty God, I want to stay close to You. Will You help me with this?

21 January

Ahab

(the father's brother)

Who and when? King of the Northern Kingdom of the ten tribes; reigned from 873 BC to 852 BC.

Want to know more? Read: 1 Kings 16:29–22:40.

Thoughts for today

Ahab was a king who rebelled against God even more than many other kings of Israel. His wife Jezebel had a very bad influence on him and was even more obstinate than her husband in her resistance against the God of Israel and in her allegiance to other gods – the Baals and the Asherahs. But they found a fierce opponent in Elijah, whose life was in great danger because of his constant criticism of Ahab and Jezebel. The prophets of Israel's God were systematically exterminated, to the point that Elijah thought: 'I am the only one of the LORD's prophets left' (1 Kings 18:22). By way of contrast: at the same time there were some 850 prophets who worshipped Baal and the Canaanite mother goddess Asherah.

The controversy between the two camps – Ahab and Jezebel and their army of prophets on the one hand, and Elijah on the other hand – came to a climax on Mount Carmel. On the surface it seemed a totally unequal fight. But things are often not what they seem. Here, the battle was not between two groups of people, but between the only living, Almighty God and the impotent man-made deities. And when push came to shove, this God was able to put the seemingly invincible opponents out of action. The tragic part of the story is that Ahab and his wife continued in their refusal to recognise the authority of God. An extra sad element is that Elijah entered a phase of depression, in spite of having experienced God's sublime power. In this respect many of us today resemble Elijah.

My prayer

Almighty God, help me to discern Your omnipotence and to trust in Your power without ever losing courage.

22 January

Ahasuerus

(Persian: sjah of the sjahs; Greek: Xerxes)

Who and when? Son and successor of Darius I on the Persian throne (486 BC to 465 BC); in secular history he was known as Xerxes.

Want to know more? Read: Ezra 4:6; Esther 1-10.

Thoughts for today

King Ahasuerus was a powerful ruler. According to Esther 1:1 he reigned over '127 provinces stretching from India to Cush' (the Upper Nile region). Even though Esther is, of course, the chief character in the book that bears her name, it gives us a clear picture of this man who became her husband, after Queen Vashti lost her royal status.

We may have many reasons to be critical of Ahasuerus, but he also had his positive side. Take, for instance, the story of the sleepless night when the king wanted someone to read for him from the chronicles of his reign. As he listened, he was reminded of how a certain Mordecai, who happened to be the uncle of Esther, had saved the king's life by unmasking a plot against him. In the aftermath of that event, the royal bureaucracy had not worked as it should have, for Mordecai was never rewarded for his extraordinary deed. We learn, however, in the sixth chapter of Esther how the king made generous amends for this mistake.

One would not want to wish serious insomnia on anyone, but it is good to have moments when we look at our own personal history. And if we then conclude that we may have failed to do something for someone that we should have done, it is never too late to do what we can to remedy our fault.

My prayer

Lord, I realise that I sometimes forget to thank people in an appropriate way. Give me, when necessary, the courage to amend my shortcomings in this respect.

23 January

Ahaz

(the Lord has seized)

Who and when? King of Judah; reigned from 741 BC to 726 BC.

Want to know more? Read: 2 Kings 16; 2 Chronicles 28; Isaiah 7.

Thoughts for today

Ahaz did not do what was right in the eyes of the Lord (2 Kings 16:2). 'He . . . even sacrificed his son in the fire' (vs. 3). When he was confronted with a political crisis, and the very survival of Judah was at stake, he had greater confidence in the gods of his political enemies than in the God of Israel.

In spite of Ahaz's determination to 'play it safe' and seek support from the king of Assyria, God did everything possible to make him change his mind. One of the first assignments God gave the prophet Isaiah was to earnestly appeal to Ahaz to put his full trust in Him. Ahaz was even allowed to ask for a sign that would confirm God's power. When he refused to ask for such a sign, God reacted by stating that He would, nonetheless, give a special token of His presence. Then follows the famous text in which God declares that a young woman would become pregnant and give birth to a boy, who would be called Immanuel. It would be a sign to affirm that God does not abandon His people.

What an immense tragedy. God did everything He could do to create a bond between Himself and Ahaz, but Ahaz turned his back on God and chose a route he considered safer. Unfortunately, he ignored all those past dealings of God with His people that indicated that it is always the safest route to expect the solution of our troubles from God.

My prayer

Thank You, Lord, for all the signs You provide that show me that You hold not only the history of the world in Your hands, but also my personal history.

24 January

Ahithophel

(the brother of foolishness)

Who and when? One of David's advisers; he became a traitor and chose the side of the enemy.

Want to know more? Read: 2 Samuel 15:12, 31; 16:15-17:23.

Thoughts for today

In ancient times people had a high regard for wise men. In the time of David, Ahithophel was one of the wise men he constantly asked for advice. 'In those days the advice Ahithophel gave was like that of one who enquires of God. That was how both David and Absalom regarded all of Ahithophel's advice' (2 Samuel 16:23).

Often wisdom is even more important than much knowledge. Wisdom is based on experience and insight. Today also, when we face serious problems, it remains important to ask the advice of people who we know have a lot of experience and a good insight, which enables them to give a balanced judgement. In the New Testament wisdom is mentioned among the spiritual gifts (1 Corinthians 12:8-10). But if we give counsel to others we must realise that this implies certain responsibilities and requires us to be totally trustworthy. This was where Ahithophel failed. David trusted him completely, but was bitterly disappointed, because he eventually decided to throw in his lot with Absalom, who wanted to usurp his father's place on the throne.

We should have a high regard for wisdom and for wise people. And we may ask God for more wisdom, for the good of ourselves and of others. However, this wisdom must always be linked with loyalty towards those who have put their trust in us.

My prayer

God of all wisdom, I thank You that You are willing to give us wisdom if we ask You for it. Give me, Father, the wisdom that I need today and help me to be the kind of person that others can completely trust.

25 January

Alexander

(defender of man)

Who and when? A coppersmith who opposed Paul.

Want to know more? Read: 1 Timothy 1:20; 2 Timothy 4:14; Acts 19:33, 34.

Thoughts for today

In his letters the apostle Paul mentions dozens of people who assisted and encouraged him. Unfortunately, some opposed him instead. Alexander, a coppersmith in Ephesus, belonged in that category. Paul warns Timothy of this man. Be careful, he tells his younger colleague, for he 'did me a great deal of harm'. The Lord will give him what he deserves, but, in the meantime, be on your guard, for 'he strongly opposed our message' (2 Timothy 4:14, 15). Paul had already mentioned another difficult character by that name in his earlier letter to Timothy, but we have no proof that they are one and the same troublemaker. In 1 Timothy Paul refers to Hymenaeus, but also mentions this other Alexander. Their faith was 'shipwrecked' because they refused to follow their conscience (1 Timothy 1:19, 20).

Note the sequence in this process: Alexander and others no longer allowed the Spirit access to their hearts. They blasphemed God and, eventually, the little faith they still had also evaporated (1 Timothy 1:20). The apostle added that he had 'handed' Alexander and those who spoke and acted like he did 'over to Satan'. This means that Paul had to conclude that Alexander and his friends had completely lost their way and could no longer be counted as members of God's family of faith. Was there no longer any hope for them, or for those who have gone through a similar process? Yes, there is, but only if there is real remorse and a radical conversion.

My prayer

Our loving God, please protect us, so that we will never oppose You to the point that You can no longer recognise us as part of Your family, unless we turn around and once again embark on a route that leads towards You.

26 January

Amnon (trustworthy)

Who and when? The son of David who wanted to have an intimate relationship with his sister Tamar; ca. 1000 BC.

Want to know more? Read: 2 Samuel 3:2; 13:1-22.

Thoughts for today

Amnon – one of David's sons – had a half-sister who was called Tamar. She was a beautiful girl and Amnon fell in love with her: 'Amnon became frustrated to the point of illness on account of his sister Tamar.' A fatal obsession took hold of him, which led to tragic consequences. Amnon sought the advice of a cousin as to how this intense desire might lead to an actual intimate, sexual contact with Tamar. A shrewd tactic enabled Amnon to ensure that Tamar would come to his private quarters. It did not take long for Tamar to discover Amnon's intentions. She tried to persuade him as best as she could not to defile her, but 'since he was stronger than she, he raped her' (2 Samuel 13:14).

Sadly, sexual violence against women has always been a fact of life and is found in all social circles. As in Amnon's case, the perpetrator is frequently someone who is well-known to the victim. Often it involves a father, uncle, brother, or close friend. In Amnon's time there were no advocacy groups or social workers to address this problem of sexual violence. Even today there are cultures where, like in ancient Israel, these evil acts are dealt with by means of honour killings rather than in a court of law. We have the privilege of living in a context where we can report these crimes to the police and let the legal system take care of them. Sadly, even in Christian families and religious environments there are Amnons who pose a threat to our Tamars. Christian communities must deal properly with victims as well as perpetrators. It is important to be alert for signals that things may possibly derail, and to provide the right kind of support to both victims and perpetrators.

My prayer

Lord, help me see how I can do my part in combating sexual misconduct.

27 January

Amos

(burden bearer, powerful)

Who and when? A prophet during the reigns of King Uzziah (788 BC to 735 BC) and King Jeroboam II of Israel (790 BC to 749 BC).

Want to know more? Read: Amos 1:1, 2; 7:10-17.

Thoughts for today

Amos was a modest person. He gives a few details about himself, but tells us nothing about him having a special status or famous forebears. He presents himself as 'one of the shepherds of Tekoa' (Amos 1:1). Nonetheless, he was not afraid to speak out, even in the face of fierce opposition. Amaziah, a priest in the sanctuary at Bethel, tried to convince King Jeroboam of Israel not to listen to Amos. This Amaziah told the prophet Amos: 'Get out, you seer! Go back to the land of Judah. Earn your bread there and do your prophesying there' (Amos 7:12). But Amos was ready with his reply: 'I was neither a prophet nor a prophet's son, but I was a shepherd, and I also took care of sycamore-fig trees. But the LORD took me from tending the flock and said to me, "Go, prophesy to my people Israel." ' Then followed a message of condemnation for Amaziah, which was abundantly clear. It predicted major disasters for him, his wife and children.

Amos may have been a farmer and not an academically educated person or a priest, but, nonetheless, he became one of the Bible writers. God looks – as we are constantly being reminded – at what is inside a person. Amos had no ambition to become famous. Titles did not interest him. The one thing he was focused on was faithfully communicating what God wanted to say through him to certain individuals or groups of people. In doing so he has left us with a magnificent example.

My prayer

Help me, Lord, to be like Amos – a faithful messenger – without demanding attention for myself.

28 January

Ananias (the Lord is gracious)

Who and when? Well-to-do member of the early church in Jerusalem. He decided to sell a plot of land and give the proceeds of the sale to the church. But he was less than transparent.

Want to know more? Read: Acts 5:1-11.

Thoughts for today

The Bible presents us with several persons with the name of Ananias. The Ananias we are dealing with today belonged, together with his wife, Sapphira, to the small company of Jesus-people in Jerusalem. Apparently, the couple were reasonably well-to-do and could afford to make a generous gesture towards the church. They decided to sell a piece of land and bring part of the proceeds to the apostles.

One would think that there would be nothing but appreciation for their generosity. However, they attempted to deceive the believers by bringing only part of the proceeds to the apostles, but wanted them to believe that they were giving to the church all that they had received for the land. They were severely punished for this deceit, and for the fact that they wanted to be respected and admired by their fellow-believers more than they wanted to be honest before God.

Unfortunately, this kind of thing is an all-too-common phenomenon. It also happens all too often that our acts of charity spring from mixed motives. We may have an affinity with the cause to which we are giving, and in which we have a strong interest, but at the same time we are eager that our generosity will not pass unnoticed! And thus the furtherance of our own reputation is an aspect that frequently plays a far-too-important role.

My prayer

Heavenly Father, I know my weaknesses and I realise that at times I am far too much concerned with my own reputation, instead of focusing all my attention on You.

29 January

Andrew

(manly, the strong one)

Who and when? One of the twelve men whom Jesus called to be His disciples. He was the brother of Simon Peter.

Want to know more? Read: Matthew 4:18-20; John 1:40-42; 6:8, 9.

Thoughts for today

Andrew is one of the lesser-known disciples of Jesus. In contrast to his brother Peter, and to James and John, he remained mostly in the background. We discover this in John 6, where we find the story of how Jesus fed a multitude of perhaps in excess of ten thousand people.

Jesus asked Philip where they would be able to buy enough bread. Jesus already knew what He was about to do, but, we are told, He asked the question 'only to test him'. In the meantime Andrew had been busy. He had already made an inventory of the food that people had brought along. He hoped that there would be enough to solve the dilemma. But the results of his enquiries were disappointing: he found only five loaves of bread and two fish. However, in Jesus' hands that proved to be more than enough to feed everybody. Jesus was happy to build on the work that Andrew had silently been doing.

The author of the gospel found Andrew's efforts so significant that he explicitly included them as part of the story. We should never underestimate the work that is done in the background. Usually everything grinds to a halt if there are no people who, unnoticed to others, make the necessary preparations. These people deserve not to be forgotten.

My prayer

Dear God, help me to find satisfaction in activities in the background while noticing what other people around me do without seeking the spotlight.

30 January

Andronicus

(the man who conquers)

Who and when? Believer in Rome, whom Paul knew personally.

Want to know more? Read: Romans 16:7.

Thoughts for today

Many Bible readers may never have encountered the name of Andronicus. He is mentioned at the end of Paul's letter to the church in Rome in a long list of men and women, who all receive greetings from the apostle. When Paul wrote this letter he had not yet been to Rome, but he hoped to go there soon, and his letter was partly intended as an introduction.

It is quite remarkable that Paul knew so many members of the church in Rome by name. Some of them he had, no doubt, met elsewhere, at some time in the past. That was also true of this Andronicus. In Romans 16:7 we read: 'Greet Andronicus and Junias, my relatives who have been in prison with me. They are outstanding among the apostles, and they were in Christ before I was.' Andronicus had a Jewish background. He had already joined the church before Paul was converted. He had a certain standing in the church and was referred to by Paul as an 'apostle'. Something else is mentioned: he had been in prison together with Paul. We are not told when and where this was, but there are several possibilities, for Paul was more than once imprisoned for his faith.

A dramatic experience as a consequence of one's faith creates a special bond. It is great to have friends and colleagues. However, when a believer shares in some meaningful spiritual experience with fellow believers, it gives their friendship an extra dimension that supersedes everything else.

My prayer

Thank You, Lord, for friends with whom I can share my faith experiences.

31 January

Aner

(waterfall or affliction)

Who and when? An Amorite who helped Abraham to rescue Lot.

Want to know more? Read: Genesis 14:13-24.

Thoughts for today

Thinking of Abraham, a number of stories from the book of Genesis almost immediately come to mind: for instance, God's promise to Abraham and Sarah that their marriage would not remain childless and that they would be the beginning of a big nation. And, of course, we think of the story of the near-sacrifice of Isaac by his father.

We discover a somewhat different picture of Abraham in Genesis 14, however, where we read about him going to war. His nephew Lot, together with his household and all his possessions, was abducted by a few clan chiefs – they are referred to as 'kings'. Abraham was told about this act of aggression just after he had pitched his tents near 'the great trees of Mamre'. Mamre the Amorite was willing to join Abraham in the raid he organised to rescue Lot. Abraham was able to field a force of 318 'trained' men from among his own servants (Genesis 14:14). The expedition was successful and Lot and his household were rescued.

At that point in time, Abraham was living among people who did not share his faith, but apparently he had been able to win the trust of people like Mamre and his brothers, Aner and Eshcol. In a time of need he could count on their help. Today many believers also live among people who do not share their religious convictions, but that doesn't mean that they have to feel completely isolated. It is important to live the kind of life that will help us win the trust of people like Aner who live around us. If we succeed in doing this, we can surely count on their help when we need it.

My prayer

Heavenly Father, help me to live the kind of life that will make me gain the trust of people around me, so that I can ask for their support when I need it.

1 February

Annas

(Greek form of *Chananja*: the Lord is gracious)

Who and when? High priest (AD 6 to AD 15); father-in-law of Caiaphas. During His trial, Jesus was brought to Annas before he was handed over to Caiaphas.

Want to know more? Read: Luke 3:2; John 18:12-24; Acts 4:6.

Thoughts for today

Caiaphas was the official high priest when Jesus was put on trial in Jerusalem. But Jesus was first brought before Caiaphas's father-in-law, Annas, who had previously been high priest. He, in fact, was still very much in control and has been described as the head of the 'Jewish mafia' of his day. He was obsessed with the thought that this dangerous Jesus had to be dealt with. According to the Jewish historian Flavius Josephus, Annas was the one who made the deal with Judas to betray Jesus. In Acts 4 we meet Annas again, when there is trouble between the apostles and the Jewish leaders.

Annas had power and influence. He was the power behind the throne. Power-hungry people are dangerous, but this applies in particular to spiritual leaders who get too much power. Religion in combination with power is a deadly mix. It was the case when Jesus was confronted with this phenomenon, and it continues to be so with many religious (Christian and non-Christian) leaders in the twenty-first century. It is bad enough when leaders have very distinct opinions and feel that everyone should agree with them. But if they are intolerant and also have the power to silence all who disagree, it can have serious consequences. Our Lord became a Victim of such a situation; and His present-day followers must still be alert for this danger, and avoid this behaviour themselves.

My prayer

Loving God, protect us against the tyranny of people who may try to force their opinions on us, and please help us never to treat others in this way.

2 February

Apollos

(Short form of Appollonius: belonging to the god Apollo)

Who and when? A learned Jew from Alexandria who became a Christian and a co-worker of Paul in the Gospel proclamation.

Want to know more? Read: Acts 18:24-28; 1 Corinthians 1:10-17; 3:1-23.

Thoughts for today

A serious discord had arisen in the church of Corinth. The conflict was about the question of who was to be regarded as the real leader of the church. Some were adamant that Paul was the number-one. Others attributed that honour to Apollos, or felt that Peter was entitled to that status. One of Paul's intentions in writing his first letter to the Corinthians was to put an end to the controversy. He wanted to impress upon the Corinthian Christians that they should not think in such terms. None of the leaders was the number-one. They had all contributed to the founding of the church and had built firmly upon each other's efforts. Therefore, the church was not the church of Paul, Peter or Apollos, but of Jesus Christ!

Apollos, no doubt, played an important role in establishing the church in Corinth. Paul said that he had been involved in the work of planting, but that Apollos made sure that the young plants were continuously watered, while God was responsible for the growth that followed (1 Corinthians 3:6). The evangelist is the 'planter' who lays the basis with his preaching: but his work will not bear much fruit if no one takes care of what has been sown and planted. Unfortunately, we often find that new Gospel contacts are not sufficiently nurtured. The work of people like Apollos is still a crucial element in our attempts to take the Gospel to the world: yet we must remember that the end result always depends on God's blessings.

My prayer

Help me, dear Lord, always to remember that the blessing comes from You, and that all those who work for You are equally important!

3 February

Araunah (the Lord is firm)

Who and when? A Jebusite who sold his threshing floor (the spot where the temple was to be built) to David.

Want to know more? Read: 2 Samuel 24:16-24; 1 Chronicles 21:18-28; 2 Chronicles 3:1.

Thoughts for today

The spot that Araunah used as his threshing floor became very important. It was the place where Solomon would build his famous temple and where, according to the Muslims, Mohammed ascended to heaven. David's choice of this place was not without reason. The prophet Gad had brought a message from God: here David was to offer his sacrifices once God had put an end to the terrible plague that had struck Israel after David had gone against God's will.

David was to purchase the plot of land where Araunah was threshing his grain. When David started his negotiations with Araunah, his first reaction was that David did not have to pay anything. That was how, in accordance with the customs of those days, the process of bargaining started, which would then lead on to a conclusion that satisfied both parties.

Araunah was supportive of David's plan to transform his threshing floor into an offering place, to such an extent that he was ready to donate the site and provide the sacrifices himself. David's response, however, must have given him food for thought, as it should for us too: for David insisted that he wanted to pay for the threshing floor, saying, 'I will not sacrifice to the LORD my God burnt offerings that cost me nothing' (2 Samuel 24:24). David realised that a sacrifice that costs nothing is not really a sacrifice!

My prayer

Make me understand, Lord, that a true sacrifice to You may cost me something!

4 February

Archippus

(master of the horse)

Who and when? A leader in the church of Colosse.

Want to know more? Read: Colossians 4:17; Philemon vs. 2.

Thoughts for today

The first verse in the letter to the Colossians states that it was written by Paul and Timothy. The Gospel had not been preached in Colosse – a city about 160 kilometres east of Ephesus, on the coast of present-day Turkey – by Paul himself. That appears to have been mainly the work of a certain Epaphras. However, Paul was well acquainted with the situation in Colosse and was aware of the difficulties in the church in that city. Reading the letter to the Colossians we find that the church was infected by some strange ideas. In fact, it would be no exaggeration to say that the Colossians were faced with a dangerous heresy. But, even though Paul issued some serious warnings (see 2:16-23), we do not know the details of this heretical teaching.

Epaphras still had an important position in this church: but that was also true of Archippus. At the end of the letter we find a message especially addressed to him: 'Tell Archippus: "See to it that you complete the work that you have received in the Lord." '

Why was it necessary to say this so explicitly to Archippus? Had he ignored his task, being too busy with other things? Or were the problems of such a magnitude that he had thrown in his towel? There may be all kinds of reasons why people who have accepted a task – in the church or in society – at a certain point in time walk away from it. That is only too human. However, if that should happen to us, hopefully there is someone to give us a little push (and hopefully we are there to give that little push to others), as a reminder of what is expected from us (or from them).

My prayer

Gracious God, send people on my path who, if needed, will remind me that I should complete my tasks, as You expect me to.

5 February

Arphaxad

(one that releases)

Who and when? Son of Shem and ancestor of Abraham.

Want to know more? Read: Genesis 10:21-31; 11:12, 13.

Thoughts for today

We are easily tempted to skip the details of the genealogies in the book of Genesis. We know, of course, that before the Flood people lived to a very high age, with Methuselah with his 969 years as the record holder. After the Flood these high ages soon became a thing of the past. However, Arphaxad, the son of Shem - one of the three sons of Noah who, together with their wives, survived the Flood - still reached the respectable age of 438 years.

One aspect that is hardly ever mentioned is when this Arphaxad was born. This was two years after the Flood. Arphaxad, therefore, grew up in a very unique world. No doubt, the ravages of the Flood were all around him. There were only a few people. Of many kinds of animals only fourteen had survived, and of the so-called 'unclean' animals only one pair had been saved in the ark. Arpharxad had few, if any, other boys to play with. And, undoubtedly, over and over again he heard the story of how his grandpa and his grandma, his father and mother and his two uncles and aunts, had been saved.

We cannot fully imagine what kind of situation Arphaxad grew up in. And this is not only true of Arphaxad. All around us we see men and women who have grown up in a world that radically differs from our own, and it is important to realise this. It helps us to have more understanding for what those people do, and be more empathetic when they behave in ways that deviate from what we are used to.

My prayer

Help me, loving Father, to think more often about the background of the people around me, so that I will find it easier to accept their way of life and love them in spite of our differences.

6 February

Artaxerxes

(owner of a pre-eminent kingdom)

Who and when? In 457 BC Artaxerxes I Longimanus sent Ezra, with a group of exiles, back to Judah to make a start with the restoration of this Jewish province.

Want to know more? Read: Ezra 7:1-26.

Thoughts for today

What Artaxerxes did in the seventh year of his reign is an important detail for people who are interested in biblical prophecy: for this is, they say, closely connected with the prophecy of Daniel about the seventy year-weeks (Daniel 9:24-27). This prophetic period, it is claimed, refers to a period of 490 years, ending with the events surrounding the ministry and death of the Messiah. The starting point of the 490 years is mentioned in Daniel 9:25: 'the issuing of the decree to restore and rebuild Jerusalem. . . .' That decree was issued by Artaxerxes.

The 'decree' that made this development possible is found in a letter Artaxerxes gave to Ezra (see Ezra 7). It is remarkable how much space and authority Ezra was given for the enterprise he was to lead. What made the king so generous? Was it a matter of political expediency? Or were there other motives? Ezra was certain that there was something more at stake. God had determined that the time had come to fulfil His promise that the exile was not to last forever. Therefore Ezra stated: 'Praise be to the LORD, the God of our fathers, who has put it into the king's heart to bring honour to the house of the LORD in Jerusalem . . .' (Ezra 7:27). For Ezra this development was not a matter of good luck. He knew that behind the scenes God was at work – as He always is.

My prayer

Almighty God, to us many things may appear to be the result of what we do, or of sheer good luck, but I know that You are ultimately in charge. I thank You for this.

7 February

Asa (healer)

Who and when? King of Judah; reigned 41 years (911 BC to 870 BC)

Want to know more? Read: 1 Kings 15:9-24; 2 Chronicles 14-16.

Thoughts for today

Asa was a 'good' king. He put a stop to all kinds of pagan practices, but permitted a few dubious things to continue. We may also criticise him for the fact that he encouraged the king of Damascus to withhold his support from King Baasha, the king of the Northern Kingdom of Israel, and to make life difficult for Baasha. The most remarkable detail about Asa is found in a short remark in 1 Kings: 'In his old age, however, his feet became diseased' (1 Kings 15:23). In 2 Chronicles 16 we learn a little more about this. 'Asa was afflicted with a disease in his feet. Though his disease was severe, even in his illness he did not seek help from the LORD, but only from the physicians' (vs. 12).

For older readers this is something they can relate to. Age often comes with mobility challenges. Fortunately, we can now get many things that help us to stay mobile, but, nonetheless, this frequent problem of limited mobility not only causes pain, but also a lot of frustration. Faced with this challenge, we consult our family doctor and are also often referred to medical specialists for further treatment. Therefore, we may wonder why Asa was criticised for consulting 'physicians'. However, in his case these 'physicians' were most likely occult practitioners who were enemies of Israel's God. Instead, Asa should have sought help from the Lord.

We must use all available medical assistance when faced with ageing and decreasing mobility, but our real well-being and true happiness depend first of all on a close 'walk' with the Lord. This, fortunately, is not affected by physical mobility challenges.

My prayer

Dear God, help us to realise that, when confronted with difficulties, we should first seek help from You.

8 February

Asahel (God has made)

Who and when? One of the Levites sent out by King Jehoshaphat of Judah (reigned from 870 BC to 845 BC) to instruct the people in the law.

Want to know more? Read: 2 Chronicles 17:8, 9.

Thoughts for today

Asahel was one of the Levites and priests who were sent out by King Jehoshaphat to teach the people all the things that the Lord had revealed in the past, and to re-acquaint them with the details of the sanctuary services in Jerusalem. Jehoshaphat had decided to bring about a religious reformation in his country. 'His heart was devoted to the ways of the LORD; furthermore, he removed the high places and the Asherah poles from Judah' (2 Chronicles 17:6). But Jehoshaphat understood that a true reformation required more than some government enforcement of the instructions God had given through Moses many centuries earlier, to return the traditional religion to its former glory. Every individual citizen had to understand what this reform meant. This is what Asahel and the ten other specifically named Levites and priests had as their task. Asahel and his colleagues therefore 'taught throughout Judah, taking with them the Book of the Law of the LORD' (vs. 9).

Present-day leaders of God's people can learn from this approach of Jehoshaphat. A revival does not automatically come about when the leaders try to impose all kinds of plans on the people, or by restating the rules more clearly in new documents or declarations. The key is that every individual feels personally addressed and invited to rededicate himself or herself to the Lord. How would it be if we, as modern Asahels, would play an active role and also 'teach throughout' the land?

My prayer

Lord, we realise that, just as in the past, Your people must be personally alerted to their responsibilities towards You. Please, let me know in what way You can use me in this process.

9 February

Asaph (gatherer)

Who and when? Belonged to a group of Levites who had important tasks in the musical aspects of the sanctuary services; contemporary of David.

Want to know more? Read: 1 Chronicles 16:1-37.

Thoughts for today

We find Asaph's name above twelve of the Psalms (50, 73-83). Asaph may have been the writer of either the text or the music, or both. We do know, however, that he was a man with musical talents and that he played the cymbal and possibly some other instruments.

Music was an extremely important element in the services of the tabernacle and (later) in the temple. A large number of singers and musicians were involved. Throughout the centuries music and hymns have been, and are still, an essential part of the Christian worship service. In some sublime way music and song can help us express our feelings and open ourselves up to the Spirit of God.

Many people say that, when they go to church, they first of all want to hear a good sermon. That is fine. But it is good to realise that originally a sermon was not part of the sanctuary service. In Asaph's days, worship was actually a matter of bringing sacrifices, participating in religious festivals and enjoying worshipful music.

Things are no different in the twenty-first century, for the church still has a great need of good poets who can provide us with beautiful and meaningful lyrics, rather than the poor and simplistic ones of some of the popular songs we are too often asked to sing. Those who assist in presenting good music, or by participating in a choir, have at least as important a role in the worship service as the person who reads the Scripture or preaches the sermon!

My prayer

Lord, give me a good ear for the kind of music and song that truly glorifies Your name.

10 February

Asher (happy)

Who and when? The eighth son of Jacob and the second son of Zilpah; one of the twelve tribes of Israel bears his name.

Want to know more? Read: Genesis 30:12, 13; 35:26; 49:20; Deuteronomy 33:24, 25; Luke 2:36.

Thoughts for today

Asher was a son of Jacob and Zilpah. Since Zilpah was a servant of Leah, it was Leah who selected the name for the newborn baby boy. She called him Asher, to indicate how happy she was. When, at the end of his life, Jacob blessed his sons, he prophesied of the good fortune Asher and his descendants would experience. 'Asher's food will be rich; he will provide delicacies fit for a king' (Genesis 49:20). Moses spoke in similar terms about the tribe of Asher: 'Let him bathe his feet in oil' (Deuteronomy 33:24). Asher's posterity lived in a fertile region of Palestine, near the coast.

The tribe of Asher is not mentioned very often in the Bible. The aged prophetess Anna, who brought praise to the newborn Jesus in the temple, was an Asherite. The tribe of Asher did not join the other tribes of Israel when, in the time of the Judges, Israel went to war (Judges 5:17). And, as far as we know, the tribe of Asher never produced an important leader.

Nonetheless, Asher had a prominent place among the twelve tribes. Moses stated that Asher received blessings that exceeded the blessings given to the other tribes. And he added: 'Let him be favoured by his brothers' (Deuteronomy 33:24). We may be grateful if our family has produced some men and women with leadership skills. But there is even more reason to be thankful when our family is loved ('favoured') by many others.

My prayer

Loving heavenly Father, let us share in the happiness you want to give to mankind, and help us live in such a way that we are 'favoured' by the people around us.

11 February

Ashpenaz

(Persian: horse's nose)

Who and when? In charge of the court of the Babylonian king Nebuchadnezzar (605 BC to 562 BC).

Want to know more? Read: Daniel 1.

Thoughts for today

Daniel and his three friends posed a serious problem for Ashpenaz when they approached him with their plea not to be forced to eat from the king's table. In his position Ashpenaz was not only responsible for the education of the Judean princes, but also for their physical well-being. When Daniel and his friends asked for these concessions, Ashpenaz no doubt saw the risks, yet was willing to give them a chance. It seems that he was willing to look the other way when the four young men went with their request to the official who was assigned to them as their daily coach. He was prepared to allow a ten-day test.

Ashpenaz must have known what was happening, but did not intervene. The reason was not that he sympathised in any way with the religious scruples of Daniel and his comrades. He had given them new names that no longer pointed to their Judean religion. But was there something that moved him to be flexible? Yes, there was. 'God had caused the official to show favour and sympathy to Daniel' (Daniel 1:9).

Ashpenaz was willing to take a risk, but by presenting their request Daniel and his friends took a much greater risk. They were not in a position to ask for favours: but they wanted to remain loyal to their God. And, when we decide to follow the example of Daniel and his friends, we can be sure that God will also help us.

My prayer

Almighty God, You are the God of Daniel, but also my God: and, therefore, I may be sure that You will support me when I decide to live according to Your principles, in spite of severe opposition. I thank You from the bottom of my heart.

12 February

Athaliah

(the Lord is exalted)

Who and when? Queen of Judah (841 BC to 835 BC).

Want to know more? Read: 2 Kings 8:26; 2 Chronicles 22:10–23:21.

Thoughts for today

We often encounter children we can describe as 'a chip off the old block'. By this we mean that the children resemble their parents in many ways. One might say that this also applied to Athaliah. She was the daughter of the cruel, merciless King Ahab, and in ruthlessness she almost equalled her father. In an attempt to secure her position she started her reign by killing 'the whole royal family of the house of Judah' (2 Chronicles 22:10). Athaliah reigned for six years before it was her turn to become the victim of a conspiracy. When she plotted to have the entire royal family killed, she was not careful enough. Joash, who was still a child, had escaped. He was hidden by Jehoiada, a priest, and was 'brought out' when he was seven years old and proclaimed king. For a number of years Jehoiada acted as regent on his behalf.

However, is stating that she was 'a chip off the old block' an adequate explanation for Athaliah's behaviour? Was her cruelty caused by her genes, or was her character strongly influenced by the environment in which she grew up? In her case the latter was most likely. We discover this in ourselves and in the people around us. However, this can never serve as a valid excuse: for, no matter how strong the influence is of the environment in which we grow up, or who our role models may be, in the end our own free will determines the direction of our life. Athaliah was not predestined to be cruel. It was her own choice. Her ultimate destiny is a powerful warning for anyone who reads or hears her story.

My prayer

Gracious God, give me the strength to make good choices and not to find excuses in the bad influences of others.

13 February

Aquila (Latin: eagle)

Who and when? Together with his wife Priscilla (or Prisca) Aquila converted to the Christian faith. He met Paul in Corinth and later in Ephesus. Later again we meet him in Rome.

Want to know more? Read: Acts 18:1-3, 18-22; 1 Corinthians 16:19; Romans 16:3.

Thoughts for today

The church needs more people like Aquila and Priscilla. They were close co-workers with Paul, as, for instance, in Corinth. There they made their home available as a 'house church' for the Corinthian believers. In those days the church did not yet meet in the kind of church buildings that would be built in later centuries; the believers met in the homes of fellow believers who happened to have a spacious house.

Aquila and Priscilla were active missionaries, but, of course, they needed enough money to make a living. They were tentmakers, and it so happened that this was also Paul's original occupation. The twelve apostles were to some extent financially supported by the church members, but there was no infrastructure to provide for a regular income for all those who 'worked for the church'. As a result many – like Paul and Aquila and Priscilla – had other jobs besides their work for the church.

Today the authorities in most countries allow official missionaries to enter their country and do missionary work. But so-called 'tentmaker' missionaries may find a way to successfully enter 'closed' countries, where their professional or practical skills are in great demand. This enables them to discreetly witness of their faith. However, in many 'open' countries the church does not have the means to hire enough men and women to reach all people with the Gospel message. If more people were willing to follow the example of Aquila and Priscilla, this would not just be a blessing for themselves, but also for many who otherwise would not hear the Good News.

My prayer

Thank You, heavenly Father, for all the 'tentmakers' of today.

14 February

Augustus

(Latin: majestic)

Who and when? Roman emperor from 27 BC to AD 14.

Want to know more? Read: Luke 2:1.

Thoughts for today

Is Emperor Augustus really a biblical personality? Admittedly, one may question this, as the emperor of the immensely large Roman Empire belongs first of all to the secular history of antiquity. However, most Bible readers know that his name is mentioned in the Bible. Each time the Christmas story is read we are reminded of him: 'In those days Caesar Augustus issued a decree that a census should be taken of the entire Roman world' (Luke 2:1). This registration was to take place in one's place of origin. For that reason Mary, in the late stage of her pregnancy, travelled with Joseph to Bethlehem, where Jesus was born.

Augustus wanted to know the state of his realm and decided to organise a census. He knew that this project would mean considerable inconvenience for many of his subjects. But it is doubtful that he ever learned that, in organising this census, he played a key role in the greatest drama of all times: the birth of our Saviour in Bethlehem – exactly as foretold in prophecy.

Even the most powerful men and women cannot have a full picture of everything that happens in the world, and often they never see the consequences of their own decisions. Nevertheless, what they do somehow fits in with God's comprehensive plan. He reaches His goal through, and often in spite of, human plans: through, or in spite of, decrees issued by a powerful emperor like Augustus, but also through or in spite of what you and I decide to do.

My prayer

I ask You, Lord, to fit the things I will say or do today into Your comprehensive plan for the saving of mankind.

15 February

Azariah

(the Lord has helped)

Who and when? One of Daniel's friends; his Hebrew name was changed into Abednego. Ca. 580 BC.

Want to know more? Read: Daniel 1; 2:13-18; 3:1-30.

Thoughts for today

We encounter in the Bible some 26 different Azariahs. However, the best-known among these was the Azariah (renamed Abednego), who, with two of his friends, was thrown into the 'blazing furnace' in Babylon. His deliverance from this burning hell was as surprising as it was dramatic. But why did Azariah end up in this hellish fire? He had refused to worship the enormous golden statue that Nebuchadnezzar, the king of Babylon, had erected. When the king heard how Azariah and two other Judean men had disobeyed his command, he gave them one final chance to save their skin.

The loyalty of Azariah and his two friends towards God was much stronger than their respect for the king. They were told: ' "If you are ready to fall down and worship the image I made, very good. But if you do not worship it, you will be thrown immediately into a blazing furnace. Then what god will be able to rescue you from my hand?" Shadrach, Meshach and Abednego replied to the king, "O Nebuchadnezzar, we do not need to defend ourselves before you in this matter. If we are thrown into the blazing furnace, the God we serve is able to save us from it, and he will rescue us from your hand, O king. But even if he does not, we want you to know, O king, that we will not serve your gods or worship the image of gold you have set up" ' (Daniel 3:15-18). What an expression of marvellous trust in God!

My prayer

Heavenly Father, give me the same unconditional trust in You as we see in Azariah and his friends.

16 February

Baanah

(meaning uncertain)

Who and when? One of the two men who killed Ish-Bosheth; he brought his head to King David and expected a reward.

Want to know more? Read: 2 Samuel 4:2-12.

Thoughts for today

Baanah and his brother Rechab, who came from the Canaanite town of Beeroth, were what we might call real opportunists. They knew that Ish-Bosheth, one of Saul's younger sons, was a sworn enemy of David. Therefore, it seemed logical to assume that they would do David a great favour if they killed Ish-Bosheth. As proof of their 'courageous' act they decided to bring Ish-Bosheth's head to David. They were certain David would give them a generous reward for doing so.

However, this was a serious miscalculation. David might have been an imperfect man, but in many respects he was also a man with principles. It is true that in those days there was often more cruelty than we experience in our time and culture (even though there is still more than enough of it), but we fail to see even a trace of idealism with Baanah and his brother. Their only concern was the reward they expected to get. David, however, reacted in a totally different manner from how they had thought he would.

In the world of crime we see that usually it is all about material gain. But we also notice many more subtle instances of opportunism, where people are only concerned about how a particular course of action will benefit themselves. This is in total contrast with the attitude of a genuine Christian. A follower of Jesus will always cling to the ideal of looking after the well-being of others.

My prayer

Dear God, forgive me for any trace of opportunism and help me to be a person with principles, who makes it his priority to be there for other people.

17 February

Balaam (devourer of the people)

Who and when? Soothsayer-prophet who was enlisted by the Moabite king Balak to curse Israel. This incident took place during the last phase of Israel's sojourn in the desert.

Want to know more? Read: Numbers 22:2–24:25; 2 Peter 2:15; Revelation 2:14.

Thoughts for today

We do not know exactly who this Balaam was. He lived in Pethor, near the River Euphrates (Numbers 22:5). It is clear that he knew about the God of Israel and that this God communicated with him. But, to phrase it euphemistically, Balaam was rather half-hearted in his attitude towards Israel's God.

Balak, the king of the Moabites, had a great fear of the Israelites. They had been successful in their wars against other nations and, apparently, Balak and his people were their next target. For that reason Balak decided to call upon Balaam to curse Israel. Considering the reward that Balak promised Balaam this seemed to be a very financially attractive assignment for him. However, in the first instance Balaam rejected the offer, for he knew that this would be against God's will. But when the request was repeated, Balaam began to go weak in the knees. He did not, however, want to give an immediate response, but first decided to seek God's counsel.

Why did Balaam ask for time in order to seek divine advice? He knew what God expected from him, but he was looking for a loophole that would enable him to accept this lucrative assignment. Seeing this, God let him follow his own course. This, however, did not mean that he went with God's blessing, as he would soon experience. His prayer was not a sincere prayer. He posed a question, but wanted to press God to give the answer that he wanted to hear.

My prayer

Dear Lord, Your Word warns us that some of Your children will be inclined to repeat this sin of Balaam. Please, protect me against this.*

**See Revelation 2:14*

18 February

Balak

(God has destroyed)

Who and when? A Moabite king in Moses' time; he employed Balaam to curse Israel.

Want to know more? Read: Numbers 22:2–24:25; Joshua 24:9; Judges 11:25.

Thoughts for today

Balak was afraid of the people of Israel, knowing how they had been victorious over other regions of the land of Canaan. He feared that they would occupy his territory, and so he decided to call upon Balaam, who enjoyed considerable fame as a soothsayer-prophet. Balaam would be paid handsomely if he was prepared to come and curse the Israelites. In that way, Balak believed, he would have a much better chance in his war against Israel.

The Old Testament often mentions the topic of curses and blessings. A blessing would result in all kinds of positive things, while someone who was cursed was doomed to experience all sorts of mishaps. God used blessings and curses in His dealings with His people (see, for instance, Deuteronomy 28). Balak wanted to use this method for his own benefit. He knew how sensitive people were with regard to this blessing-and-curse mechanism. But in his case it was based on pure superstition. He used it as part of his strategy of psychological warfare.

Balak did not understand the deeper meaning of God's blessings and curses for Israel. He did not see that God's blessings – and His curses – depend on how human beings relate to Him. That was how it was in Balak's time and how it still is in our day. At the end of Christian worship services the pastor often pronounces God's blessing. It is intended for all, but if we want to be truly blessed we must open our hearts and minds to this divine blessing!

My prayer

Dear God, I realise that things go wrong when I turn my back on You, and that I need Your blessing. Help me today, Lord, to open my heart for the blessings You have in store for me.

19 February

Barabbas

(son of a father)

Who and when? A political agitator who was imprisoned by the Romans; a contemporary of Jesus.

Want to know more? Read: Matthew 27:15-26.

Thoughts for today

Barabbas's full name as mentioned in some manuscripts of the Gospel of Matthew was Jesus Barabbas. Herod had put him in prison, because he was perceived as a very dangerous agitator who incited the people to rebel against the Romans. He should have had the least chance of receiving amnesty: yet this is what happened. When Pilate gives the people the choice whether he shall free this Jesus Barabbas or the other Jesus, whom they see before them, they listen to the Jewish leaders and shout that they want Jesus Barabbas to walk free!

This was the choice the crowd was given: Jesus, the Prince of peace, who wanted to change the world by first changing the hearts of the people, or this other Jesus who had opted for the use of violence. The Jewish leaders preferred this criminal, Jesus Barabbas, rather than the peace-loving Jesus, who had so caringly healed so many of their countrymen. In actual fact, this peace-loving Jesus was far more radical than Jesus Barabbas. There would be no place for these Jewish leaders in the kingdom that Jesus was going to establish, if they did not want to live by the norms of this new kingdom.

In our society we also hear many voices that encourage us to turn our backs on Jesus. If most people would decide to follow Jesus a totally different world would ensue. But it would be a world that would harm their interests. However, let us never forget that true happiness is only found in the world of Jesus of Nazareth.

My prayer

Help me today to keep my ears closed to the voices around me that urge me to choose a different Jesus.

20 February

Barak

(lightning)

Who and when? A military leader in the war of Israel against the Canaanites; twelfth century BC.

Want to know more? Read: Judges 4; 5.

Thoughts for today

Barak was a contemporary of Deborah, who functioned as one of the 'judges' for the twelve tribes of Israel after they had settled in the 'promised' land. Unfortunately, the original inhabitants were still quite powerful, which meant that there was almost constant warfare. Barak was told by Deborah that he was to assemble an army in order to teach the Canaanites a decisive lesson. Barak, however, did not fancy this idea. He said to Deborah: 'If you go with me, I will go; but if you don't go with me, I won't go' (Judges 4:8).

Barak's attitude was not just a matter of respect for Deborah. He was afraid he was not up to the task. Deborah, being the 'judge', had a lot of authority and, therefore, she was to come along. Deborah agreed, but warned Barak that a woman would receive all the credit for the victory!

Humanly speaking, Barak had some good reasons to be afraid: but he should have known better. Deborah was not just an ordinary woman. She was a prophetess, who was known to be a mouthpiece of God; and she had said to him: 'The Lord, the God of Israel, commands you' (4:6).

We often feel there are solid reasons to refuse a particular task: but we should not hesitate when we are confronted with a clear command from God. In that case we can confidently put our worries aside, and trust that the God who has given us this task will also give us the strength we need to accomplish it.

My prayer

Lord, help me to see what You want me to do and let me not be afraid to take up that task.

21 February

Barakel

(God has blessed)

Who and when? The father of Elihu, the fourth person to address Job, who probably lived in patriarchal times.

Want to know more? Read: Job 32:2, 6.

Thoughts for today

The book of Job raises many questions, such as: who was the author? We do not know. There is a tradition that ascribes it to Moses, a view that Ellen G. White supported in an article that she wrote in *Signs of the Times,* 19 February, 1880. But even if this view is correct, it does not make Job a contemporary of Moses. There are lots of indications that the story of Job must be placed in the era of the patriarchs. The reference to the background of Elihu, the youngest of the four 'friends' of Job, who is the last before God to address the man who was hit by so much misery, confirms this dating. Elihu is the son of Barakel, who came from Buz, a place that was named after a son of Nahor, a brother of Abraham (Genesis 22:20-22). But what use is it for us to know that Barakel was the name of Elihu's father?

The only thing we may conclude from this reference to Barakel is that we seem to meet a family that was living close to God. The name Barakel seems to point in that direction. And when he gets a son himself, he chooses the name Elihu, which means: 'He is my God.' Apparently, God played an important role in this family.

We often see how nasty characteristics and bad customs are handed down in a family from the parents to the children. But, fortunately, there are also (even today) happy families that succeed in transmitting their faith and trust in God to the next generation.

My prayer

Lord, help me to do all I can to pass my faith in You on to the next generation.

22 February

Barnabas (son of consolation)

Who and when? A Levite, originally from Cyprus; he introduced Paul to the church in Jerusalem; went with Paul on a missionary journey.

Want to know more? Read: Acts 4:36, 37; 9:26-31; 15:25-41; Colossians 4:10.

Thoughts for today

We can say many good things about Barnabas. He was a gifted preacher of the Gospel. But he also had his problematic moments. During Paul's first missionary journey Barnabas was not the only person to accompany the apostle, but his nephew John Mark had also gone along. Unfortunately, John Mark quit halfway. Then, about two years later, when Paul wanted to embark on his second missionary journey, Barnabas was once again ready to join Paul. This, however, did not happen, because Barnabas insisted that John Mark should also be part of the team. Paul was dead set against this idea, as a result of which a bitter controversy ensued, causing Paul and Barnabas to go their separate ways.

Analysing what exactly caused the friction, it would seem that Paul wanted to play it safe. He did not want to risk the success of his project by taking someone along who in the past had deserted his colleagues. Barnabas, however, wanted John Mark to have a second chance. Paul was, above everything else, thinking of the success of the *enterprise,* while Barnabas was concerned about John Mark as a *person.*

Both perspectives are valid; but perhaps Barnabas made a better choice than Paul. Christ also gives us new chances, even when we have repeatedly failed miserably. Does that not tell us that His disciples also ought to be prepared to give a second chance to people who may, in some earlier situation, have disappointed them?

My prayer

You, O Lord, are the God of new chances. Make me willing to give people who have disappointed me a new chance.

23 February

Bartholomew

(son of Tolmai)

Who and when? Almost nothing is known about him. He is also referred to as Nathanael.

Want to know more? Read: Matthew 10:2-4; John 1:43-51; Acts 1:13.

Thoughts for today

Let us assume that Bartholomew and Nathanael are indeed one and the same person. Philip told Nathanael that he had met the Messiah. He was interested, but the details given by Philip made him suspicious.

According to Philip, this Messiah was the son of Joseph and came from Nazareth. But didn't everybody know that not much good had ever come from that place? Nazareth was not a village, far out in the countryside, but was situated near an important road. It saw many caravans passing by, and this apparently led to many unsavoury situations. This was why Nazareth had a bad reputation. And would this be the place of origin of the Messiah? That was hard to believe. Jerusalem, OK. Bethlehem, OK. But Nazareth . . . ?

We can hardly blame Bartholomew/Nathanael for his suspicions; but prejudices are an all-too-frequent phenomenon. Most of us are aware of our prejudices with regard to people in other parts of the world, or adherents of other religions. We may even have negative feelings towards the people in other regions of our own country. As soon as we find out that someone comes from a different region, we may be tempted to see them in a negative light and feel that we must be careful, because you never know. . . . The story of Bartholomew gives us cause to question such attitudes!

My prayer

Heavenly Father, I realise that I am sometimes affected by prejudices. Help me to put these aside and to let myself be pleasantly surprised.

24 February

Bartimaeus

(son of Timaeus; Greek: highly esteemed)

Who and when? Blind beggar near Jericho; was healed by Jesus.

Want to know more? Read: Matthew 20:29-34; Mark 10:46-52; Luke 18:35-43.

Thoughts for today

When, just outside Jericho, a blind beggar shouted to get Jesus' attention, the Lord called the man to Him and asked him: 'What do you want Me to do for you?' That question was rather like an open door, and the reply would not have surprised any of the bystanders. Of course, Bartimaeus wanted nothing more intensely than to recover his sight. There had been a time when he could see. The Greek word that is used indicates that this visually disabled person was not blind from birth.

There were many blind people in Jesus' day. Once in a while Jesus healed some of them. Such healing miracles were a sign of Jesus' coming kingdom. With the arrival of His reign all blind people would no longer be blind, the deaf would be able to hear and the lame would be able to use all their muscles. While on earth, Jesus did not only concern Himself with physical blindness, but He also saw the spiritual blindness of His contemporaries. He warned the people about its dangers: 'Can a blind man lead a blind man? Will they not both fall into a pit?' (Luke 6:39.)

Today, as well, spiritual blindness is endemic. It is a serious condition that must be treated by the great Healer. This is His advice: 'I counsel you to buy from me . . . salve to put on your eyes, so that you can see' (Revelation 3:18).

My prayer

Almighty God, You are able to heal physical blindness as well as spiritual blindness. Help me to see things more sharply, especially where they concern Your plans for me.

25 February

Baruch

(blessed)

Who and when? Friend and private secretary of the prophet Jeremiah. Ca. 600 BC.

Want to know more? Read: Jeremiah 32:6-16; 36; 43:1-3; 45:1-5.

Thoughts for today

The Lord decided to send a message to King Jehoiakim through His spokesman, the prophet Jeremiah, who dictated to Baruch, his secretary, what God wanted to tell the king. Most likely Jeremiah would have preferred to go to the temple and to read there aloud what God had told him: but for Jeremiah the temple was forbidden territory. Therefore, Jeremiah told Baruch to go to the temple precinct on a busy day and to read to the people the content of the scroll that he had dictated to him (Jeremiah 36:6). As could be expected, the message, which dealt with the end of Judah as an independent nation, had an enormous impact. The audience correctly assumed that the king would not be amused, and they advised Baruch and Jeremiah to go into hiding for some time.

We also know of some other moments in Jeremiah's career when Baruch played an important role. Being a prophet was not without danger, and the same was true for someone in the employ of a prophet. God was well aware of this. This is why He did not only speak with His servant Jeremiah, but also with Baruch. God knew that Baruch would experience many troubles, and therefore He communicated directly with him. The people would have to face many difficulties, but God said, 'Wherever you go I will let you escape with your life' (45:5). This is what God has said to every 'Baruch' throughout the ages, and we are no exceptions today: whatever role you play in God's work, God sees you and cares for you.

My prayer

Dear God, I trust that You will protect me, just as You protected Baruch. I thank You for this.

26 February

Barzillai (the iron one)

Who and when? A Levite and the respected ancestor of one of Israel's priestly families; son-in-law of a loyal friend and supporter of David.

Want to know more? Read: Ezra 2:61-63; Nehemiah 7:63, 64.

Thoughts for today

Valid personal documentation is essential for identification. If in doubt, ask an asylum seeker who has no passport, birth certificate or other important documents. Or ask people who claim to be descendants of important people and try on that basis to claim special privileges. If people have no documentation, it is a challenge for the authorities to allow them to get settled or to confirm that they are entitled to inherit property or possessions.

When groups of Judeans were given permission to return from Babylon to Jerusalem, a similar problem presented itself. The descendants of Barzillai, his clan members who shared the name of their distant ancestor, were convinced that they were true Levites, even though they had no documentation to prove this. Unfortunately, this meant that they could not function in the temple as fully authorised priests. In our day and age the only solution may be a special government decision, as for instance a general amnesty. In the days of Ezra there was another last resort to solve a problem. They had to wait for a priest who could pronounce a judgement by consulting the two stones (the Urim and the Thummim) that were attached to the breastplate of the high priest (Ezra 2:63). We have no way of knowing how things went for the Barzillai group, but I am sure that God somehow ensured that justice was done.

My prayer

You know, heavenly Father, that in our world we often face problems because of rules and regulations. Help us to understand that we cannot live without rules, but help us also to find a solution when we find ourselves the innocent victims of particular regulations.

27 February

Bathsheba

(daughter of an oath)

Who and when? Wife of the Hittite Uriah; later the wife of King David, after he had eliminated her former husband.

Want to know more? Read: 2 Samuel 11:1-12:25.

Thoughts for today

King David had an eye for beautiful women. One day, when walking on the roof of his palace, he noticed how a beautiful woman was taking a bath in her garden nearby. What followed after this discovery would forever soil his reputation.

David usually got what he wanted, whatever it would take. He made a plan to eliminate Bathsheba's husband - a Hittite man who served in his army - and so Bathsheba could become his wife and the mother of his son Solomon.

It remains unclear whether Bathsheba was just a victim of David's lack of scruples, or whether she was actually delighted to become the wife of the king, with all the privileges this brought her. However, in David's case there was no excuse. The temptation was formidable, but through his faith in God he could have received the strength to resist it and to let his principles rule over his impulses.

We also face countless temptations, often of a sexual nature. We can give in to these temptations, but we can also ask God for the inner strength to remain true to our principles rather than to follow our impulses.

My prayer

Heavenly Father, help me to keep my desires and impulses in check. I ask You to give me the strength to follow the principles that are based on Your instructions for me.

28 February

Belshazzar

(Akkadian: Bel, protect the king)

Who and when? Last Babylonian king; co-reigned with his father Nabonidus (from 555 BC to 539 BC).

Want to know more? Read: Daniel 5.

Thoughts for today

Just imagine: you are having a good time at a big party and then, suddenly, a mysterious hand appears that writes some mysterious words on the plastered wall. That is what happened in the palace of Belshazzar, when suddenly the Aramaic words *Mene, mene, tekel, parsin* were there for all to read. The prophet Daniel was summoned to explain the meaning of these words to King Belshazzar: God had 'numbered' the days of Belshazzar's reign. He was 'weighed in the scales' and 'was found wanting', and, therefore, his kingdom was to be given to the Medes and the Persians. God saw the immoral life of Belshazzar and how this particular party was also an utterly decadent occasion. Moreover, Belshazzar provoked the God of Israel by using the objects from the temple that Nebuchadnezzar had taken to Babylon during this orgy. Enough was enough, and God wanted to communicate this in a way the king would never forget.

In our time we often see large screens on which all kinds of messages are projected, sometimes in languages we do not understand. God does not use this modern technology to communicate with us. And He does not need to do so, for we find His messages in His Word, from which we learn that God weighs our words and actions 'in His scales'. And there may also be a moment for us when God says: 'Enough is enough.' Belshazzar's experience remains a warning that we must make sure that we never reach that point of rebellion against God.

My prayer

You know who I am and what I do. I plead with You, Lord, that, when You 'weigh' me in Your 'scales', I will never be 'found wanting'.

29 February

Benaiah

(the Lord has built)

Who and when? Commander in David's army; renowned for his extraordinary courage.

Want to know more? Read: 2 Samuel 8:18; 23:8-39; 1 Chronicles 11:10-46.

Thoughts for today

In 1 Chronicles 11 we find a list of more than thirty fearless men. Had they lived in our day and age they would each have had a good chance of scoring high in a competition for the title of 'the strongest man on earth'. We learn, for instance, of a certain Jashobeam, who 'raised his spear against three hundred men, whom he killed in one encounter' (1 Chronicles 11:11). Another, Abishai, was able to do the same. Benaiah also was a 'valiant fighter' (vs. 22), even though he was not the absolute champion. 'He struck down two of Moab's best men.' Some biblical scholars think that these 'best men' were, in fact, Moabite princes. Benaiah also killed a lion, and he defeated an Egyptian who rivalled Goliath in height and was armed with 'a spear like a weaver's rod' (vss. 22, 23).

Benaiah was not only a very strong and courageous man, and therefore of considerable value in David's camp, but he also manifested great loyalty. When at a certain point in time other important military leaders deserted David, Benaiah continued to support his king. And he also remained loyal to David's successor, King Solomon. One must conclude that his loyalty was in fact more important than his muscle power and military prowess. People may have many extraordinary talents, but if they cannot be trusted these talents may be a threat rather than a blessing.

My prayer

I thank You, Lord, for the talents You have given me. But help me to excel, first of all, in loyalty and trustworthiness.

1 March

Benhadad

(son of the god Hadad)

Who and when? One of the rulers over the Aramean kingdom of Damascus (885 BC to 865 BC); contemporary of Baasha and Ahab (kings of Israel) and Asa (king of Judah).

Want to know more? Read: 1 Kings 15:16-22.

Thoughts for today

The average Bible reader may find it a challenge to remember the history of Israel after the period of David and Solomon in every detail. Following Solomon's reign the kingdom was divided into Israel (the northern kingdom of the ten tribes, with Samaria as its capital) and Judah (the southern kingdom of the other two tribes, with Jerusalem as its capital city). Time and again these two kingdoms became pawns between the major powers that surrounded them: Egypt, Assyria and, a little later, Babylon. In addition they also had to reckon with regional powers such as, for instance, Aram.

Perhaps the worst aspect was that the two brother-nations, Israel and Judah, were often at each other's throats, sometimes with the assistance of a foreign power. This happened, for instance, when King Baasha had a quarrel with King Asa of Judah and Asa called upon Benhadad, the king of Aram, to come to his rescue. Benhadad was prepared to do this, but for a considerable price, while earlier he had seemed a loyal ally of Baasha. Maybe Baasha should have chosen his friends a bit more carefully; but the problem went deeper: had Israel and Judah not repeatedly strayed away from their God, things would have turned out much better for them.

My prayer

Loving and righteous God, You can be trusted, while human beings are often opportunistic, without genuine loyalty. Help me to be free of all forms of opportunism and to follow through when I have promised to help someone.

2 March

Benjamin

(son of my right hand)

Who and when? Youngest son of Jacob and Rachel; ancestor of the tribe of Benjamin, one of the two tribes that would later form the southern kingdom of Judah.

Want to know more? Read: Genesis 35:18; 41-45; 1 Samuel 9:21; Joshua 18:11-28.

Thoughts for today

The Benjaminites formed one of the smallest of the twelve tribes (1 Samuel 9:21), but they had a special place – just as Benjamin had a privileged position among the twelve sons of Jacob. Moses expressed this special status of the tribe of Benjamin with these poetic words: 'Let the beloved of the LORD rest secure in him . . . and the one the LORD loves rests between his shoulders' (Deuteronomy 33:12). Some prominent biblical personalities were Benjaminites: Ehud, King Saul, and Saul of Tarsus. And – not to forget – the city of Jerusalem was in the area of Benjamin (Joshua 18:28).

The position of Benjamin gives us food for thought. Numbers are usually an important factor in determining the importance of a group of people. Small groups are often not very prominent or influential. However, God has a different way of measuring. We are reminded of the words of Jonathan, when he stated that the Lord may save through many but also through just a few (1 Samuel 14:6). Christian communities that are in a minority position should not think that they cannot have any influence because they are so few in number. The important point is not how numerous a group of people are, but whether God blesses them so that, like the tribe of Benjamin, they belong to the 'beloved' of the Lord, and may 'rest secure in Him'.

My prayer

Loving Father in heaven, I thank You that You are not primarily interested in size and numbers, but rather in the relationship we have with You.

3 March

Bezalel

(in the shadow of God)

Who and when? Artisan from the tribe of Judah; commissioned by Moses to make artefacts for the tabernacle.

Want to know more? Read: Exodus 31:1-11; 35:30-36:7.

Thoughts for today

Do you have an artistic talent? Do you play a musical instrument or do you write short stories? Do you quilt or are you fond of embroidery? Do you paint watercolour paintings, or do you like to model with clay? Or do you belong to the large group of people who know how to enjoy art, from the past and the present? Often the world of art has been regarded as mostly taboo for Christians. It has often been suggested that Christians must produce things that are useful! Many Christians tend to regard the making of things that just please the eye, without having any practical use, as a waste of time. And, if you are to be involved with art in some way, it should preferably be with something related to the church and religious worship. Some have concluded this from the assignment given to Bezalel and his colleague Oholiab. They were multi-talented artisans who were involved with the construction of the tabernacle - the sanctuary of the people of Israel after their exodus from Egypt. We are emphatically told that they were 'filled . . . with the Spirit of God, with skill, ability and knowledge in all kinds of crafts' (Exodus 31:3).

This applies to all our talents - also to our artistic gifts that we have received from God. We must develop those talents as much as we can, and should never use them in such a way that God is dishonoured by what we do or create. There is, however, no reason to think that everything must have a religious application: but, if we claim to be children of God, we will, of course, consider how we can also use our gifts in the context of our faith community.

My prayer

Thank You, Lord, Giver of all talents, for all the skills and abilities I have received from You. Help me to use them in a way that You can bless.

4 March

Bildad (Bel loves)

Who and when? One of the friends of Job; possibly a descendant of Shuah, a son of Abraham and Keturah (Genesis 25:2).

Want to know more? Read: Job 2:11-13; 8; 18; 25; 42:7-10.

Thoughts for today

Together with Eliphaz and Zophar, Bildad came to Job to comfort him in his misery. After they had remained silent for a considerable time, all three of these men (and later also the younger Elihu) tried to explain why Job had become the victim of so much misfortune. Bildad repeats most of the arguments of Eliphaz, who was the first of the three to speak: God does not punish arbitrarily. When such terrible things happen, as in Job's case, the person concerned must certainly have committed some very serious sins. Bildad takes the argument even a little further: the fact that Job's children were also killed must mean that they too were guilty of some major mistakes. 'Does God pervert justice?' Bildad asks (Job 8:3). Job's children perished because of their own sins, he maintains (Job 8:4).

Like countless people before him and after him, Bildad was in search for a solution to the problem of suffering. Bildad also sought to answer the question that was posed by Rabbi Harold Kushner in his best-selling book *When bad things happen to good people*: why do some people have to suffer so much misery? Bildad was unable to give a satisfying response to that question. In fact, no human being can: for evil is not just a problem; it is, first of all, a *mystery*. There will be a time when the mystery will be unveiled: but until then Bildad, and Job, and all of us, must hang on to our faith in God. He alone has the answer, and when His time comes He will share it with us.

My prayer

Help me always to trust that You are a God of love, even in moments when we are confronted with loss and suffering.

5 March

Bilhah (meaning uncertain)

Who and when? Rachel gave her maidservant Bilhah to Jacob as her concubine, in order to get additional children to her name through the services of her servant.

Want to know more? Read: Genesis 30:1-8; 35:22; 46:22-25; 1 Chronicles 7:13.

Thoughts for today

The society in which Jacob lived differed in many ways from the world that God had in mind when He created everything. There were not meant to be such differences as those between masters and slaves, or between the status of men and women, who were intended to be equals. And we may also assume that God did not want any couple to remain childless.

By the time of Jacob things had changed dramatically. When Jacob married Rachel his father-in-law, Laban, gave his daughter a female slave named Bilhah as a gift (Genesis 29:29). A relentless jealousy erupted between Leah and Rachel when Leah bore Jacob a number of sons, while Rachel remained childless. Rachel could not think of any other solution for this problem than to ask Jacob to share his bed with her servant Bilhah and through this 'detour' to ensure posterity in her own name. This plan resulted in the birth of Dan and Naphtali. Bilhah reappears some time later in the story of Jacob and his sons, when Jacob's oldest son commits adultery with her (1 Chronicles 5:1).

Our time has other customs, many of which do not correspond with God's original intentions either: but, fortunately, it will not be long until God's ideal for us will be fully restored!

My prayer

O God of all ages! When I realise how we humans have made a mess of so many things, I long even more for a restoration of Your original model.

6 March

Blastus

(shoot)

Who and when? Chamberlain of King Herod (Agrippa I)

Want to know more? Read: Acts 12:20-23.

Thoughts for today

The story in which Blastus plays a role has a very contemporary ring to it. To begin with, there was an economic boycott. Tyre and Sidon - two coastal cities - depended for their food supplies on King Herod. At this particular point in time we are dealing with Herod Agrippa I. His decision to boycott the two cities was very effective and led to a serious shortage of food. The rulers of Tyre and Sidon had no choice but to seek peace with Herod and restore their earlier relationship.

The authorities of Tyre and Sidon desperately needed some institution that could intervene, or some individual who could plead their case with King Herod. They found such a person in Blastus, a 'trusted personal servant' of the king. Whatever his official role, he had direct access to King Herod, and they were able to secure his support (vs. 20). It is not very difficult to guess how they did this. Bribery was extremely common in the ancient world (and, unfortunately, it remains a very widespread phenomenon in our day and age).

Blastus succeeded in convincing Herod to receive representatives of the two city states. The king was keen to use this opportunity to stress his own importance and gave an enthusiastic speech to the people: but, when he claimed divine honour for himself, God intervened and 'an angel of the Lord struck him down'. Blastus was present, and had a part in these unsavoury events. He is a sorry example for all time of those who abuse their position and influence.

My prayer

Almighty God, help me never to abuse my position of influence.

7 March

Boaz

(power)

Who and when? Rich inhabitant of Bethlehem; relative of the deceased husband of Ruth; he later married her; they are both mentioned in the genealogy of David – and of Jesus.

Want to know more? Read: Ruth 2-4.

Thoughts for today

When Naomi returned, with her daughter-in-law Ruth, from Moab to the region in Palestine from where she originally came, the famine which had made her flee was largely over. However, the two women were still faced with extreme poverty. Ruth had no choice but to go to the fields where the grain was being harvested, and to make use of one of the ancient rules in Israel: poor people were allowed to pick up what the harvesters left behind.

'As it turned out,' Ruth 'found herself working in a field belonging to Boaz,' so the Scriptures tell us (Ruth 2:3): but was this really a matter of coincidence? This Boaz 'was from the clan' of Ruth's deceased husband. Initially, Ruth was not aware of this, but Boaz had already heard about Ruth and knew how she had cared for her mother-in-law. He also knew that she had decided to serve the God of Naomi. Boaz realised that, according to the rules that applied in those days, he was one of the men who were eligible to marry Ruth. Ruth was totally unaware of this when she first went to Boaz's land. She saw it as a mere coincidence that she had found a spot where the workers were nice to her.

Often there are things we see as mere coincidence: but when, at some later time, we look back, we can clearly see how God has directed events in our lives.

My prayer

Thank You, Lord, that my life is not just a chain of coincidences, but that You are always in control of things.

8 March

Caiaphas (a searcher)

Who and when? High priest from AD 17 to AD 37. Son-in-law of Annas, the previous high priest.

Want to know more? Read: Matthew 26:57-68; Acts 4:5-22; John 11:45-53; 18:12-28.

Thoughts for today

The conflict between Jesus and the Jewish religious leaders further escalated after the resurrection of Lazarus. Caiaphas – the representative of the high priestly family who was in charge in those particular years – played an important role in planning to kill Jesus. In the deliberation that took place Caiaphas spoke the remarkable (and prophetic) words that it is good that one life is sacrificed if that benefits all the people. Shortly after this took place Caiaphas was to play a key role in the process that led to the death of Jesus.

His statement shows what kind of opportunist Caiaphas really was. The sanctity of a principle was not important for him. He rather followed political strategies and satisfied his power-hungry heart. If you happen to be a religious leader, this also means that you have to make compromises and ignore injustice: is that right? Honesty may sound like a good idea in theory, but some think that it is not always practical and feel that one has to be pragmatic! No wonder that Caiaphas and Jesus were in totally different camps. Jesus was truth and honesty personified. He was motivated by love, not by power or expediency: and that is what He expects from His followers.

My prayer

Almighty God: give me the will and the courage not only to be pragmatic, but always to follow my principles first.

9 March

Cain (one acquired)

Who and when? Firstborn son of Adam and Eve; the first murderer.

Want to know more? Read: Genesis 4; Hebrews 11:4.

Thoughts for today

Many people would like to get a place in the annals of history as the 'first' to accomplish a particular feat. Who was the first man to reach the North Pole? Several candidates compete for that honour, but in all likelihood the first person to actually stand on the North Pole was Robert Edwin Peary; but we will never be totally sure. Who was the first European to reach 'the new world'? Was it indeed Christopher Columbus in 1492? Perhaps so, but there are numerous other theories. Who invented printing? Was it the Dutchman, Laurens Janszoon Coster? Or does the German, Johannes Gutenberg, qualify for that honour?

However, there is no uncertainty about some other 'first' places. Neil Armstrong was without any doubt the first man who, in 1969, set foot on the moon. Likewise, there is no uncertainty about who was the first murderer. That was Cain. He did not kill his brother as the result of an unfortunate set of circumstances. Nor was it something that started as an insignificant difference of opinion which then ran completely out of control. Neither was the victim an anonymous person who happened to be in the way. It was premeditated murder: and, worse still, it was fratricide. 'Now Cain said to his brother Abel, "Let's go out to the field." And while they were in the field, Cain attacked his brother Abel and killed him' (Genesis 4:8).

Cain was the first: but this did not entitle him to a place in some gallery of honour. It meant his downfall. Not all first places are desirable!

My prayer

Lord, You know how we often aspire to be first. Make us aware that it is not always good to aspire to be the first or the best.

10 March

Caleb (dog)

Who and when? One of the twelve spies who were dispatched from Kadesh-Barnea to explore the 'promised land'.

Want to know more? Read: Numbers 13; 14; 32; Joshua 14:6-14.

Thoughts for today

The people who in a miraculous way had left Egypt under Moses' leadership had arrived at the borders of Canaan. Before taking possession of the 'promised land' it seemed wise to explore what could be expected. For that purpose twelve men – one from each tribe – were chosen to inspect the unknown. This was the assignment Moses gave them: ' "Go up through the Negev and on into the hill country. See what the land is like and whether the people who live there are strong or weak, few or many. What kind of land do they live in? Is it good or bad? What kind of towns do they live in? Are they unwalled or fortified? How is the soil? Is it fertile or poor? Are there trees on it or not? Do your best to bring back some of the fruit of the land." It was the season for the first ripe grapes' (Numbers 13:17-20).

Caleb was one of the men who were sent out with these instructions. Together with Joshua he came back with a minority report. While ten of the twelve 'spies' lamented the impossibility of ever taking possession of this land, Joshua and Caleb said: 'Do not rebel against the LORD. And do not be afraid of the people of the land, because we will swallow them up. Their protection is gone, but the LORD is with us. Do not be afraid of them' (Numbers 14:9). The faith of Caleb and Joshua was rewarded. Forty years later they were the only ones of the twelve who had been sent out to explore the 'promised land' who eventually settled in it.

My prayer

Let me realise, almighty God, that I must always depend on Your help, but also that with that help I can do the humanly impossible.

11 March

Chloe

(young sprout)

Who and when? Member of the church in Corinth in the days of Paul.

Want to know more? Read: 1 Corinthians 1:11.

Thoughts for today

Paul was not the kind of evangelist who held a short campaign, established a group of believers and then quickly moved on without ever looking back. He continued to feel a definite responsibility for the people he had brought to Jesus Christ. He would visit them again when he was in the area, would send a fellow apostle to find out about the state of the new church, or would write them a letter. He also followed that pattern with regard to the church in the Greek city of Corinth. Paul wrote a number of letters to these new Christians, two of which found their way into the New Testament.

Of course, two thousand years ago, it was much more complicated to stay in touch with people who lived far away than it is today, in our time of emails, Facebook and WhatsApp. Nonetheless Paul would receive regular messages through people who had travelled to places he himself had visited earlier. An example was how he received news from Corinth. He got this through Chloe, and then through 'some of Chloe's household'. This news was so disconcerting that Paul decided to write a long letter to the Corinthians. We may assume that Paul did what he could to check whether the news that had reached him was correct: for there is a world of difference between gossip that has no basis in fact and alarming messages that demand an immediate response. Gossip is not worth paying any attention to, but when we receive messages that demand our input and reaction we must do what we can to respond promptly and adequately – especially when it concerns people we see as our friends and/or fellow-believers.

My prayer

Help us, Lord, to react in the right manner when we get news about people who are dear to us.

12 March

Christian

(follower of Jesus Christ)

Who and when? Since the first century AD millions of people have referred and still refer to themselves as Christians.

Want to know more? Read: Acts 11:26.

Thoughts for today

The word 'Christian' is not a proper name in the Bible. Nonetheless, it is a name that may not be omitted in a book like this. About three billion people in today's world claim to be 'Christian'. For many of them this has only little significance. They want to make it clear that they are not Muslim, Buddhist or Hindu, but do believe there is 'something'. Their parents and grandparents were Christians, and thus this is what they are also. However, this does not mean that they have ever considered what this word really means.

Almost two thousand years ago, the first small groups of people who became convinced that Jesus was more than just an ordinary person - and that it was true that after three days He came back to life, after having been put to death on a cross - had no special name. But then, in the Syrian city of Antioch (in present-day Turkey), the name 'Christian' was introduced. People saw the difference between the followers of Christ and the other citizens of their city. The fact that these people followed Jesus Christ made them a class apart.

In the days of the apostles the name 'Christian' had a deep significance. It was more than just a label. It was a confession of faith: I connect my life with Christ. I recognise Him as the Lord of my life. Today the word 'Christian' has lost much of its original meaning. Realising this should give us an incentive to put our own Christian identity under a magnifying glass. Are we just Christians in name? Is our Christian identity mostly a matter of tradition and culture? Or are we, just like the people in Antioch, genuine followers of the Christ?

My prayer

Lord, help me to be a real follower of You - not just in name, but in all I do.

13 March

Cleopas

(the whole glory)

Who and when? One of the two disciples who, after Jesus' resurrection, met Him on the road to Emmaus.

Want to know more? Read: Luke 24:13-35.

Thoughts for today

Totally disheartened, Cleopas is on his way from Jerusalem back to his home in Emmaus. Someone accompanies him. Was it perhaps his wife? Then, suddenly, there is a third Person who asks why both of them look so sad. 'What are you discussing together?' He asks. They reply in utter amazement: 'Are you only a visitor to Jerusalem and do not know the things that have happened there in these days?'

However, the unknown Man then proceeds to show that He has complete background information. He explains to Cleopas and the other disciple the meaning of the recent events. He tells them, on the basis of scriptural evidence, what had to happen with Jesus, but also that, after what happened, not everything is lost. Not at all. After some urging to stay for a meal, Jesus accepts the invitation: and during the meal everything falls into place. Their visitor is not just any visitor: the risen Lord is with them. It is an experience they will never forget.

Was there ever such a moment when you suddenly knew: the Lord has come into my life!? He has been looking for me and, happily, at last I have recognised Him! If not, do not despair, for even today the Lord may decide to walk alongside you for a while on your journey through life, and will let you know that He wants to be there for you.

My prayer

I pray, risen Lord, that You will come into my life and show me who You are.

14 March

Cornelius (of a horn)

Who and when? A commander over one hundred Roman soldiers in Caesarea. Peter acquainted him with the Gospel and baptised him.

Want to know more? Read: Acts 10.

Thoughts for today

Cornelius was a Roman citizen but he believed in the God of the country where he served. He was in charge of the garrison in the port city of Caesarea. God wanted Cornelius to know more about Him, after he had prayed for 'more light'. In a vision Cornelius received instructions on how he could find someone who would help him in his spiritual quest. He was to send men to Joppa, a town some 50 kilometres from where he lived. The apostle Peter was staying there at a location that was specified.

Cornelius did not hesitate. He sent 'two of his servants and a devout soldier who was one of his attendants' (Acts 10:7) to Peter with the request that he would come with them. This brought Peter no mean embarrassment. Could he go and share the Gospel with a non-Jew?

Immediately another question presented itself. Why did Peter have to go to Caesarea? Could the angel who had given Cornelius instructions in his vision, of how he could get in touch with Peter, not also have provided the information that Cornelius was seeking? Of course, the angel could have done this. It was possible for God to instruct His angels to proclaim the Gospel to all human beings. But that is not how God operated in the first century, and neither is it His method in our day and age. He wants to use people to tell other people about Jesus and His plan of salvation. This applied to Peter and it still applies to all of us.

My prayer

Lord, remind me today, when I meet other people, that I have a responsibility to use every opportunity that presents itself to tell them about You.

15 March

Crescens (growing)

Who and when? An associate of Paul who was given an assignment in Galatia, an area in Asia Minor.

Want to know more? Read: 2 Timothy 4:10.

Thoughts for today

Paul wrote his second letter to Timothy during his imprisonment in Rome. Within thirty years the good news had spread to a large part of the Middle East and even further. The churches that had been established remained in touch with each other. This was through letters, but also through personal visits. At the end of the second letter to Timothy we get an interesting glimpse of the network that existed (4:9-13). Paul wants Timothy to visit him as soon as possible in Rome, together with John Mark, and to visit Troas en route. In the meantime Titus has left for Dalmatia (modern-day Croatia) and Tychicus has been sent to Ephesus. Paul also mentions that Crescens has left for Galatia. Some manuscripts of the New Testament do not refer to Galatia, but to Gaul. This reading is not totally implausible, since there are other traditions that inform us how the Gospel reached France at a very early date.

In our time of fast and cheap means of communication it seems as if travel is no longer so important. Indeed, using Skype and the streaming of committee meetings and larger gatherings can be a great advantage, but these things can never completely replace personal contact. Those of us who have children, parents or friends in far-away countries do not only want to send emails, but also want to be physically with them from time to time. In a church, also, personal contact cannot be missed. Paul had already understood this important fact.

My prayer

We thank You, Lord, for the many possibilities we have today to communicate with others over short and long distances. But let us never forget the importance of personal contact.

16 March

Cyrus (Persian, Kores: shepherd)

Who and when? Cyrus, also known as Kores, was king over Medo-Persia; put an end to the Babylonian empire (539 BC).

Want to know more? Read: 2 Chronicles 36:22, 23; Isaiah 44:28; 45:1-13; Ezra 1:1-4; Daniel 1:21; 6:28; 10:1.

Thoughts for today

Isaiah lived and worked as a prophet in the eighth century BC. About two centuries later, in the first year of his rule, Cyrus allowed the Judeans to return to Jerusalem (Ezra 1:1). But Isaiah had already prophesied about the decision that Cyrus would take, even mentioning him by name! This is what Isaiah said about Cyrus: 'He is my shepherd and will accomplish all that I please; he will say of Jerusalem, "Let it be rebuilt," . . . This is what the LORD says to his anointed, to Cyrus, whose right hand I take hold of to subdue nations before him . . . so that you may know that I am the LORD, the God of Israel, who summons you by name' (Isaiah 44:28; 45:1, 3).

Not all prophetic statements were predictions, but here is one that clearly was. At some future time there would be a man named Cyrus/Kores, who would be called by God to play an important role in God's plan for His people. God stated through Isaiah: 'I will strengthen you [Cyrus], though you have not acknowledged me' (Isaiah 45:5). How are we to interpret these words? Did Cyrus not have his own will and could he perhaps have refused to let God's people leave Babylon? We could ask many difficult questions. However, we can be certain that in one way or another God's plans are executed. It is as the old spiritual tells us: 'He's got the whole world in His hands!'

My prayer

Thank You, Lord, that You know all things from the beginning and that You even use people who do not know You to expedite Your plans.

17 March

Dan (judge)

Who and when? Dan was the fifth son of Jacob and the first of Bilhah, the servant of Rachel.

Want to know more? Read: Genesis 30:5, 6; 49:16, 17.

Thoughts for today

We know very little about Dan. He was one of Jacob's twelve sons. When Jacob's favourite wife, Rachel, could not conceive, she arranged that her servant Bilhah would provide offspring in her name. Rachel could not live with the idea that her rival Leah gave birth to one son after the other, while she was denied that privilege.

From Genesis 49 – the chapter that relates how Jacob at the end of his life blessed all his sons – we do not get a very positive picture of Dan. Jacob compares him with 'a serpent by the roadside' (vs. 17). Might that be the reason why the name 'Dan' does not figure in the symbolic description of God's people at the end of time? In Revelation 7 God's people are pictured as the 144,000 who have remained loyal to their Lord. They come from all the tribes of Israel, but Dan is left out, along with Ephraim.

In Judges 18 we find that Dan's posterity, the tribe of Dan, was guilty of horrible forms of idolatry. Is this why the name Dan was omitted in John's symbolic list of all who belong to the people of God? Ancestry or status plays no role in the question of who are regarded by God as His people. The only things that count are whether (a) we have accepted by faith His offer of salvation; (b) we have been honest in our dealings with those around us; and (c) we are loyally serving God in the way He has instructed us. When this is not the case, we disappear into nothingness, just like Dan!

My prayer

Lord, I want to remain Your loyal disciple and want to be part of that great multitude that will enter Your eternal Kingdom.

18 March

Daniel (God is my judge)

Who and when? A prominent prophet. He was a Judean prince who had been deported to Babylon in 579 BC. He occupied high positions at the Babylonian and Persian courts respectively, with his career stretching over 67 years.

Want to know more? Read: the book of Daniel, especially chapters 1-6.

Thoughts for today

Daniel and three other young men were enrolled in an intensive course of Babylonian language and culture as soon as they had arrived from Judah. The Babylonian king wanted them to become fluent in the Chaldean language and they would be trained for diplomatic service.

It must have been difficult for someone like the young Daniel to be forced to leave his family and his country. He was wrenched away from all that he had been used to, and suddenly found himself in a totally new environment, where he could not understand the people, had to get accustomed to strange food, and had to adapt to many completely new customs. He was not even allowed to keep his own name, but was renamed Belteshazzar.

Although he was prepared to do his best to adapt to his new situation, it was still quite risky for Daniel to openly state that he did not want to forsake his religion. He wanted to remain obedient to his God, even if that was against the rules of the court. This required an enormous degree of courage. Fortunately, Daniel was able to show that kind of courage and commitment to his God. He soon experienced that God had not abandoned him in this foreign land, but would help him time and time again. This is what God is like. He expects us to remain loyal to Him, but will help us when we meet obstacles on our journey with Him. We may experience this even today.

My prayer

Heavenly Father, help me to remain loyal to You, even when I find obstacles in my way.

19 March

Dathan (strong)

Who and when? Together with his brother Abiram and the Levite Korah, Dathan rebelled against Moses' leadership.

Want to know more? Read: Numbers 16; 26:5-11.

Thoughts for today

Many people find it difficult to accept the authority of others, especially when they regard themselves as more qualified for that role. Even in ancient times this was already a fact of life. Together with his brother Abiram and the Levite Korah, and some 250 supporters, Dathan resisted the leadership of Moses and Aaron. This group consisted of 'well-known community leaders who had been appointed members of the council' (Numbers 16:2). Moses sent word to Dathan and his brother that they were to come to him and give account of their rebellion. However, they refused. Who, after all, were these men, Moses and Aaron, that they could order them around!

We must relate to people 'above' us. Those who cannot accept the authority of superiors will have problems. Even though before God we all share the same status, in society we have very different roles.

In the church we must also recognise that some men and women have a leading role, and that we must respect them in those roles. Admittedly, not all men and women are so directly appointed by God as happened in the case of Moses and Aaron, but we may have the confidence that the right men and the right women will get the right responsibilities, as long as a faith community observes careful procedures and asks for the guidance of the Holy Spirit. We may be disappointed when we are not chosen, or the people we had preferred are passed by, but God expects us to respect those who have been chosen and not to compete with them or make their life difficult. The story of Dathan has not lost its relevance for our time.

My prayer

Heavenly Father, forgive me if I have not always shown due respect for the men and women who lead the church on Your behalf.

20 March

David (beloved)

Who and when? The youngest son of Jesse; was anointed king by the prophet Samuel; succeeded Saul as Israel's king. David authored many of the Psalms. He reigned from ca. 1011 BC to ca. 971 BC.

Want to know more? Read: 1 Samuel 16 to 1 Kings 2; Psalm 51.

Thoughts for today

There are but few persons to whom the Bible has devoted more chapters than it has for David. In the New Testament Jesus has, of course, first place, but in the Old Testament Abraham, Moses and David are the champions. David was a gifted and multifaceted leader, who put his country and his people on the map around 1000 BC. He was a musician and a great poet. He was courageous and undaunted on the battlefield. He developed Jerusalem as his capital, built a representative palace and made preparation for the building of a magnificent temple complex.

However, David also made some very serious mistakes. Just think of the way in which he eliminated Uriah and made Bathsheba his wife (2 Samuel 11); the census that he organised against God's express will (1 Chronicles 21); and the other low points in his life that we could mention. But, in spite of this, he is referred to in the Bible several times as a 'man after [God's] own heart' (1 Samuel 13:14; Acts 13:22).

David was an imperfect person: but God was very close to him and forgave him his mistakes. That gives all of us great hope, because we have all committed serious wrongdoings; but He will never abandon us, as long as we always return to Him.

My prayer:

Lord, I make many mistakes, but I want to be someone 'after Your own heart'. I thank You for the inspiring story of David. It convinces me that You will never abandon me.

21 March

Deborah (bee)

Who and when? Prophetess and judge, who held court under the Palm of Deborah, between Ramah and Bethel; ca. 1100 BC.

Want to know more? Read: Judges 4 and 5.

Thoughts for today

Deborah was a strong and courageous woman; but she was also a prophet: that is, someone who communicated messages from God. At a given moment she had a message for Barak, a judge: namely, the time had come for Israel to wage war against the Canaanites. Barak considered this a risky plan, but did not want to refuse point-blank. He said this in response to Deborah: 'If you go with me, I will go, but if you don't go with me, I won't go.' Deborah agreed to go with him, but she warned Barak that a woman would get most of the credit for the victory they were going to gain.

The battle ended in favour of Israel. King Jabin and his people were 'destroyed' (Judges 4:24). But this is not the end of the story: 'On that day Deborah and Barak, son of Abinoam, sang this song: I will sing to the LORD. . . .' This song is to be found in the fifth chapter of the book of Judges. In many translations it starts with the words: 'Praise the LORD' (Judges 5:2).

Deborah had done a great work: but she did not want the credit for her victory. The enemy did not 'quake' before her, but 'before the LORD, the God of Israel' (5:5). She also mentioned Barak several times, and Jael, another woman who also played an important role. That clearly shows what kind of woman Deborah was. She was a hero. The people had seen her in action. That was enough.

My prayer

Dear God, protect me against the temptation to claim all the credit for myself, without giving due recognition to others. And make me always realise that You are the One to whom we owe all the victories we gain.

22 March

Delilah

(coquette)

Who and when? A Philistine woman who seduced Samson, which, eventually, became his downfall.

Want to know more? Read: Judges 16:4-22.

Thoughts for today

Four different women play a role in the Samson drama. The one, however, who has caught the imagination of so many people is the Philistine woman Delilah. Samson proved too strong for the Philistine soldiers, but was, in the end, brought down by this woman.

Did Delilah love Samson? Or were the feelings one-sided? Delilah was not forced to betray her friend: but, when the Philistines asked for her help to bring their arch-enemy to his knees, she could not resist the offer the five Philistine city kings made to her. Each of them would give her eleven hundred shekels of silver – altogether a nice little fortune. If you do not know the story, just read it and discover how Delilah, after a few failures, succeeded in robbing Samson of his strength and delivering him to the Philistines.

Perhaps Delilah did have sweet feelings for Samson and was not just a cunning betrayer. But, whatever the case, her love for Samson was not strong enough for her to reject the attractive reward. Love for money and luxury superseded her feelings for a human being. Today also, many people prioritise their interest in money and possessions, and push their feelings for their fellow human beings into the background. The best remedy against this tragic course of affairs is to involve God in all aspects of our lives. That is the only safe route to keep our value system in the right order!

My prayer

Lord, help me to have my priorities straight, and to always put people above money and possessions.

23 March

Demas

(abbreviated form of Demetrius: belonging to Demeter)

Who and when? An associate of Paul, who was with him during his house arrest in Rome, but later deserted him.

Want to know more? Read: Colossians 4:14; Philemon 24; 2 Timothy 4:10.

Thoughts for today

Demas owes the fact that his name is well-known to a negative decision. Ever since, he has been lumped together with many others who at a given point in their lives came to a similar decision. Paul writes: 'Demas, because he loved this world, has deserted me' (2 Timothy 4:10). There came a moment when Demas could not continue. He had been with Paul for a considerable time and remained loyal to him even when the apostle had lost his freedom of movement because of his house arrest in Rome.

Let us not, however, judge Demas too harshly. Paul's career was at a low ebb. How long was Demas to persevere? Life with Paul seemed to have lost all its attraction. This kind of thought must have occupied his mind. When most of the pleasant things seem to have disappeared from their lives, many people reach the place where they feel they have to be realistic and must let go of earlier ideals.

Have you never been in a situation similar to that of Demas? Was there never a moment when you wondered whether you would stay in the church? Or should even give up on your faith? If you have never yet experienced this, chances are that at some future moment you will. The name of Demas remains a warning for all of us not to surrender our ideals, even when black clouds darken the horizon of our lives. When you are close to giving up, do not seek the power to persevere in yourself, but rather in the only true Source of power!

My prayer

Dear God, give me the power to persevere and to stay with You, even if for a while things in my life look rather dim.

24 March

Demetrius

(belonging to Demeter, the goddess of agriculture)

Who and when? A silversmith in Ephesus, who saw his business threatened by Paul's activities.

Want to know more? Read: Acts 19:23-40.

Thoughts for today

Coming to faith in Jesus Christ can have momentous consequences. If Demetrius had converted to Christ he would have been obliged to change his profession. It would have become impossible for him to continue with the manufacturing and sale of miniature Artemis temples, since that would have been understood as a denial of the decision to become a Christian. But it would also have serious consequences for his business if many fellow-citizens of Ephesus would accept the message of Paul and his two colleagues. No wonder that Demetrius protested against their missionary activities. He did so by using a pious pretext. What Paul and his friends were doing, he said, was utterly offensive towards the great goddess of Ephesus, and this was something to be prevented by all means. However, the bottom line was his fear that he would lose his income.

We cannot deny that the conversion to Christianity of a major percentage of the population in a particular area may have serious social (and, thereby, also economic) consequences. From a Christian perspective most of these consequences are positive. But those who become the victims of the changes that occur may have a different view. However, if a society becomes truly Christian, in the long run everyone will benefit. If Demetrius had become a Christian, he would also have found a solution for his problem. He would have experienced that a life with Jesus Christ was far superior to continuing his trust in idols.

My prayer

Help me, dear Lord, never to allow my religious convictions to be compromised by financial concerns.

25 March

Dinah (who has received justice)

Who and when? Daughter of Jacob and Leah – the only daughter amid twelve sons; was raped by Shechem in the place with that same name; her brothers Simeon and Levi took revenge in a despicable manner.

Want to know more? Read: Genesis 34.

Thoughts for today

Genesis 34 does not make for happy reading. It is one of the horror-stories of the Old Testament, in which the lowest human instincts emerge. The story is a chain of violent sex, murder, revenge, betrayal and egoism. It is challenging to determine who exactly are the heroes and the villains in this story. In any case, the men from Shechem and the sons of Jacob both fall into this latter category.

Jacob's reactions are very dubious. He seems intent in keeping his hands clean. He remains a spectator and does not show any aversion to the atrocities that are committed by Simeon and Levi.

The violence they use is what we today would call totally disproportionate. Jacob is mostly worried about his own safety and his own reputation. He says: 'You have brought trouble on me by making me a stench to the . . . people living in this land' (Genesis 34:30).

And Dinah? Her voice isn't heard anywhere in the story. In that respect little has changed in the past few thousand years. Unfortunately, we are usually much more worried about the perpetrators of sexual violence than about its victims!

My prayer

Lord, help me, when I see terrible things happening around me, not primarily to worry about my own safety and my own reputation, but to do whatever I can to turn the tide of violence.

Dionysius

(pertaining to the god Dionysus/Bacchus)

Who and when? Listened to Paul in Athens; became a believer.

Want to know more? Read: Acts 17:34.

Thoughts for today

Paul was not very successful in Athens. As was his custom, he visited the local synagogue and engaged in dialogue with the Jews and the 'God-fearing Greeks' (Acts 17:17). He also entered into debate with those he met in the marketplace: philosophers of different 'schools' of thought, who called him a 'babbler'. In Athens Paul found himself in an environment where many different gods and goddesses were worshipped. In a meeting of the Areopagus he used this situation as a point of departure for explaining the Gospel. The Areopagus was a court of justice that met in the immediate vicinity of the famous Acropolis. Paul tried to meet these people at their own level, and even cited some of their famous poets: but what he said had little impact. His remarks about a resurrection, in particular, met with a lot of mockery.

However, Paul did reap some results. Some people became Christians. 'Among them was Dionysius, a member of the Areopagus, also a woman named Damaris, and a number of others' (vs. 34). We might compare this evangelistic outreach with modern-day attempts to share the Gospel message with secular people. Paul accepted the challenge, even though the harvest remained very modest. However, some traditions tell us that this Dionysius became the leader of the church in Athens. Today, also, we must not avoid 'difficult target audiences' in our world, even if we may expect just a few converts.

My prayer

Lord, give us the perseverance to keep on witnessing, even when we see only very modest results.

27 March

Diotrephes

('fed' by Zeus)

Who and when? False teacher in an unknown church.

Want to know more? Read: 3 John vs. 9.

Thoughts for today

Have you ever heard of Diotrephes? John mentions him in his short letter to his 'dear friend Gaius' (3 John vs. 1). John's opinion about Diotrephes is rather negative. This man wants to be first in this church to which John is writing, and he wants to have nothing to do with John. 'I will call attention to what he is doing, gossiping maliciously about us. Not satisfied with that, he refuses to welcome the brothers. He also stops those who want to do so and puts them out of the church' (vss. 9 and 10).

Pastors and elders with long experience in various churches can sympathise with John. Almost every congregation has one or more people like Diotrephes, who want to be in charge. They are seldom open to advice from others and usually speak negatively about the leaders of the church. Their comportment sometimes chases others away from the church. It is only small comfort to know that this phenomenon was already known in apostolic times. Dealing with such a situation demands a considerable range of social skills, but in the end it demands, more than anything else, patience and love.

When we - sometimes with good reason - feel irritated by fellow believers, we must not forget that we ourselves are also far from perfect and may at times test the patience of others. Moreover, we must always remember that God has unending patience with all of us: and let us always decide to keep those who act like Diotrephes did in our prayers.

My prayer

Help me, Lord, to be patient with difficult people, knowing that You have so much patience with me!

28 March

Doeg

(timid)

Who and when? The Edomite Doeg supervised the herds of King Saul. He happened to be in the sanctuary in Nob when David received the 'showbread'.

Want to know more? Read: 1 Samuel 21:1-7; 22:9-19.

Thoughts for today

It appears that the Edomite Doeg was worshipping in the sanctuary in Nob when David called there. While Doeg was there, he witnessed how the priest Ahimelech, in an extraordinary gesture, handed the consecrated bread to David, who was constantly on the run from King Saul.

Doeg told Saul about this when he met the king, shortly after this incident. The king then accused Ahimelech and his family of high treason and ordered that they should be killed. Ahimelech had helped the arch-enemy of the king, and Saul felt that this treacherous act deserved the death penalty. The soldiers of Saul's bodyguard were told to execute Ahimelech and his family.

The bodyguards, however, refused to obey their king. They did not want to touch the priests of the Lord. The only person who was willing to accept this grisly assignment to kill eighty-five people was Doeg. How could someone sink that low! Throughout history we find people who seem to have lost their conscience; and, tragically enough, there are also always leaders who tolerate the actions of those people or even use them for their own purposes. That made Saul perhaps even guiltier than Doeg!

My prayer

Lord, help us never to allow people around us to do terrible things without us even protesting against it.

29 March

Dorcas

(Greek: gazelle; also referred to as Tabitha)

Who and when? A pious, socially active woman in Joppa who was brought back to life by Peter.

Want to know more? Read: Acts 9:36-43.

Thoughts for today

In many countries in the not-too-distant past most Adventist churches of some size had a Dorcas department. It was more or less expected of the women in the church to be members. They would come together to knit and sew, and often they were also active at home making items 'for Dorcas'. The things they produced found their way, often through the diaconate department, to families with a very tight budget. Later, the items were increasingly sold through bazaars or in yard sales, with the proceeds going to some charity.

Today hardly any Dorcas associations have survived, and, as a result, the name 'Dorcas' is not as well-known to the average church member as it was in the past. That is unfortunate, for the story of this woman in Joppa can still inspire us in our day and age. When she died, people continued to speak of the good work she had done. We may assume that her work on behalf of others was already known before her death, but even more so when, after her miraculous return to life through the ministry of Peter, she could continue to help others.

The traditional Dorcas activities no longer fit in the way we live, but her idea, that women (and men) must do what they can to relieve the suffering of the weakest and most unfortunate in our society, must remain alive. Dorcas understood that this is an important aspect of what it means to be a follower of Jesus.

My prayer

Thank You, Lord, for the inspiration someone like Dorcas still brings to us.

30 March

Drusilla

(feminine form of the Roman name Drusus)

Who and when? The Jewish wife of the Roman procurator who governed Judea and Samaria on behalf of the Romans from ca. AD 52 to ca. AD 60.

Want to know more? Read: Acts 24:24-27.

Thoughts for today

Felix, the husband of Drusilla, is a historical figure who is mentioned in non-biblical sources. He married three times. His first wife was Drusilla, a granddaughter of Antony and Cleopatra. His second wife had the same name. She was the daughter of King Herod Agrippa I. For this Drusilla, her marriage with Felix was also her second marriage.

Drusilla met Paul when he was incarcerated in Caesarea. We read in Acts 24 that Felix and Drusilla came to the prison to talk with Paul. We can only guess what moved them to do so. It was certainly not very common that the wife of a Roman official would visit a prisoner. Had she become interested in this man who had lost his freedom because of his religious convictions? Did her Jewish ancestry play a role? Whatever the reason: she wanted to know more about this Jesus.

During his ministry Paul did not confine himself to relating a few anecdotes about the activities of Jesus. He crossed all the 't's and spoke 'on righteousness, self-control and the judgment to come'. There is no indication that Paul's words had any impact on Felix and Drusilla. Nonetheless, they will – just as all of us – have to face that 'judgment to come'. Perhaps at some later time Drusilla and her husband Felix gave further thought to these words of Paul. And who knows whether, because they may eventually have taken these words to heart, they will be declared forgiven and saved in that future judgement.

My prayer

I realise, dear God, that I do not have to fear the judgement as long as I commit myself to You. I want to thank You for this.

31 March

Ebed-Melech

(servant of the king)

Who and when? An Ethiopian eunuch in the employ of King Zedekiah (reigned from 597 BC to 586 BC). Played an important role in the rescue of Jeremiah from a deep pit.

Want to know more? Read: Jeremiah 38:7-13; 39:15-18.

Thoughts for today

Ebed-Melech is an example of extraordinary courage. He hears that his master, King Zedekiah, has allowed the enemies of the prophet Jeremiah to throw him into a deep pit. There is no water in this cistern, but the prophet 'sank down into the mud' (Jeremiah 38:6). Not an enviable situation; the more so, since Jeremiah has nothing to eat. Ebed-Melech picks up his courage. He goes to the king and speaks his mind. What has happened here, he says, is a crime. How could His Majesty allow this?!

The king gives Ebed-Melech permission to pull Jeremiah from the cistern. This, apparently, is not without danger, for he takes thirty men along to do the job. The story contains a few interesting details about how they hoisted the prophet from the muddy depth of the pit. Jeremiah is then given lodgings in the barracks of the palace guard.

Later this servant of the king is told that he will be saved when in the very near future Jerusalem will be taken and destroyed by the Babylonians. It shows that God does not forget our courageous acts on behalf of other people, even though at the moment when we perform these acts we do not know what will follow them.

My prayer

Faithful God, I also want to be courageous when I see that other people are treated unjustly. Help me in such moments not to think only of myself, but give me the guts to stick out my neck for others.

1 April

Eglon

(circle or chariot)

Who and when? A cruel Moabite king in the time of the judges; was killed by the judge Ehud.

Want to know more? Read: Judges 3:12-30.

Thoughts for today

The biblical story does not show much sympathy for this Moabite king. Eglon was both feared and hated by the Israelites. After having conquered Jericho, he cruelly oppressed Israel for some eighteen years. The chronicler who preserved the stories of the judges for us interpreted this as a divine punishment for all the wicked things God's people had done. But after some time God intervened and 'gave them a deliverer' (Judges 3:15).

When Ehud, the liberator, arrives to pay the taxes that are due to Eglon, he succeeds in arranging a private audience with the Moabite king. After Ehud has been ushered into the presence of the king, and all servants have left them, the king excuses himself for a toilet visit, before their meeting begins. Ehud uses this opportunity to attack the king with his sword. The king is very obese and cannot dodge the attack or defend himself. The palace security is apparently far from watertight and Ehud is able to escape. This event becomes the prelude for an attack on Moab. 'That day Moab was made subject to Israel, and the land had peace for eighty years' (Judges 3:30).

Some immediately see God's hand in all kinds of unexpected events. However, in most cases some very human factors also play an important role. Yet somehow God is involved, although it may take some time before that becomes visible.

My prayer

Father in heaven, give me the confidence that, somehow, You are also involved in many of the 'strange' things that may happen to me today.

2 April

Ehud

(union)

Who and when? The judge who killed the king of Moab.

Want to know more? Read: Judges 3:12-20.

Thoughts for today

Yesterday we saw how, through a shrewd plan, Ehud, the judge, was able to eliminate the Moabite King Eglon. The story shows us that many things that happened in those ancient times were facilitated by small-scale events. This explains how Ehud could rather easily penetrate the 'palace' of his enemy. But the story also mentions all kinds of very human details. We learn, for instance, that Eglon suffered from serious obesity. And we also hear how he was struck down during a sanitary pause.

Ehud is described as being left-handed, a seemingly unimportant detail that is hardly worth recording. On closer inspection, however, it begins to make sense. Right-handed people would conceal their swords or daggers on the left side of their bodies for quick access. Ehud had fooled the guards by keeping his weapon on the right side and using his left hand to stab the king, something that portrays him as a real human being of flesh and blood.

The men and women of the Bible were people such as we are. It is an aspect of the way in which the Bible is written that brings God's Word closer to us. God wants to be involved with people of flesh and blood - then, and also now. He touches the lives of ordinary people, with all their peculiarities and in all the situations, often strange, in which they find themselves; and - whether we are right-handed or left-handed - God's hand can guide us if we allow Him to do so.

My prayer

Lord, You know me with all my special characteristics and habits. I thank You that I may come to You, just as I am, and can ask for Your guidance.

3 April

El Roi

(the God who sees)

Who and when? One of the names of God in the Old Testament.

Want to know more? Read: Genesis 16:7-14.

Thoughts for today

When Hagar is in the wilderness, together with her son Ishmael, she does not know what to do. But she finds comfort in the thought that God sees her, even in this terribly difficult situation. She addresses God with a meaningful name: El Roi. She says: ' "You are the God who sees me," for she said, "I have now seen the One who sees me" ' (Genesis 16:13).

Hagar was glad that God sees everything – that He is the El Roi. This is in sharp contrast to what many people experience when they realise that God sees everything; for this means that nothing remains hidden from Him, and that all their poor decisions and the things they mismanaged through the years, and all they still do wrong, are registered with God. For many people, the idea that God sees everything is frightening rather than comforting.

Hagar described God as a 'God who sees'. She knew that this kind of seeing was not a matter of control and judgement. The fact that God sees us means that He cares for us and that we can always count on His help. He keeps His eyes on us, not out of mistrust or to catch us in some mischievous act, but because He loves us. He sees us, just as parents want to keep their small children within their sight, because they want to protect them and come to their aid whenever they need them.

My prayer

I thank You, heavenly Father, that You are a God who sees me, because You love me. It puts me at ease that You never lose me from Your sight.

4 April

El Shaddai

(God the Almighty)

Who and when? One of the names given to God in the Old Testament.

Want to know more? Read: Exodus 6:2, 3; Psalm 91:1.

Thoughts for today

The names of the men and women of the Bible often have a deep significance. Parents did not just choose a name for their child that happened to be in fashion. Instead they wanted to express their hopes and expectations for their newborn son or daughter in a specific name. The Bible informs us that God also has a name, or rather many different names. Many of these names are combinations of El and some other word. The word 'El' means 'god'. It is a generic term that may be used for the gods of other nations as well as for Israel's God: but when it is used in connection with Israel's God we usually find it combined with a word that highlights one of God's characteristics. God is, for instance, often addressed as 'El Shaddai'. Most probably 'Shaddai' means 'unlimited power'. Therefore, 'El Shaddai' means 'God Almighty'.

When we think about God, His power is one of the characteristics that immediately come to mind. But how do we understand His unlimited power? As human beings we know that our power is painfully limited. We must constantly face our lack of power and the limitations of our possibilities: and, thus, we cannot imagine what 'almighty' really means. Can God do anything He wants to do? If we answer that question in the affirmative, we inevitably wonder why He does not intervene in the many things in this world that go so wrong.

There are many questions we cannot solve. But we can be sure that God's limitless power and love are the guarantee that eventually all will be well - with this world and with each of us individually. Thank You, God, that You are the El Shaddai.

My prayer

Thank You, almighty God, that, with all our limitations, we may always come to You, the Almighty One.

5 April

Eldad

(God has loved)

Who and when? One of the seventy elders chosen to assist Moses.

Want to know more? Read: Numbers 11:24-29.

Thoughts for today

When Moses had to face yet another crisis, because the Israelites once more complained bitterly about their circumstances, he called the seventy elders, who had been appointed as supervisors of the people, to the tent of meeting. God promised that He would, at this occasion, reveal Himself to Moses in a very special way. His Spirit would rest on Moses, and in part also on the seventy elders.

Eldad was one of the seventy elders. For some reason he, and a certain Medad, decided not to go to the place where Moses wanted them to go, but to remain in the camp. However, against all expectations, these two men were also touched by the Spirit and began to prophesy (vs. 26). This was reported to Moses, and Joshua became quite upset. He felt that Moses should not let this pass. Moses, however, felt that he did not need to punish them. His reaction was: 'I wish that all the LORD's people were prophets and that the LORD would put his Spirit in them!' (Vs. 29.)

Joshua wanted order and obedience. Moses emphasised the positive side of what happened, even though Eldad and Medad had not followed his instructions. Moses made clear that a leader does not have to feel immediately threatened when some people treat the rules somewhat creatively. The ultimate goal must remain the priority. In this incident the most important aspect was that as many people as possible would be touched by the Spirit.

My prayer

Almighty God, let Your Spirit touch us in the way You have chosen.

6 April

Eleazar

(God has helped)

Who and when? Third son of Aaron; consecrated as priest; a leader among the Levites.

Want to know more? Read: Exodus 6:23, 25; 28:1; Numbers 3:32; 20:22-29.

Thoughts for today

Together with his father and brothers, Eleazar served as priest during the sojourn of the people of Israel in the wilderness, before they could enter the 'promised land'. He eventually succeeded his father as high priest after his father's death.

Why did Eleazar become the new high priest, and why did he play an important role in the allocation of the land of Canaan (Joshua 14:1)? He had three brothers: Nadab, Abihu and Ithamar (Exodus 6:23). Ithamar was the youngest of the four, and it stands to reason that he was not the first in line to succeed his father: but Nadab and Abihu were older than Eleazar. They were, however, already dead when their father Aaron died. God had punished them because they had been very negligent with regard to the instructions He had given. 'They offered unauthorised fire before the LORD,' we read in Leviticus 10:1-11.

Sometimes life takes an unexpected turn. When people take the wrong decision or make serious mistakes it can have grave consequences - for themselves and for others. Nadab and Abihu abused the opportunities that God had given them. Fortunately, Eleazar had a different attitude and remained loyal to God during his entire life.

My prayer

Heavenly Father, help me to remain loyal to You, and not to make catastrophic mistakes and throw away the opportunities You have given me.

7 April

Eli

(God is exalted)

Who and when? Priest and judge in the sanctuary at Shiloh; ca. 1050 BC.

Want to know more? Read: 1 Samuel 1-4; 1 Kings 2:27.

Thoughts for today

Eli is one of the most tragic figures in the Bible. That is true, in particular, of how his life ended. In 1 Samuel 4:12-18 we find him sitting on a bench at the roadside, near the city gate, waiting for news about the battle between the Philistines and Israel. He is now almost one hundred years old; he is obese and nearly blind. Then a messenger arrives with devastating news: the ark of the covenant will not return to Shiloh, since it has been taken as loot by the Philistines. But that is not all: his two sons, Hophni and Phinehas, have been killed on the battlefield. Overpowered by emotion, Eli falls to the ground and dies.

Most likely, Eli was a good person in many respects. But he was faced with at least one enormous problem. His sons were increasingly involved with things that were totally wrong. The Bible does not mince words when describing them: they 'were wicked men' (1 Samuel 2:12). That was bad enough in itself, but Eli simply did not have the courage to bring them to heel. He did not stop Hophni and Phinehas from officiating in the sanctuary; and so things went from bad to worse.

The story of Eli teaches us that we should never allow things that are absolutely wrong to continue. Instead we should do what we can to deal with them. If we fail to do so, a chain of events may be set in motion with fatal consequences. Eli received a number of warnings, which he did not heed. May the Lord keep us from making the same kind of mistakes.

My prayer

Help me, heavenly Father, to stand up against evil things and, as much as I can, resist the wickedness around me.

8 April

Eliashib

(God restores)

Who and when? A high priest after the Babylonian captivity; he played an important role in the restoration of Jerusalem's walls. Circa 445 BC.

Want to know more? Read: Nehemiah 3:1-32; 13:1-14.

Thoughts for today

If our only knowledge of Eliashib had been from Nehemiah 3, we would have had a rather positive impression of him: but later on we discover that he had far too close ties with the people who wanted to thwart the work of those who had returned from Babylon. However, in our meditation for today we will focus mainly on the first phase of his ministry. In Nehemiah chapter 3:1 we read: 'Eliashib the high priest and his fellow priests went to work and rebuilt the Sheep Gate.' Taking part in the rebuilding of the defence structures around the city was not usually part of the job description of the high priest; but in a time of crisis he was, together with many other spiritual leaders, prepared to roll up his sleeves and do heavy manual labour.

There are people – and there always have been – who will never do anything that is not part of their formal task. They will say: 'I was not hired to do that.' Of course, the terms of a labour contract must always be taken seriously. But there are occasions when we must temporarily forget about those contractual terms, and together with others put our shoulders under some urgent work. When special circumstances arise, we should not regard ourselves as too good or too important to help, even if it concerns the kind of work that is normally not something we would get involved with.

My prayer

Heavenly Father, make it clear to me when I must get involved, even if it concerns things that are not part of my 'normal' task. Help me to be prepared to join others in doing what needs to be done.

9 April

Eliezer

(my God is a helper)

Who and when? Servant of Abraham; ca. 1900 BC.

Want to know more? Read: Genesis 15:1-6; 24.

Thoughts for today

There are at least ten biblical persons with the name Eliezer. The best-known among them is the servant of Abraham. He was a servant, but at the same time someone who was very close to his master. Abraham had even thought of the possibility of making Eliezer his heir, when it looked as if he would not have any posterity of his own (Genesis 15:3). There is no further mention of this Eliezer by name, but we have good reason to assume that he was the one charged by Abraham to go in search of a suitable wife for his son Isaac.

Eliezer was given a difficult task: to find a wife for the son of his master - someone who would have a similar cultural background. Abraham did not want a Canaanite girl as his daughter-in-law, but someone from his own native area. We learn from the description of Eliezer's journey and his approach to his assignment how creative he was. But there is also another aspect that draws our attention. Eliezer is pictured as a man of prayer. When, together with his entourage, he arrived in the region where his master had his roots, he first communed with God: 'O LORD, God of my master Abraham, give me success today, and show kindness to my master Abraham' (Genesis 24:12), and then he sketched a desired scenario.

It is important to devise solid plans when we have to deal with a problem, but God is always the first One to be consulted. Only then can we move ahead with confidence.

My prayer

Help me, Lord, never to forget to involve You in my plans.

10 April

Elihu

(he is my God)

Who and when? The fourth discussion partner of Job, who joined the 'friends' towards the end of the story.

Want to know more? Read: Job 32–37.

Thoughts for today

When the three 'friends' of Job have had their say, Elihu appears on the scene. He is younger than the others and says he knows his place. This was proper in a society in which age was respected and wisdom was thought of as mainly the domain of the elderly. But little remains of his reticence once Elihu starts speaking. He has become extremely irritated by what Job's friends have said, as well as by the arguments Job has put on the table in his own defence. But, surprisingly enough, he advocates a similar theory. He sees Job's misery primarily as a corrective measure, whereby God wants to call Job to order. 'God is exalted in his power. Who is a teacher like him? Who has prescribed his ways for him . . . ?' (Job 36:22, 23.) God 'does great things beyond our understanding' (Job 37:5).

Job does not respond any further to what Elihu adds to the accusations Eliphaz, Bildad and Zophar have already bombarded him with; and neither is Elihu mentioned in the divine response at the end of the book of Job. It seems that he was less important in God's eyes than in his own. In our day and age we would not object when a young person joins a discussion after several participants have already had their say: but, whatever our age, we must be hesitant in suggesting that we have the one and only correct solution for a complex problem. Unfortunately, we meet many people who claim to be modest, but are rather the opposite in actual practice. In fact, it is striking to see how many people, like Elihu, are immodest in their modesty!

My prayer

Help me, Lord, to be modest and not to pretend that I have a quick solution for problems that have been too difficult for others to solve.

Elijah (the Lord is my God)

Who and when? A prophet in the time of Ahab (reigned from 873 BC to 852 BC) and Jezebel. Resisted the cult of Baal.

Want to know more? Read: 1 Kings 17-19; 2 Kings 2:1-18.

Thoughts for today

During a long period of famine God sent His servant Elijah to a widow in Zarephath, near Sidon. Elijah asked her for some water and a piece of bread. However, the poor woman had nothing left to give away. She only had a little residue of oil and a handful of flour, enough to make one small loaf of bread for herself and her son. After that she and her son would be doomed to die from hunger. Elijah tested her faith. He asked her to go ahead and bake the bread and then share it with him. He promised her that God would perform a miracle for her. As long as the famine continued, the oil and the flour would, in some miraculous way, be continuously replenished.

The woman showed an unbelievably strong faith. She did what the man of God had asked her, trusting that the Lord would keep His promise. But let us not forget that Elijah's faith was also heavily tested. It must have been terribly difficult for him to ask this poor woman to give him the last tiny quantity of food she still had, and to trust that God would indeed do for her what he had told her. And every new day demanded an act of faith from Elijah, as he shared the last food with the woman and her son. Giving is often difficult, but accepting something that you know the other cannot afford to give can be even more awkward: and yet it can bring a real blessing to the giver as well as the receiver of the gift.

My prayer

You, Lord, who are so generous, help me to give when I am asked to, but also to be a gracious receiver when others think of me, even in difficult circumstances.

12 April

Elimelech

(my God is king)

Who and when? Husband of Naomi, originally from Bethlehem. Circa 1300 BC.

Want to know more? Read: Ruth 1:2, 3; 2:1-3; 4:3-9.

Thoughts for today

Elimelech had a beautiful name. His parents must have been pious people. They gave their son this name because they wanted to express their trust in God. The question is whether Elimelech, as he grew into adulthood, let himself be guided by this motto his parents had given him for his entire life.

Some have suggested that Elimelech should have stayed in Judah when the famine broke out. He should not have gone to the pagan land of Moab; for could God the Almighty One not have cared for Elimelech and his family in Judah? After all, look at what happened to his family, it is further argued. Elimelech died in Moab; and his two sons, who married Moabite women, died there as well. Should Elimelech not have believed what, at some later time, the psalmist put in such moving words: 'The days of the blameless are known to the LORD . . . in days of famine they will enjoy plenty' (Psalm 37:18, 19)?

Often it is easy to say in retrospect what course of action would have been best. The Bible does not tell us that Elimelech sinned by moving to Moab to survive the famine. He simply wanted to care for his family. True, his family had to face serious difficulties, but many good people also meet one disaster after the other. When that happens, we ought to refrain from any judgement, as if we know what causes people's misery. Elimelech experienced what many others have also encountered: in spite of their caring attitude, they may have to face a lot of misfortune. However, Elimelech's name remains a forceful reminder that, in spite of everything, God is King!

My prayer

O God, may we always trust in You, knowing that, in spite of many tragic occurrences, You are the King over everything.

13 April

Eliphaz

(my God is pure gold)

Who and when? One of the 'friends' who visited Job when he was struck by disaster. The story of Job is to be dated in the period of the patriarchs.

Want to know more? Read: Job 2:11-13; 4; 5; 15; 22.

Thoughts for today

Eliphaz is one of Job's friends who have come from a considerable distance. He is the first one, Eliphaz, having come from Teman, and is probably an Edomite. How Job and Eliphaz became friends is not recorded. Together with two other 'friends' Eliphaz decides to visit Job, as soon as they have heard about all the calamities that have been poured out over Job. After having sat together for a full week, face-to-face with Job's distress, the discussions begin. Eliphaz is the first one to speak after Job breaks the silence. In three discourses he tries to explain the 'why' of Job's suffering. Eliphaz refers to a special experience – possibly a dream – he has had. This experience had made the fundamental reason of Job's misfortune clear to him (Job 4:12-21). As he continues speaking, his arguments become ever sharper. He is very dogmatic in his reasoning. He feels he has the right to speak his mind, for God revealed the situation to him! It boils down to this: whatever tragedy comes to us, it is the direct result of the things we have done wrong.

Eliphaz is not the first, nor the last person to think along these lines. Admittedly, there is a relationship between sin and the suffering that we may have to endure because of it: but there is not the kind of direct link that Eliphaz argues there is. And there is another problem with the way Eliphaz operates. When people are struck by pain and misery, they do not need dogmatic theories. They need love and comfort. In that area, however, Eliphaz had very little to offer.

My prayer

I thank You, Lord, that You are the great Comforter. Teach me how I may comfort people in need, instead of judging them.

14 April

Elisha (God is salvation)

Who and when? Elisha was the successor of the prophet Elijah. He was active in the Northern Kingdom during the reigns of Jehoram, Jehu, Jehoahaz and Joash, from circa 852 BC to circa 798 BC.

Want to know more? Read: 2 Kings 2:13–8:20.

Thoughts for today

Elisha is one of the important prophets of the Old Testament. But, like Elijah, he did not leave any writings for us. Be that as it may, the stories of the miracles they performed and their constant efforts to make the people return to the worship of the true God, rather than of Baal, belong to the best-known parts of the Bible.

One of the most fascinating stories is that of the transition of the prophetic office from Elijah to his disciple Elisha. In the presence of Elisha, Elijah was taken from this earth in a spectacular manner. 'In a whirlwind' he was taken up to heaven, leaving Elisha on his own. His first challenge was to cross the River Jordan. He repeated what Elijah had done, earlier that day: with his cloak he struck the water, which 'divided to the right and to the left'. Thus Elisha was able to cross the Jordan with dry feet.

The first question Elisha asks, after he has been left behind and is alone, is very striking: 'Where now is the LORD, the God of Elijah?' (2 Kings 2:14.) Elisha realises that with the cloak of Elijah he had not received some magical wonder-working power. In his work he was to rely on the same God in whom Elijah had put his trust. In the narratives that follow it becomes clear that Elisha did, indeed, put his trust in God. That makes him such a great role model for us.

My prayer

We plead with You, O God, that You always be present in our lives, as You were in the life of Elisha.

15 April

Elizabeth

(Greek, derived from the Hebrew *Elisheba*: my God has sworn)

Who and when? Wife of the priest Zechariah; at an advanced age she became the mother of John the Baptist.

Want to know more? Read: Luke 1:5-80.

Thoughts for today

They were not permitted to quietly enjoy their old age. Just as her husband Zechariah, Elizabeth was 'well on in years' (Luke 1:7) and she had come to terms with the fact that she would not have any children. Nonetheless, she did become pregnant. It happened, just as 'the angel of the Lord' had told her husband while he was performing his service in the temple. The fact that, for the duration of her pregnancy, her husband was unable to speak did not make life any easier for them. For five months Elizabeth lived in reclusion.

In the sixth month of her pregnancy this elderly expectant mother was visited by Mary, who was a relative of hers (1:36). Mary had also become pregnant, in an even more unusual way: and, at the very moment when Mary arrived at Elizabeth's house, the baby in her womb announced its presence in a way it had not done before. In her excitement Elizabeth exclaimed: 'Blessed are you among women, and blessed is the child you will bear! But why am I so favoured, that the mother of my Lord should come to me?' (1:42, 43.)

John the Baptist was as yet unborn, but his mother was already indicating by this remarkable response that he was to be the 'forerunner' of Jesus. Elizabeth expressed this in her words of greeting when she called Mary 'the mother of my Lord'. Elizabeth experienced blessings she had not in any way foreseen. Let us not forget that this is how God sometimes works!

My prayer

Dear Lord, at times when I wonder whether things in my life will ever take a turn for the better, help me always to remain open to Your surprises.

16 April

Elkanah

(God has created)

Who and when? The father of Samuel; circa 1000 BC; although originally a Levite, he was regarded as 'from the hill country of Ephraim', where he lived.

Want to know more? Read: 1 Samuel 1.

Thoughts for today

Elkanah played a secondary role in the Samuel story. He was Samuel's father and Hannah was Samuel's mother. As was quite common in those days, Elkanah had another wife, Peninnah. Elkanah had a number of children with Peninnah, but the relationship with his favourite wife Hannah had remained childless. Bible readers know the story of Hannah – how she came to the sanctuary in Shiloh, where she knelt for a silent prayer: much to the irritation of Eli, the priest, who thought that Hannah was intoxicated. When this misunderstanding had been cleared up, Eli prophesied that, within a year, Hannah would give birth to a son. It happened as predicted, and when Samuel was still a toddler he was brought to the sanctuary, because Hannah had dedicated him to God.

Where is Elkanah in this story? He remains in the background. After having received the promise that she would bear a son, Hannah went home with Elkanah. We read: they 'went back to their home at Ramah. Elkanah lay with Hannah his wife, and the LORD remembered her' (1 Samuel 1:19). But there is more to say about Elkanah. Every year he went to Shiloh to worship his God, and he made sure that the members of his family, who went with him, could also bring their offerings. When Samuel was born, Hannah did not go there that year – but, as soon as he was weaned, she went to give the child to the Lord. In the meantime Elkanah made his annual pilgrimage to Shiloh. The fact that Hannah could not accompany him did not stop him from going without her and bringing the Lord his annual offerings.

My prayer

I thank You, Lord, for the example of Elkanah. Help me also to be regular in the way in which I bring You my sacrifices.

17 April

Elymas

(not a proper name, but a title: sorcerer)

Who and when? A sorcerer in Paphos (Cyprus), who opposed Paul and tried to keep the Roman proconsul from becoming a believer.

Want to know more? Read: Acts 13:4-12.

Thoughts for today

In Paphos, a place in the southwestern part of the isle of Cyprus, Paul had to face aggressive opposition. At first the situation looked very promising. Sergius, the Roman proconsul, heard about Paul and Barnabas and called them for a visit, since he was eager to know more about their message. However, among the attendants of Sergius was a certain Bar-Jesus. He was a Jewish sorcerer and, according to Acts 13:6, a 'false prophet'. People usually called him Elymas, meaning 'seer' or 'magician'. This Elymas did his utmost to convince Sergius not to listen to Paul.

Paul did not mince words in his comments. He turned on this practitioner of the occult and said in very plain language: 'You are a child of the devil and an enemy of everything that is right! You are full of all kinds of deceit and trickery. Will you never stop perverting the right ways of the Lord?' (Vs. 10.) Elymas was severely punished by God: the so-called seer became blind, unable to see anything.

When in our day and age we want to take the Gospel to those around us, we may also discover that there are those who try to hinder or even destroy our work. Perhaps we cannot deal, or do not want to deal, with these people in quite the same way as Paul did. But it is still true that people cannot work against God's messengers with impunity. God will take care of them, just as in the past!

My prayer

Help me, dear Lord, to react in the proper way when people get in my way as I try to interest someone in Your message.

18 April

Enoch

(dedicated one)

Who and when? The father of Methuselah. He lived in a close relationship with God. His time on earth ended when God 'took him away'.

Want to know more? Read: Genesis 5:21-24.

Thoughts for today

Okke Jager (1928-1992), a Christian-Reformed pastor in the Netherlands, wrote a beautiful poem about Enoch. He took his cue from the simple words in Genesis 5:24: 'Enoch walked with God.' In this poem Enoch is pictured as a friend of God. They often met in person to talk and pray together. Then, one morning, God proposed to Enoch that they should go for a walk. And off they went. They walked much further than Enoch had expected. In fact, he saw that they had come closer to where God lived than to his own home. Enoch expressed his worries about getting home again safely.

Then God said to Enoch: 'Well, in the future you will come and live with Me for ever. Why don't you just come with Me and stay with Me from now onwards?' And that is how (expressed in very human terms) Enoch disappeared from the face of the earth after having lived for 365 years.

It is a simple story and does not answer our curiosity about what exactly happened to Enoch. But we owe him the beautiful metaphor of 'walking' with God. It suggests closeness, trust, friendship and many more things. It is a kind of closeness that ought to be the envy of every Christian.

My prayer

Loving heavenly Father, may I walk with You today?

19 April

Enosh

(man, mortal)

Who and when? Son of Seth and thus the grandson of Adam and Eve. Lived before the Flood, when people still reached a very high age.

Want to know more? Read: Genesis 5:6-11.

Thoughts for today

In my country the life expectancy for a man now stands at just over 79 years. For women the figure stands at almost 83. This is much higher than a century ago. Two hundred years ago people lived on average no longer than around forty-five years. But even the average ages of today differ greatly from the ages people reached just after the world had been created. Adam reached the age of 930, and his son Seth lived to be 912 years, while his grandson Enosh died at age 905.

It was God's original intention that man would live forever. However, man used his free will to be disobedient and this resulted in a totally different scenario. Human beings gradually degenerated after the Flood, when the average life expectancy dropped sharply. This trend continued. In some African countries people do, on average, still live about fifty years. In many countries, especially in the Western world, better food and hygiene, and improved living circumstances, have improved the life expectancy rates. Nowadays it is no exception for men or women to become centenarians!

A long life is a blessing, as long as we remain reasonably healthy and find meaning in life: but we will not equal Enosh in age. That is to say: not as long as we live on this side of death. But a world is coming in which age will cease to be important, since immortality will have replaced mortality. It is hard to imagine what that will be like. But we may trust the divine assurance that one day this will be glorious reality.

My prayer

Thank You, eternal God, for the promise that I will be forever with You.

20 April

Epaphras

(short form of Epaphroditus: beloved)

Who and when? Believer in Colosse; co-worker with Paul.

Want to know more? Read: Colossians 1:7; 4:12, 13; Philemon 23.

Thoughts for today

I have never been a prison inmate. Therefore, I do not know what being incarcerated does to you and to those around you, and I can only guess what kind of stigma you experience after getting out from jail. Most ex-detainees are not eager to tell others about their experience. Paul, however, did not keep it a secret that he was a regular inmate; but in his case there was a specific reason why he regularly ended up behind bars. That reason was his faith. His preaching caused so much resistance that his enemies were, time and time again, successful in getting him locked up. Often Paul was not the only victim, but was incarcerated together with others for the same alleged crime. This was a source of encouragement for him; and in several of his letters he mentions his joy that people visited him while he was in prison.

One of Paul's fellow prisoners was a certain Epaphras. This man has given his name to an organisation in the Netherlands that arranges for visits to Dutch citizens who are in prison in other countries. Most of the circa 2,000 Dutch prisoners in foreign jails have not been arrested because of their faith, but for smuggling drugs or for other criminal practices. It is great that there are people who care about these (mostly) men and (some) women and will make sure they get regular visits. And this applies, of course, also to prisoners in their cells in our own country. Paul would certainly have encouraged this kind of activity. It is good to remember that Jesus regards looking after prisoners as something we do 'as to Him' (Matthew 25:31-46).

My prayer

Lord, today I want to pray for all people who are imprisoned. May they sense that You have not forgotten them.

21 April

Epaphroditus

(beloved)

Who and when? Co-worker with Paul in Philippi.

Want to know more? Read: Philippians 2:25-30; 4:18.

Thoughts for today

Epaphroditus was worth his weight in gold. He was with Paul before he was sent back by the apostle to Philippi. It seems to have been a dear wish of Epaphroditus to reconnect with the believers in Philippi. Did he perhaps originally come from this city? Or had he previously worked there for some time? In any case, the Christians in Philippi knew him well, and, no doubt, they heard that he had gone through a period of ill health: 'Indeed he was ill, and almost died. But God had mercy on him' (Philippians 2:27).

Paul refers to Epaphroditus as 'my brother, my fellow-worker and fellow-soldier' (2:25). These were no empty words. Paul adds that Epaphroditus has been sent to him 'to take care of [his] needs'. Paul appeals to the members of the church in Philippi to joyfully welcome Epaphroditus. They should show their appreciation for the enormous commitment of this man. 'Honour men like him, because he almost died for the work of Christ, risking his life to make up for the help you could not give me' (vss. 29, 30).

There are still men (and women) like Epaphroditus, who serve the church with great commitment, who bring enormous sacrifices and disregard their own interests. We must show our appreciation for the work of such men and women and 'honour' them.

My prayer

Lord, we thank You for men and women who, like Epaphroditus, are willing to commit themselves to Your work in this world. Remind us that we should always 'honour' them.

22 April

Esau (hairy)

Who and when? Sold his birthright to Jacob, his younger twin brother. After a long period of estrangement the two brothers were reconciled.

Want to know more? Read: Genesis 25:19-34; 26:34–28:9; 32:3-33:16; Hebrews 12:16.

Thoughts for today

It would be fair to say that the educational strategy of Isaac and Rebekah was far from perfect. Isaac gave Esau preferential treatment, while for Rebekah Jacob was number one. Esau was the firstborn of the twins, which, according to the customs of those times, gave him special rights. But, with the assistance of his mother, Jacob succeeded through deceit to rob his brother of these rights. As a result Jacob had to flee, while Esau eventually decided to live in Seir, near the Dead Sea.

In spite of the fact that major issues had arisen between the two brothers, in the end the situation changed for the better. When Jacob returned, with a substantial entourage, from Mesopotamia, and had gone through the Jabbok experience, Esau was prepared to let go of the past. The story ends (Genesis 35:29) with the report that Jacob and Esau together buried their old father (who died at age 180).

Bitter conflicts between family members are, unfortunately, not uncommon. Often it appears to be impossible to build a bridge between the two parties: yet we must never give up, but rather keep working for reconciliation. The fact that the abyss between Jacob and Esau could be bridged is proof that reconciliation is never impossible, whatever the conflict in the family is about.

My prayer

We come to You, the Prince of Peace, and plead with You to help us in bridging the gap between us and others, or between people around us.

23 April

Esther

(star)

Who and when? A girl of Jewish descent; became queen at the Persian court (in Susa) during the reign of Ahasuerus (also known as Xerxes I), who ruled from 486 BC to 465 BC.

Want to know more? Read: Esther 1-10.

Thoughts for today

Esther saved her people from genocide by informing her royal husband about the ghastly plot that her uncle had uncovered. If you have not read the Esther story for some time, I recommend that you do so and re-acquaint yourself not only with Esther, but also with people like Mordecai and Haman.

The book of Esther is not just a tale of a *beautiful* young woman who, through an unexpected range of events, became queen. It is also the story of a *courageous* woman, who was prepared to risk her life by bringing the situation of her people to the attention of the king, and by accusing one of the most powerful men in the empire of high treason. Undoubtedly, she remembered the fate of her predecessor, Queen Vashti, who fell into total disgrace after having angered her husband.

Esther was willing to risk her own future for the sake of her principles and her people, which makes her a powerful example for us today. We may also get into a situation in which it is risky to speak our minds, or to take action, because it could start a chain of events that might cause us all sorts of problems. In such circumstances, it is essential that we have courage and full trust in God to do what our conscience tells us we should do.

My prayer

Heavenly Father, give us the courage and the trust in You to speak up when needed, and to be willing to accept major risks in defence of what is right.

24 April

Ethan

(permanently)

Who and when? A man who was famous for his wisdom; a contemporary of King Solomon; ca. 950 BC.

Want to know more? Read: 1 Kings 4:31; Psalm 89.

Thoughts for today

King Solomon owed part of his fame to his wisdom. 'God gave Solomon wisdom and very great insight, and a breadth of understanding as measureless as the sand on the seashore' (1 Kings 4:29). There were but few contemporaries who (almost) equalled Solomon in wisdom. The author of 1 Kings could only think of a few names: three brothers – Heman, Calcol and Darda – and the Ezrahite Ethan (4:31). Solomon was wiser than these four men, but they were also well known for their perception. We have no further information about the three brothers, but we know that Ethan wrote Psalm 89.

In ancient times wisdom was rated very highly. Wisdom stood first of all for the ability to distinguish between good and bad, and for the insights that result from the daily experience and communion with God. 'The fear of the Lord is the beginning of wisdom' (Proverbs 9:10). As we come closer to our own times, *knowledge* seems to have become more important than *wisdom*. Science is based on the gathering of knowledge. Today, in the twenty-first century, knowledge is still essential, but *information* now seems to be top of the bill. We are often told that it is not so important to know a lot of things, as long as we know where to find that knowledge when we need it. No one will deny that knowledge and information are of great value. But having much knowledge and dispensing a wealth of information does not automatically make us wise. Today, as in ancient times, we ought to show our appreciation for wise people like Ethan.

My prayer

I thank You, all-wise and omniscient Lord, that You have given me the ability to gather knowledge and information, but help me also to constantly seek for wisdom.

25 April

Eunice

(blessed with victory)

Who and when? A Jewish woman, married to a Greek man; mother of Timothy.

Want to know more? Read: Acts 16:1; 2 Timothy 1:5.

Thoughts for today

Paul had a very close relationship with young Timothy. At first he was Timothy's mentor; later they were fully equal partners in the Gospel work. Timothy could not have wished for a better trainer and a more competent role model. But the basis of what and who Timothy was had been laid much earlier. Paul was aware of the kind of upbringing Timothy had received. He knew both Timothy's mother Eunice and his grandmother personally, and had discovered that they were deeply committed believers. We do not know whether these two women were still alive when Paul wrote his letter to Timothy, but we do know that their faith lived on in their son and grandson. The fact that the father and grandfather are not mentioned does not mean that they did not play any role in Timothy's life, or that they did not positively influence his spiritual development. However, in many cultures – and that is true even today – the mother has the most significant role in the upbringing of the children. And often the grandmother plays an important part too. They tend to have a decisive influence on the beginning of the faith development of young children.

Increasingly we hear that parents want to give their children total freedom in matters of faith. Of course, each child will have to make its own choices, also in the area of faith. But anyone who was born in a family where faith ranks as a top priority, and who has a mother like Eunice, of whom it may be said that she had 'sincere faith' (2 Timothy 1:5), may count himself or herself as greatly blessed.

My prayer

Thank You, heavenly Father, for all mothers with 'sincere faith'.

26 April

Euodia

(safe journey; fragrance)

Who and when? Church member in Philippi.

Want to know more? Read: Philippians 4:2, 3.

Thoughts for today

Euodia and Syntyche are mentioned by Paul in one breath. There was a problem between these two women in Philippi. This is what we are told: 'I plead with Euodia and I plead with Syntyche to agree with each other in the Lord. Yes, and I ask you, loyal yokefellow, help these women who have contended at my side in the cause of the gospel, along with Clement and the rest of my fellow-workers, whose names are in the book of life' (Philippians 4:2, 3).

Euodia and Syntyche were apparently embroiled in a conflict. We are not told what the issue was. It may have been quite unimportant, but it had severely damaged their relationship. Paul calls upon them to bury the hatchet and asks a 'loyal yokefellow' (who remains anonymous) to mediate. Paul wants to see the peace restored, for together with him Euodia and Syntyche have worked hard in the Gospel work.

Paul wants to see a different kind of mentality, not only with these two sisters in the faith, but with all readers of his epistle - including those in the twenty-first century: 'Finally brothers, whatever is true, whatever is noble, whatever is right, whatever is pure, whatever is lovely, whatever is admirable - if anything is excellent or praiseworthy - think about such things. Whatever you have learned or received or heard from me, or seen in me - put it into practice. And the God of peace will be with you' (vss. 8 and 9).

My prayer

Dear Lord, You are the Prince of Peace. Help me to be a worthy representative of You and, where possible, to work for peace between people who are estranged through conflict.

27 April

Eutychus

(fortunate)

Who and when? A boy who fell from a window during Paul's sermon in Troas.

Want to know more? Read: Acts 20:7-12.

Thoughts for today

Many young people find sermons rather sleep-inducing. Whether that was true for this Eutychus remains anybody's guess. In any case, Eutychus was unable to keep his eyes open during Paul's farewell speech in Troas. That would not have been so bad, were it not for the fact that he sat on the sill of an open window. When he fell from the window he landed in an unfortunate way and died instantly.

We do not know how late it was. In all likelihood this special service was held on a Saturday evening, after the sun had set. In Bible times this would have been counted as the beginning of the first day of the week. Paul had planned to depart early next day. The accident caused a lot of commotion. The end of Paul's work in Troas could have been marred forever by this tragic event. But the boy was miraculously restored to life!

What lesson can we draw from this incident? The main lesson is not that we should find a safe place as soon as we become sleepy during a sermon. It is rather that God is always able to change a tragedy into a blessing! He can do so in many different ways. Keep in mind: God will often intervene with very happy surprises.

My prayer

Thank You, dear God, that You will intervene at the time and in the manner that You choose, when we are exhausted and lack the energy to remain attentive.

28 April

Eve

(the one who gives birth)

Who and when? The first woman, created to be Adam's partner. Together with Adam she was charged to care for the world God had created.

Want to know more? Read: Genesis 2:18–4:2, 25.

Thoughts for today

In many denominations the discussions continue about the question of whether Adam and Eve were created fully equal. How this question is answered has major consequences: for instance, for the role of women in the church and their right to be appointed in all church offices. Moreover, the fact that Eve ate from the fruit and also tempted Adam to join her in this sinful act has through the centuries continued to hang over the heads of women. When debating these issues, reference is often made to some statements by Paul that, some feel, suggest a difference in status between Adam and Eve.

It is, however, important to focus on how God wanted things to be originally. Certainly, the consequences of the 'Fall' cannot be denied. But, as we journey towards 'Paradise restored', we are entitled to do what we can to diminish or remove those negative consequences. That childbirth would henceforth be a heavy burden does not imply that we may not take any measures to make the birthing process less painful!

Adam and Eve were created as fully equal partners. Together they were charged with caring for God's creation. Disciples of Christ know that, through faith in Him, all inequalities between people, which over time have arisen, must be removed: 'There is neither Jew nor Greek, slave nor free, male nor female, for you are all one in Christ Jesus' (Galatians 3:28).

My prayer:

Help me, heavenly Father of all humankind, that I may make a contribution towards making the words of Galatians 3:28 a reality in the context where I live.

29 April

Evil-Merodach

(Babylonian: man of the god Marduk)

Who and when? The son and successor of Nebuchadnezzar on the throne of Babylon; reigned from 562 BC to 560 BC.

Want to know more? Read: 2 Kings 25:27-30; Jeremiah 52:31-34.

Thoughts for today

What kind of man was Evil-Merodach? According to extra-biblical historical sources he was an extremely cruel tyrant who, after having been on the throne for only two years, was murdered by his brother-in-law (Nergal-Sharezer).

Second Kings 25, however, gives us quite a different picture of this Babylonian ruler. When he began his reign he pardoned King Jehoiachin of Judah, who had been incarcerated in a Babylonian prison for some thirty-seven years. It may well be that Daniel, who in this period held a high position at the Babylonian court, played a role in this gesture of goodwill. In any case, the biblical story does not tell us of cruelty. Evil-Merodach spoke to Jehoiachin 'kindly . . . and gave him a seat of honour higher than those of the other kings who were with him in Babylon.' For the rest of his life Jehoiachin 'ate regularly at the king's table' (2 Kings 25:28, 29).

What portrayal of Evil-Merodach should we believe? He may have had two very different sides to his character. Perhaps, like the Babylonian historian Berossus, those who claimed that he was so cruel were strongly prejudiced against him. Often we do well to suspend our judgement about other people - past and present - since we simply do not have enough information to form a balanced opinion.

My prayer

As the great God, You are the One who judges without prejudice. We usually cannot come to a definitive conclusion since we do not have enough information. Remind us, Lord, when needed, that we should suspend our judgement.

30 April

Ezekiel (God will strengthen)

Who and when? A priest called by God to serve as His prophet. He was among the Judeans who, in 597 BC, were deported to Babylon.

Want to know more? Read: the Bible book of Ezekiel; for his calling, see Ezekiel 1:1-3:15.

Thoughts for today

Even a very cursory reading of the book of Ezekiel makes clear that Ezekiel received a very complicated assignment. This first impression becomes many times stronger when we read the entire Bible book that bears his name more carefully.

The calling of this priestly prophet was an impressive event. God knew that Ezekiel needed to get a glimpse of the other world in which God Himself lives, if the prophet was to have the strength needed for his immense task. 'Son of man,' God said, 'I am sending you to the Israelites, to a rebellious nation' – but he was not to be afraid of all the awful things they would say, for, even though they were like 'briers and thorns', God would give Ezekiel the power he needed, and 'they will know that a prophet has been among them' (Ezekiel 2:3-6). His calling was, all in all, an event that defied description. Afterwards Ezekiel sat 'overwhelmed' for seven days among his people (3:15).

Not all of us are called by God to be His prophets, like, for instance, Ezekiel, Isaiah or Daniel. And yet, as God's children, we all have a prophetic calling and must speak on behalf of our Lord. This may result in some very negative experiences when people treat us as if we are 'briers and thorns': but, if we live close to God, we may from time to time be granted a glimpse into that other world; and that gives us the power and the courage to do what God asks us to do.

My prayer

Help me, Lord, to be a spokesperson for You. And may I cause people around me to know that 'a prophet' has been among them.

1 May

Ezra (God has helped)

Who and when? Advisor in Jewish affairs at the court of the Persian king Artaxerxes. He received the assignment to return with a group of exiles to Jerusalem and begin the rebuilding of the city and the temple (457 BC).

Want to know more? Read: Ezra.

Thoughts for today

Ezra is described as 'a priest and teacher' (Ezra 7:11). Although he was clearly a multitalented man these two qualifications were probably the most defining features of this important Old Testament figure: to which is added that he 'was learned in matters concerning the commands and decrees of the Lord for Israel'.

Another important quality of Ezra was that he trusted in God and also wanted to stimulate others to have that same trust. When he left Babylon, he declined the offer of the Persian king to provide him with an armed escort (Ezra 8:21-23). He wanted to impress on his fellow travellers that their enterprise depended in all aspects on God's blessing and protection; and Ezra was also a man of prayer (Ezra 10:1).

Many positive things may be said about Ezra. They may be summarised in these words: Ezra was the kind of spiritual leader the people in Israel needed at that point in time. Such leaders are needed in all periods of history – certainly also today, both in society and in the church. Those who are at a given moment called to such a leadership role find in Ezra a leadership model that may continue to inspire them.

My prayer

Thank You, dear Lord, for leaders like Ezra. May he be a source of inspiration for us when we are called to a leadership role, in whatever position and at whatever level.

2 May

Felix (happy)

Who and when? A Roman official in Judea and Samaria, known for his cruelty (ca. AD 52 to ca. AD 58); Paul was his prisoner.

Want to know more? Read: Acts 24.

Thoughts for today

At first sight Felix seemed to be a powerful man, while Paul sat in prison, unable to do his work: but perhaps the reality was not as it appeared to be. Perhaps in reality Felix was a moral weakling, while Paul was a man with superior moral strength.

Felix had been in Palestine long enough to be wary of the political 'games' that Jewish leaders often played. He was also familiar with the 'Way', the new movement that proclaimed Jesus as Saviour, and was obviously curious about its teachings. Perhaps this is why he kept Paul in prison under less severe restrictions than would normally have been the case.

From time to time he commanded that Paul be brought to him for questioning. Paul, however, used these opportunities to tell Felix about the Gospel in very straightforward language. What he said must have made a deep impression on Felix, who began to worry 'about doing right, about self-control, and about the coming judgment' (Acts 24:25, CEV).

Felix appears to have been a cowardly man. But he was also corrupt, silently hoping that Paul and his friends would bribe him into granting the apostle a pardon (Acts 24:26). So, then, who was truly free, and who was the real prisoner? Felix was imprisoned by his cowardice and corruption, while Paul, in spite of his chains, enjoyed freedom in Christ.

My prayer

Let me, dear God, enjoy the freedom that results from fully trusting You.

3 May

Festus

(Latin: festal)

Who and when? Representative of the Romans in Judea.

Want to know more? Read: Acts 25; 26.

Thoughts for today

Porcius Festus succeeded Felix as the Roman procurator of Judea. His job came with an awkward heritage. He was confronted with a prisoner his predecessor had been unable to deal with. As soon as Festus had assumed his position, the Jewish leaders were ready to point out that Paul's case should have his immediate attention. They had a shrewd proposal. They suggested that Paul be put on transport from Caesarea to Jerusalem. That would provide them with an excellent opportunity to kill the apostle en route!

The Roman Festus had great difficulty in understanding what this business with Paul was all about. He summarised the matter as follows: there were, apparently, 'some points of dispute . . . about their own religion and about a dead man named Jesus whom Paul claimed was alive' (Acts 25:9). That was indeed the core of the issue. The tragedy was that the Jewish leaders, in spite of the fact that they had been eyewitnesses to the results of miracles performed by His followers, refused to accept that Jesus had risen from the dead. And there was also the sad aspect that Festus did not want to find out whether Paul was perhaps right in his insistence that Jesus was alive.

As ever before, we see today great numbers of people who, like Festus, do not know how to deal with Jesus. Christians are convinced that Jesus did not remain in the tomb, but rose from death on the third day. However, to many this remains a strange hocus-pocus. Our situation needs people like Paul who, with courage, persist in saying that Jesus is indeed alive!

My prayer

I thank You, Lord, for the certainty that You are alive, and that I may tell others about this.

4 May

Gad

(good fortune)

Who and when? Prophet; counsellor of David.

Want to know more? Read: 2 Samuel 24.

Thoughts for today

God often gave His prophets very uncomfortable assignments. This was also true for 'Gad the prophet, David's seer' (2 Samuel 24:11). David and Gad were well acquainted; the prophet was part of David's entourage before he became the king (1 Samuel 22:5). Nonetheless, his task was far from easy. King David had committed a grievous sin against God by persisting with this census. Now Gad was commissioned to tell David what God thought of his action. To make the assignment even more awkward, Gad was also to announce a terrible punishment for David. The king could choose from three options: several years of famine, three months of fleeing from an enemy, or three days of plague in his country. David went for the third option, which resulted in the death of seventy thousand people!

We may count ourselves fortunate that we are not, like Gad, told to go to the perpetrator of a wicked action with such a terrifying menu of options. Neither should we, at our own initiative, approach people to tell them how 'wrong' they were and that God will punish them. Yet, as Christian believers, we do have a responsibility for those people who seem to have landed in a spiral of evil and misery. We cannot simply close our eyes. We must find the courage to go to such people and warn them – with the real risk that they will react very negatively towards us. Such a step requires careful thought and prayerful preparation. But we cannot, like Cain, shrug our shoulders and utter such a sarcastic response as 'Am I my brother's keeper?' (Genesis 4:9.)

My prayer

Heavenly Father, give me the tact and the courage to warn other people when they clearly make very wrong choices.

5 May

Gad

(good fortune)

Who and when? Son of Jacob and Zilpah, the servant of Leah. Ancestor of the tribe of Gad, one of the twelve tribes of Israel.

Want to know more? Read: Genesis 30:9-11; 49:19.

Thoughts for today

When Leah could not bear any more children for Jacob, she gave, as was customary in those days, her servant Zilpah to her husband, in order that he might, through her, have more posterity. Leah's plan worked. Zilpah became pregnant twice and gave birth to two sons. Leah was excited when Gad was born. She regarded the little boy as her own son and gave him a fitting name: Gad. She explained her choice with these words: 'What good fortune!' (Genesis 30:11.)

Genesis 30 tells us how the two wives of Jacob – Rachel and Leah – lived in an atmosphere of deadly jealousy. Both wanted to give Jacob many children, preferably sons. In this process the servants Bilhah and Zilpah were enlisted. For Leah as well as for Rachel, happiness equalled a large family, but Rachel lagged behind Leah. She was Jacob's favourite wife and they tried hard enough to have offspring. Jacob, however, understood that some things cannot be forced. When Rachel said to Jacob: 'Give me children, or I'll die,' Jacob rightly replied: 'Am I in the place of God . . . ?' (Genesis 30:1, 2.)

Many people confuse 'being fortunate' with 'being blessed'. We may always ask for God's blessing. He will give that blessing in His way and at His time: and when His blessings come it is important not to regard these as good luck or as 'being fortunate'!

My prayer

Please, Lord, remind me that I should not chase good fortune, but must trust that You will bless, in a manner of Your choosing and at Your time.

6 May

Gaius

(happiness)

Who and when? The addressee of the third letter of John.

Want to know more? Read: 3 John.

Thoughts for today

Gaius was well known to the apostle John. We do not know where he lived, nor when exactly he received this short letter from John. The apostle kept this epistle rather short, since he hoped to see Gaius soon again in person. In fact we do not know much about this Gaius other than that he exercised the gift of hospitality. Itinerating 'brethren', who travelled from one church to another to strengthen these churches, could always find a place to sleep in Gaius's home.

In the biblical culture hospitality was seen as extremely important. Of course, hospitality was often also a great necessity. Travellers could not expect to find a nice hotel or comfortable motel in every town or village of some size. Many also needed physical care after having travelled for days. This was also true for the animals that served them on their journey. For itinerating Christian leaders it was important to know that they would find hospitable church members like Gaius in the places they would visit – the more so since Christian travellers often ran significant risks when proclaiming their message.

In our day and age pastors do not expect to stay for a few days with church members after having preached in the church in their city. However, it is still a privilege to experience hospitality. This does not only apply to pastors. Anyone who visits a church, whether in his own country or abroad, hopes to meet a hospitable Gaius, and hospitality is also a positive element in many other situations. In our time of mostly superficial Facebook friends, real hospitality is often sadly neglected.

My prayer

Help us, heavenly Father, to show hospitality to people within and outside the faith community to which we belong.

7 May

Gallio

(he that sucks)

Who and when? Brother of the Roman philosopher Seneca; was proconsul in Corinth in AD 51-52. Declared Paul to be not guilty.

Want to know more? Read: Acts 18:12-17.

Thoughts for today

During his career Paul got to know a number of Roman officials. Unfortunately, this was often because he was accused by his enemies of circulating dangerous ideas. This also brought him, for instance, before the tribunal of Gallio in Corinth. This man did not want to waste much time in listening to the accusations that were brought against Paul. Since the argument involved 'questions about words and names and your own law', Gallio told the Jewish leaders to 'settle the matter yourselves. I will not be a judge of such things' (Acts 18:15). When Paul left the tribunal building as a free man, the crowd (which, apparently, had followed him) set upon a certain Sosthenes, a leader of the local synagogue, who had played a role in the opposition against Paul.

Gallio saw what happened, but did not intervene when this Sosthenes was severely beaten up.

Gallio should have acted differently. He should have made clear to the Jewish enemies of Paul that religious disagreements may never be resolved by violence. And when Sosthenes was attacked by the people, he should have been protected by Gallio. Religion and violence should never go together, and religious disputes should never lead to angry physical attacks. Diversity of opinion should never cause oppression, but should always be dealt with in the spirit and the love of Christ.

My prayer

Loving Father, I want You to help me to reflect Your love when I am faced with people who do not agree with my way of worshipping You.

8 May

Gamaliel

(God has rewarded)

Who and when? Legal scholar and member of the Jewish Sanhedrin; spoke positively of the apostles; teacher of Paul.

Want to know more? Read: Acts 5:33-42; 22:3.

Thoughts for today

In general, the New Testament is not very positive about the Pharisees and the other Jewish legal scholars. However, Gamaliel, a famous scholar from a family of even more famous legal specialists, was an exception. When the apostles were arraigned before the Sanhedrin, Gamaliel strongly advised the members of this council to set them free. 'For,' he said, 'if their purpose or activity is of human origin, it will fail. But if it is from God, you will not be able to stop these men; you will only find yourselves fighting against God' (Acts 5:38, 39).

There is an ancient tradition that Gamaliel later converted to Christianity. However, any biblical evidence is absent. Nonetheless, we can only have a lot of respect for this wise man. He dared to speak his mind, even when he defended a minority position. And what he said held water: it is impossible to halt God's work. Gamaliel saw sufficient reason to keep the possibility open that the work of the apostles might, in fact, be the work of God.

Going against majority opinion may be risky. It is not the best way to make friends and it may seriously damage your career. For Gamaliel these aspects were not important enough to remain silent. His courage is a great example.

My prayer

Loving Father in heaven, give me the courage to speak my mind, even if that would make me very unpopular.

9 May

Gedaliah (the Lord is great)

Who and when? After Zedekiah had been dethroned and deported by Nebuchadnezzar, Gedaliah was installed as governor of Judah. He was assassinated after just a few months.

Want to know more? Read: 2 Kings 25:22; Jeremiah 40:7-41:18.

Thoughts for today

The name Gedaliah is not very common, but I discovered that there is a youth choir in a town near where I live with the name Gedaliah. In the Jewish community the name is much better known. On the third day of the month Tishri (September/October) the *Tzom Gedaliah* is celebrated. It is a day of fasting in remembrance of the last governor of Judah before the Exile. He reigned for a short time over the remnant of the Judean nation, before the curtain finally fell over Judah as an independent political entity.

Gedaliah did his very best to salvage what he could: but groups of Judeans emerged from their hiding places, wanting to profit from the new situation that had arisen. This made the position of Gedaliah very shaky. Shortly after he had taken office, an army officer named Johanan informed him that a certain Ishmael was plotting an attack on his life. He advised Gedaliah to eliminate this Ishmael. Gedaliah did not follow this counsel, which sadly resulted in his death. Perhaps history would have taken another turn if Gedaliah had taken the warning to heart; but perhaps we see in Gedaliah a man who did not want to make the mistake of brutally removing all his real and alleged opponents. Whatever was the case, there no longer was a future for a free and independent Judah. And only Judah itself was to blame for its misfortune.

My prayer

Father in heaven, give us the insight we need to deal with warnings that relate to things that are directed against us.

10 May

Gehazi (meaning uncertain)

Who and when? Servant of the prophet Elisha, who was active in the Northern Kingdom (ca. 850-800 BC).

Want to know more? Read: 2 Kings 4:12-8:5.

Thoughts for today

I must admit I have often felt some sympathy for Gehazi. I am sure that being the servant of a prophet was not a highly paid job. Suddenly there seemed to be an unexpected bonus. His boss received a visit of a prestigious general from Syria, who sought healing from a serious skin disease; and, indeed, this general Naaman was saved from his fatal disorder. No wonder this man was extremely grateful. He had brought a wagonload full of gifts and wanted to leave these with Elisha: but, in spite of Naaman's pressure, Elisha refused to accept any gifts.

Gehazi sees all this. We can hardly blame him for his lack of understanding for Elisha's reaction. It stands to reason that he regretted the prophet's categorical refusal to take any gifts, and that, therefore, he would not share in anything either: but what follows is indefensible. Gehazi follows Naaman, without telling Elisha, and with his smooth talking he succeeds in getting some precious objects from the general, which he then hides from Elisha.

Gehazi was not the first person, nor the last, who tried in a cunning way to seek a personal benefit when the opportunity seemed to present itself. Not all who did so were punished in the same severe way as Gehazi was. But playing the kind of tricks of which Gehazi was guilty always brings trouble. The only safe course is honesty. That is as true today as it was in the past.

My prayer

Lord, may I never give in to the temptation to avail myself of some benefits in dishonest ways.

11 May

Gershom (sojourner)

Who and when? Oldest son of Moses and Zipporah; born in Midian; ancestor of a clan of the Levites. One of his posterity was a priest in the sanctuary in Dan (Judges 18:30).

Want to know more? Read: Exodus 2:21, 22; 18:2-7; 1 Chronicles 23:14-16.

Thoughts for today

How was it to be born and to grow up as the son of Moses? Let us try to reconstruct the situation. Gershom's father, Moses, was originally a Jewish boy, but later an Egyptian prince. He had to flee from Egypt after he had killed an Egyptian in a fit of rage. Gershom was born in the region where his father had found refuge and married the daughter of the Midianite priest, Jethro. Gershom was their firstborn. He received a meaningful name. His father Moses said: 'I have become an alien in a foreign land' (Exodus 2:22).

In Midian the family lived in a desert-like environment. Moses looked after the sheep and the goats of his father-in-law, until the Lord called him to return to Egypt with the assignment to free his people from the yoke of the pharaoh. Gershom was in the midst of all these events. And, after the exodus, once again he had to be satisfied with life in the desert.

It can be a good thing to try to picture what other people around us have had to experience. Often we are just focused on our own problems, but these are frequently insignificant when compared to what others are going through. It helps to relativise our own situation when we think of what others have experienced, and to be more understanding of them.

My prayer

Dear God – You who see everything – help me to be more attentive to what other people have to go through, rather than thinking only of my own plight.

12 May

Geshem

(born in the rainy season)

Who and when? Arab; opponent of Nehemiah; one of the leaders of the tribal federation in the Syrian-Arabian desert. Ca. 445 BC.

Want to know more? Read: Nehemiah 2:19; 6:1-7.

Thoughts for today

When Nehemiah arrived in Jerusalem to lead out in the rebuilding of the walls of the city and of the temple - which had suffered serious delays - he was faced with strong opposition. This hostility came mainly from leaders of the various populations in the region. Among them were Sanballat of Samaria, with his Ammonite ally Tobiah, and Geshem, the prince of the Kedar Arabs.

First they tried to undermine the morale of Nehemiah and his people by ridiculing them. Next, Geshem and two other opponents of Nehemiah tried to keep them from their work. They asked him to meet with them in Kephirim, some fifty kilometres from Jerusalem. The reason given was the need for consultation, but in reality they had other plans with Nehemiah. Therefore, Nehemiah's answer remained the same: 'I am carrying on a great project and cannot go down' (Nehemiah 6:3).

All too often we see a similar pattern. When we are trying to focus on an important work, which demands all of our concentration and even sacrifice, there are usually people like Geshem who do their utmost to keep us from our task, often with seemingly reasonable arguments. This happens especially when we are busy with the things of God. Our answer should then be an echo of the reply of Nehemiah: 'I have an important work to do. I cannot abandon that.'

My prayer

Almighty God, I pray that You give me the resolve not to let people like Geshem keep me from any important work that You have given me.

13 May

Gideon

(hewer-feller)

Who and when? One of the most important judges; leader in Israel's war against Midian; twelfth century BC.

Want to know more? Read: Judges 6-8.

Thoughts for today

God called Gideon in a time of national crisis in order to give short shrift to the enemies that were a constant threat to Israel. God sent an angel to underline the seriousness of this call: but, in spite of this, Gideon was not immediately convinced that he was suited for the task God wanted to entrust to him. He asked for a sign that would confirm that God had indeed spoken to him. However, even when he received that sign, he was still not sure and asked for a second sign. Only then was Gideon prepared to go to battle.

Of course, once he had decided to start the war he wanted to recruit an army with maximum strength. But God had a different plan. He persuaded Gideon that His divine power would be the decisive factor in the coming military campaign, and that Israel's success would not primarily depend on human courage and meticulous preparation – however important these may be. God said: 'You have too many men for me' (Judges 7:2). After Gideon had dismissed as many as 22,000 men, God told him his army was still far too big. In the end there was a group of no more than three hundred men (Judges 7:8). With this tiny army Israel won the victory over the Midianites and the other enemies. As a result 'the land enjoyed peace for forty years' (Judges 8:28). With God on our side we can always be sure of victory.

My prayer

Lord, when I meditate on the inspiring story of Gideon, I realise I depend all too often on my own efforts and forget that everything depends on You.

14 May

Gog (prince)

Who and when? Symbolic name for a distant enemy of Israel.

Want to know more? Read: Ezekiel 38; 39. Revelation 20:7-10.

Thoughts for today

Ezekiel 38 begins with these words: 'The word of the LORD came to me: "Son of man, set your face against Gog, of the land of Magog, the chief prince of Meshech and Tubal. . . ." ' Some other translations render this text as follows: 'Gog in the land of Magog, the prince of Rosh.' Many readers of Ezekiel probably skip sections like these, as many of their elements are rather puzzling. There has been endless speculation about this prophecy of Gog and Magog: especially in circles where the founding of the State of Israel in 1948 is seen as a prophetic fulfilment, and the name 'Rosh' is interpreted as referring to Russia. Ezekiel 38 was believed to explain how in the time of the end Russia would lead a federation of powers to try to wipe Israel off the map. The American president Ronald Reagan supported this view.

During the time of the Cold War Russia was seen as the ultimate threat to world peace. Since then, however, Russia has seen a significant reduction in her power and global prestige. Besides this, the theory that Ezekiel refers to Russia is pure speculation. This type of approach to the prophecies has caused a lot of confusion. Since the speculated fulfilments have not occurred, the confidence of many people in Bible prophecy has been severely shaken. The prophet Ezekiel used 'apocalyptic' language, and the meaning of many of the symbols he uses remains unclear to us in the twenty-first century. But the underlying message is crystal clear: our world will come to an end; this will cause indescribable trouble – but God continues to be in charge, and, therefore, the victory of good over evil is guaranteed.

My prayer

I thank You, almighty God, that You pull the ropes in this world, and that this will become totally clear as the end of time draws near!

15 May

Goliath

(meaning uncertain)

Who and when? The Philistine giant who was slain by the young David. Ca. 1000 BC.

Want to know more? Read: 1 Samuel 17:1-54.

Thoughts for today

In the story about Goliath we are faced with a man with a height of almost three metres. Or perhaps he measured 'only' about 2.6 metres, if we take our cue from other ancient Bible manuscripts. Whatever his exact height, the word 'giant' is certainly applicable. As a special warrior he represented the Philistines. To avoid large-scale bloodshed on both sides two warriors would sometimes fight each other. The nation of the winner would thereby be considered to have gained the victory.

Goliath challenges the enemy Israel to battle, but no one is willing to meet the challenge – until David steps forward. He has felt so irritated by the blasphemies of the Philistine giant that he volunteers to fight Goliath. Goliath sees this as an enormous insult! However, the boy David – not carrying any armour and with only a sling and a few stones – kills the giant. How in God's name was this possible? The answer is found in the words of this question. Only in the name of God, and through His help, was this possible!

Are there any 'giants' in your life? Challenges that surpass anything you might, humanly speaking, be able to handle? Do not be disheartened. Trust that God will enable you to get through. Use what you have, even if it is the equivalent of a simple sling and a few small stones, and ask God to steer your hands so that you may conquer your 'giants'.

My prayer

Lord, You know the 'giants' in my life. Let me be like David and make me victorious by always trusting You.

16 May

Habakkuk

(water mint; or possibly derived from a word that means 'to embrace')

Who and when? Lived and prophesied at the end of the seventh century BC; we owe the Bible book of Habakkuk to him.

Want to know more? Read: Habakkuk 2:1; 3:2.

Thoughts for today

'I will stand at my watch and station myself on the ramparts; I will look to see what he will say to me' (2:1). This is perhaps the best-known verse from the three chapters of the book of Habakkuk. The prophet lived in a turbulent period of the history of the Southern Kingdom of Judah. The Babylonians, a 'ruthless and impetuous people' (1:6), are about to establish the New Babylonian Empire, and Judah will need to face up to this dire situation.

Habakkuk keeps his eyes open. He stations himself 'at his watch', so that he will observe what is happening. His special interest is, however, in what God might want to tell him. For that is his task: to communicate messages from God to His people.

In fact, our role at the beginning of the twenty-first century is very similar to that of Habakkuk. It is important to carefully analyse what is happening in the world and to observe that the hands of the divine clock are relentlessly moving forward. It is crucial that we never forget that we are living in 'the time of the end', and how – as God's children – we are entrusted with a prophetic message for mankind. What does God have to say to *us*, for *our* world? This is the question we must constantly ask ourselves. And linked to this is another vital question: how can we effectively communicate this message to the people around us?

My prayer

Almighty God, we know that this world will soon come to its end. Help us discern the signals that confirm that the final resolution of all problems is near; and endow us with the skills to communicate this to others in a convincing manner.

17 May

Hadad

(name of a Semitic storm god)

Who and when? An Edomite who became a powerful opponent of Solomon, after a significant part of the Edomite people had been killed by Joab, the chief commander of David's army.

Want to know more? Read: 1 Kings 11:14-25.

Thoughts for today

'The Lord raised up against Solomon an adversary, Hadad the Edomite, from the royal line of Edom' (1 Kings 11:14). How do we interpret these words: 'The Lord raised up'? It is not difficult to understand that Hadad became Solomon's enemy. There had been a war with Edom. When the fighting had ended, Joab, the top military leader in David's army, decided to bury the dead. But he did more than that. He remained in Edom for six months, until his men 'had destroyed all the men in Edom' (vs. 16). Hadad was still a boy when he escaped with some court attendants to Egypt, where he received asylum from the pharaoh. The Egyptian ruler was kindly disposed towards Hadad, gave him a piece of land and even allowed him to marry one of his daughters. One would think that Hadad would consider himself fortunate, considering that things had ended for him in the way they did, and that he would be content to continue living quietly in Egypt. But his roots were elsewhere and he wanted revenge. When David had died and Solomon had ascended to the throne, Hadad decided to return to his country and to fight Solomon in whatever way he could.

God 'raised up an adversary'. That is to say: God did not prevent Hadad from taking revenge on David's successor. It is very difficult – if not impossible – for us, as human beings, to determine what God should, or should not, have done. The bad things that happen around us are usually the result of the decisions (often wrong) of men and women. God may allow these to occur, but at the same time He assures us that evil remains within certain constraints. Some day, however, everything will turn out for the better.

My prayer

I trust You, Lord, knowing that, whatever happens, You are in control.

18 May

Hagar (flight)

Who and when? Hagar was a servant of Sarah, the wife of Abraham. When Sarah was advanced in years and had given up hope of ever becoming pregnant, she arranged for Abraham to have posterity through her servant Hagar. Hagar gave birth to Ishmael.

Want to know more? Read: Genesis 16; 21.

Thoughts for today

When the unthinkable happened and when in her old age Sarah did, after all, give birth to a son, she could no longer tolerate Hagar and her son Ishmael and didn't want them anywhere near her. The situation eventually became so unbearable for Sarah that she demanded that mother and son be sent away permanently. Abraham reluctantly agreed, under God's instruction, and they were sent off into the wilderness together.

In Genesis 21 we find Hagar in the desert of Beersheba. She has nothing left to drink and realises that both she and Ishmael will not survive. She is sitting 'about a bow-shot away' from her son, unable to watch him die. She 'began to sob' and we read that 'God heard the boy crying' too. At that point an angel appears, who tells Hagar: 'Do not be afraid. God has heard the boy crying. . . .' Everything will be OK. And now notice: 'Then God opened her eyes and she saw a well of water' (Genesis 21:19).

Had that well been there all along? Or did God create it for this special occasion? We do not know, and neither is it of importance. The point is that we often do not see the solution to our problems until God opens our eyes. Sometimes He will only do so at the very last moment, when we are at the end of our tether. We can only guess why He waits so long. But perhaps it is to make an even stronger impression on us that in the end we are totally dependent on God, and this trust in Him should make us even more grateful for all He constantly does for us.

My prayer

Lord, when I see no way out in the midst of the problems that engulf me, open my eyes to the possibilities and solutions You have for me.

19 May

Haggai (born on a feast day)

Who and when? A prophet in Judah; we owe one of the books from the series of 'minor' prophets to him. Contemporary of Zerubbabel and of the prophet Zechariah. Active around 520 BC.

Want to know more? Read: Ezra 5:1; 6:14; Haggai 1; 2.

Thoughts for today

Haggai lived in a turbulent time. He was a messenger of God in the period after the exile. Around 538 BC a substantial group of exiles had returned from Babylon to Jerusalem. With good courage those who had resettled in Palestine had begun the rebuilding of the nation. However, opposition had arisen from many sides, and the rebuilding of Jerusalem, and especially of the temple, had suffered serious delays. The prophets Haggai and Zechariah played an important role in these developments.

More often than not God's people hardly paid attention to God's messengers, but things were different at this particular time. We read that the people and the leaders listened to the prophet Haggai (Haggai 1:12). The two chapters of the document bearing his name contain five messages. All of these underline the same assurance. We read in 1:13: 'Then Haggai, the LORD's messenger, gave this message of the LORD to the people: "I am with you, declares the LORD." '

It was a simple message, but it was all the returned exiles needed. Their task was far from easy, but God was with them. This was the secret of their eventual success. And that has always been the secret of the success of all those who are prepared to listen to the prophetic word.

My prayer

Thank You, Lord, that You want to be with me – also today.

20 May

Ham

(hot)

Who and when? The youngest son of Noah.

Want to know more? Read: Genesis 5:32–10:20.

Thoughts for today

Undoubtedly, Ham and his two brothers helped their father Noah in the construction of the enormous ship that also saved them, when everything on earth disappeared in the Flood. Ham was one of the eight people who God decided were good enough to make a new start in the world after the Flood. Ham's reputation, however, was soon tarnished because of an incident that happened shortly after the Flood. Noah had planted the first vineyard and had enjoyed the fruits of his labour to excess. While in a drunken state, sleeping off his intoxication, his youngest son found him in his tent, and 'saw his father's nakedness' (Genesis 9:21). In between the lines we gather from the biblical story that Ham did not handle this situation too gracefully.

Traditionally many have concluded that (a) Ham became the ancestor of the dark population of Africa; and that (b) because of Ham's wrong behaviour the black people on this earth are forever cursed. Many despicable theories and racial prejudices have been the result. However, a careful reading of the story of Ham reveals that a judgement was pronounced not over Ham, but over his son Canaan (Genesis 9:25-27). Moreover, there is absolutely no ground whatsoever for the kind of racial theories that suggest that a dark skin is a reminder of God's disapproval. Not only is all racism that is based on the story of Ham without any basis, but any kind of racist prejudice runs contrary to the Gospel message, which tells us that all men and women are fully equal in Christ.

My prayer

You are the Father of all of us. Help us to see all people as Your children, all of whom You love in equal measure with Your limitless love.

21 May

Haman

(well disposed)

Who and when? A high official at the court of the Persian king Ahasuerus (or Xerxes); reigned from 486 BC to 465 BC.

Want to know more? Read: Esther 3:1-8:2.

Thoughts for today

Antisemitism is a horrible phenomenon. In the last century it led to the Holocaust, in which at least six million (mostly Jewish) people were systematically murdered. But antisemitism was not a Nazi invention. We know of many earlier attempts to eliminate all the descendants of Jacob from the face of the earth. Haman was responsible for one of these attempts.

Haman had reached an important position at the Persian court and was a close confidant of King Ahasuerus. He used every opportunity he saw to emphasise his own importance, and he expected that others - even the highest functionaries - would kneel before him. However, a certain Mordecai found this unnecessary and refused to do what Haman expected of him. From the moment Haman heard about this he hated Mordecai with a vengeance. That hatred acquired an extra dimension when he was made aware of the Jewish background of Mordecai. It made Haman into a fanatical antisemite and he decided that the entire Jewish people was to be eradicated.

This is how antisemitism and racism work. An entire nation may be stigmatised, and this sometimes results in a threat to its very existence. Risking her own life, Queen Esther was able to stop the danger that Haman represented. Like Esther, we should be determined - even if this might cause problems for us personally - to combat antisemitism and racism.

My prayer

Give us, O God, the courage always to do what we can to stop antisemitism and racism.

22 May

Hannah

(graciousness)

Who and when? An aged prophetess who was constantly in the temple and praised God for the birth of the Saviour.

Want to know more? Read: Luke 2:36-38.

Thoughts for today

In Bible times the prophetic office was not reserved for men. Hannah is one of the New Testament prophetesses who is mentioned by name. She must have been a remarkable woman, who refused to go into retirement, although she was far past retirement age. After she had married (perhaps at the age of around 15), she had lived with her husband for only seven years, 'and then was a widow until she was eighty-four' (Luke 2:37): but in spite of her age she was a daily visitor to the Temple and spent a major part of her time in fasting and prayer. This explains why she was there when Joseph and Mary brought their forty-day-old child Jesus to the temple, in compliance with the Jewish purification rites.

Because of her prophetic gift Hannah saw in them more than just a typical couple visiting the temple with their child, as could probably be seen in the temple on a daily basis. The uniqueness of the event was further confirmed by what she had heard Simeon, a 'righteous and devout' man (vs. 25), say to Mary. Hannah 'gave thanks to God and spoke about the child to all who were looking forward to the redemption of Jerusalem' (vs. 38).

Whatever our age, all of us have daily opportunities to praise God and to speak freely about 'the child' that was born some twenty centuries ago as our Saviour.

My prayer

Lord, show me the opportunities that present themselves today to speak about You and the delivery from all evil that You are soon going to bring about.

23 May

Heman

(faithful)

Who and when? A Levite serving as a musician in the temple at the time of David.

Want to know more? Read: 1 Chronicles 15:17-21; 16:41, 42; 25:1-6.

Thoughts for today

Heman was one of the thousands of Israelites who belonged to the tribe of Levi and were therefore qualified to serve in the temple. He was one of the musicians who were 'set apart . . . for the ministry of prophesying, accompanied by harps, lyres and cymbals' (1 Chronicles 25:1). In addition Heman had other gifts. He was also 'the king's seer', who was able to pass on and explain divine messages (vs. 4). And, in passing, the author of the Chronicles also mentions that Heman had fourteen sons and three daughters!

We meet Heman also in the introduction to Psalm 88, where the psalm is referred to as a 'maskil' (antiphonal song, i.e. sung alternately by two choirs or two singers) of Heman the Ezrahite. This psalm is sometimes regarded as the most melancholic of all psalms. But who is the person about whom Heman writes his psalm: 'O LORD, the God who saves me, day and night I cry out before you. May my prayer come before you; turn your ear to my cry' (vss. 1, 2)?

Do these words reflect Heman's own sentiments? Or did he think about David and what his king must have experienced when things were difficult? We do not know. But, in any case, these words also fit with what many of us experience – when we cry for help until we no longer have words for our feelings. Sometimes we may want to echo the statement by Heman: 'I am confined and cannot escape' (vs. 8). Fortunately, this is not the only psalm in our psalter. The next psalm begins with the beautiful words: 'I will sing of the LORD's great love for ever . . .' (89:1).

My prayer

Let us rediscover Your love, dear God, especially when we go through periods of despair.

24 May

Herod

(Greek: son of a hero)

Who and when? Herod the Great was responsible for the massacre in Bethlehem.

Want to know more? Read: Matthew 2.

Thoughts for today

In the New Testament we hear of a number of men who shared the name, 'Herod'. Today we meet number one: Herod the Great. He ruled over Judea, and the Romans had allowed him to call himself 'king'. He enjoyed his royal status and wanted to stay on his throne as long as possible. At the first indication that there might be competition for this royal privilege he stood ready with draconic measures. When he heard through some 'magi' from the East that a royal child might have been born in Bethlehem, he wanted to make sure that this child would not survive. For that reason he commanded that all little boys in and around Bethlehem who were below the age of two were to be killed.

Today there are, fortunately, not many leaders who are so chained to their position that they would go as far as this cruel King Herod. But we see ample evidence that many people, once they have received a taste of power, do not easily surrender their position. Even in countries that claim to be democratic, many leaders find it difficult to step down from their place of authority and may resort to all kinds of tricks to remain in power.

Most of us ordinary people also face the constant temptation in everyday life to choose the path of self-interest, and often many among us are quite willing to cheat if needed. This is in complete contrast to the way of life that we were taught by the One who could not even be eliminated by Herod the Great.

My prayer

God of love, help me not to see the people around me primarily as competitors.

25 May

Herod Agrippa I

(Greek: son of a hero)

Who and when? Grandson of Herod the Great; ordered the apostle James to be beheaded and Peter to be put in jail; reigned over Judea from ca. AD 41 to ca. AD 44.

Want to know more? Read: Acts 12.

Thoughts for today

Since the New Testament mentions a number of different Herods it is easy to become confused. Herod Agrippa I was in power at the time when the church in Jerusalem was solidly placed on the map. This Herod was an enormous opportunist. He had several church leaders put in prison, and even killed James, the brother of John. When he saw how this brought him increased popularity with the Jews, he also incarcerated Peter.

The story of Peter's deliverance is well known. Herod wanted to be absolutely certain that he wouldn't escape, and had arranged that Peter would be guarded by sixteen sentries. However, those sixteen soldiers could do nothing against the 'angel of the Lord'! While Peter was locked up and was heavily guarded, the church members continued to pray fervently for him.

God decided to teach Herod a painful lesson. He did not intervene to put an end to the sufferings of James, but showed in the miraculous deliverance of Peter that Herod could not continue his evil practices at will. The early church found great inspiration in what happened. Apparently, God still wanted Peter to have an important role in the preaching of the Gospel. At that point, Herod could have repented and accepted the apostolic message, but, unfortunately, there is no indication that this ever happened.

My prayer

Thank You, Lord, that I may know that You are almighty.

26 May

Herod Agrippa II

(Greek: son of a hero)

Who and when? Last of the Herodians. Was consulted in the court case against Paul.

Want to know more? Read: Acts 25:13–26:32.

Thoughts for today

We have already met Herod Agrippa I (Acts 12:1), who was the persecutor of the apostles. Herod Agrippa II appears later on the scene. After having ruled on behalf of the Romans over Chalcis (a small area in the Lebanon region), he was promoted to be the caretaker of a large part of Palestine. In Acts 25 we meet him on a visit to Jerusalem, where he became acquainted with Paul.

What kind of person was this Herod? I must admit that I feel an instinctive revulsion when I hear the name of Herod. The name 'Herod' is forever linked to the massacre in Bethlehem, and connected with the murder of John the Baptist, with Jesus' trial and the unlawful execution of the apostle James. Different Herods were responsible for these evil actions, but is there any reason to think that Herod Agrippa II was different? We must be careful not to jump to conclusions. The Bible has nothing negative to say about this Herod. He is correct in his dealings with Paul, takes his time to listen to him and decides that Paul is innocent and could have been a free man, if he had not appealed to the emperor.

In other words: we must suspend our judgement about this Herod. We have no solid reason to think that he was a villain like the other members of the Herodian dynasty. That may, however, not be easy, for prejudices tend to be difficult to ignore.

My prayer

You are the God who sees what is in our hearts and is able to judge all people fairly. Help me always to be careful in my judgement of others.

27 May

Herod Antipas

(Herod, in the place of the father)

Who and when? One of the sons of Herod the Great; vassal of the Romans; ruled over Galilee and Perea at the time of Jesus' ministry and death.

Want to know more? Read: Matthew 14:1-12.

Thoughts for today

What we read about Herod Antipas resembles to some extent the Old Testament story of Jephthah, who made a rash promise that would cause great misery. Herod Antipas swore an oath that he would give his stepdaughter Salome whatever she would ask. Her mother prompted Salome to ask for the head of John the Baptist. John had already been a prisoner for some time and Herodias, the wife of Herod, hated him with a vengeance. Herod was keen to get rid of John but knew that this prophet was still very popular with many people. For that reason he was afraid to execute him (vs. 5).

It put Herod in a quandary when his stepdaughter asked for the head of John the Baptist. He was 'distressed', we are told (vs. 9), but did not dare to back out, since he had made his rash promise in the presence of a large number of guests. He would lose face in a big way if he were to break his oath now.

How much injustice has been done, and how much trouble has been caused – through all times and in all cultures – because people were afraid to lose face! It continues to be an immense problem and, unfortunately, many people do not realise that it is advisable to back away in time from some unwise or evil act, even if that means losing face.

My prayer

Help me, dear Lord, not to make any rash promises. But give me the courage, if needed, to suffer loss of face if that prevents me from doing something very wrong.

28 May

Herodias

(female form of Herod: heroic)

Who and when? Granddaughter of Herod the Great; was married to her uncle Herod Philip; later cohabited with Herod Antipas. She plotted the death of John the Baptist.

Want to know more? Read: Matthew 14:1-12.

Thoughts for today

The Herod-clan were, generally speaking, not a nice bunch of people. Herod the Great was guilty of the massacre in Bethlehem (Mathew 2:16, 17) because he was afraid that the royal child, who was found by the magi from the East, would grow up to be a contender for the throne. Herodias, his granddaughter, was first married to a relative, her uncle Herod Philip, but after some time had traded him in for his half-brother Antipas.

Both Herodias and her new partner Herod Antipas, with whom she now cohabited, hated John the Baptist. The main reason was that he had had the audacity to sharply condemn their relationship. Antipas had thrown John in jail, but, in view of John's popularity with the masses, he had been reticent to have John executed. In the meantime Herodias kept conspiring to find ways to get rid of John.

The opportunity arose when, during a party in the palace, Antipas was so excited about a dance by the daughter of Herodias that he told her to make a wish. Incited by her mother, she asked for the head of John the Baptist. It was the tragic finale of a chain of sad events. It remains a vivid warning that wrong decisions and impulsive promises can easily cause situations to escalate, with terrible consequences.

My prayer

Loving God, keep me on the right path and protect me from wrong decisions and impetuous promises that may set in motion a chain of miserable events.

29 May

Hezekiah

(the Lord has strengthened)

Who and when? King of Judah; reigned from 726 BC to 696 BC.

Want to know more? Read: 2 Kings 18–20; Isaiah 36–39.

Thoughts for today

By and large the Bible is quite positive about Hezekiah's rule, even though he did not leave a perfect track record. He lived in a time of political crisis and had to make a crucial decision: with which of the main powers of his day would he align himself? Fortunately, he eventually realised that only God would be an effective ally. As we read about his internal struggle we discover that Hezekiah knew about the power of prayer.

Later in the story we once again meet a praying Hezekiah. This is after he has heard from the prophet Isaiah that he will succumb to a fatal illness, and that he had better put his affairs in order. Hezekiah then fervently prays for healing. Once again the prophet Isaiah has a message for him: fifteen years will be added to his life. When Hezekiah wonders how he can be sure that this promise will come true, God gives him an extraordinary sign. 'The LORD made the shadow go back the ten steps . . . on the stairway of Ahaz' (2 Kings 20:11).

God presents us with lots of inexplicable things. What to think of a shadow that creeps backwards? And what to make of this life extension of fifteen years? Why did Hezekiah get this extra lease on life, and why does God not give this same extension to the terminal cancer patients we know? In vain we look for answers. However, if we contemplate the main patterns of the Hezekiah story we can take courage. As long as we go to God when we are in difficulties, we may expect surprising interventions on our behalf.

My prayer

Loving Father, we thank You for the example of Hezekiah. Help us also to find our way towards You, trusting that, when life seems grim, You can do surprising things for us.

30 May

Hilkiah

(my portion is YHWH)

Who and when? High priest at the time of King Josiah (639 BC to 609 BC). He found the book of the law in the temple.

Want to know more? Read: 2 Kings 22:1–23:30.

Thoughts for today

King Josiah was one of Judah's 'good' kings. He was one of the few rulers who tried to bring his people back to the worship of YHWH and to reform the nation's religious scene. Josiah gave the order that the necessary repairs to the temple be made. In order to finance these works, the donations given by the worshippers were used. While making a thorough search in the closets in the temple an unexpected discovery was made: the high priest Hilkiah found a scroll that had not been seen for a long time. It was, in all likelihood, a scroll containing the book of Deuteronomy or a part thereof. Hilkiah immediately gave the scroll to Shaphan the scribe, who took the scroll to the king and read its content to him. For Josiah this was a good enough reason to call his people together in order to re-acquaint them with God's law.

This story about the discovery made by Hilkiah is quite remarkable. Just imagine: in the temple, of all places, the scrolls containing the Word of God had been lost. Just suppose that you go to church and there is nowhere a Bible to be found. Fortunately, there will not be many places where that is the case. But, rather tragically, we find that many Christians no longer read the Bible as much as they used to. For many – old and young – the Bible is becoming a book they are not familiar with. It is high time that we rediscover the Word of God!

My prayer

Thank You, Lord, for Your Word. Help me to make sure that it will never get lost in my life.

31 May

Hiram (brother of the exalted one)

Who and when? King of Tyre; ally of David and Solomon; provided materials and labourers for the construction of the royal palace and the temple in Jerusalem.

Want to know more? Read: 2 Samuel 5:11; 1 Kings 5:1-7:51; 9:10-14; 1 Chronicles 14:1.

Thoughts for today

We might get the impression that Hiram was a kind man who was eager to help his neighbour David, and later his son Solomon, when they needed assistance with a few prestigious projects. Fortunately, in Hiram's days there were many more cedars in Lebanon than there are today. It was no problem to deliver large quantities of this quality wood. Hiram could also export the kind of stone that was required; and he was able to provide the thousands of labourers needed for the transport of all these heavy building materials over uneven terrain over a long distance.

Hiram was indeed a nice man, but he was also very businesslike. He wanted ample compensation for his service to David and Solomon. We read in 1 Kings 5 about the enormous quantities of olive oil and grain that were shipped to Tyre. In addition, some twenty towns in Galilee were later handed over to Hiram. When Hiram went to inspect these towns, he was far from content. He asked Solomon: 'What kind of towns are these you have given me, my brother?' (1 Kings 9:13.) Of course, Hiram was entitled to ensure that all business agreements were executed correctly; and David and Solomon were duty-bound to show absolute honesty in their commercial transactions. That is what God still expects, also from us. Christians must be totally trustworthy and transparent in the way they do business.

My prayer

Help me, O God, that it may always be clear that I serve You from the way I do business.

1 June

Hophni

(Egyptian word: tadpole)

Who and when? Son of Eli; priest in Shiloh at the time of Samuel; brother of Phinehas.

Want to know more? Read: 1 Samuel 1:3; 2:12-26; 4:2-22.

Thoughts for today

Eli was unable to control the behaviour of his two adult sons. This was at least partly the result of a rather poor upbringing. Yet, like their father Eli, they served as priests of the Lord. However, when people came with their offerings, they ignored the instructions God had given them for their sacred task. When the worshippers came with their sacrifices, Hophni and Phinehas first took the best parts for themselves. The writer of 1 Samuel does not mince his words: 'Eli's sons were wicked men' (1 Samuel 2:12). We learn about some of the details of their sinful behaviour: they 'slept with the women who served at the entrance to the Tent of Meeting' (2:22). Of course, this was talked about. Eli accused his sons: 'I hear from all the people about these wicked deeds of yours' (vs. 23).

Through the ages God's cause has suffered most from the evil acts of spiritual leaders who should have given an example. This was not just true in Old Testament times or in the days of Jesus. It was also all too visible in the immoral practices that were common in the medieval church and in the scandals caused by clergy in our day and age.

'This sin of the young men was very great in the LORD's sight' (vs. 17), and that is also true of similar behaviour in our time. God wants us to have respect for holy things and requires a high moral standard from those who profess to serve Him.

My prayer

Loving Father, forgive me if I have ever handled holy things without respect.

2 June

Hosea (the Lord saves)

Who and when? One of the 'minor' prophets. We owe the book of Hosea to him. Contemporary of Isaiah, Amos and Micah (ca. 750 BC to ca. 725 BC).

Want to know more? Read: Hosea.

Thoughts for today

The relationship between the Lord and Israel is the central theme of the fourteen chapters of the Bible book that bears the name of the prophet Hosea. This relationship is compared to that between a man and his wife. Israel is like a wife that is continually unfaithful and runs after other lovers. Hosea is given a number of ways in which to imprint that message on the minds of the people. Even his private life plays an important role. God tells him to marry a woman of loose morals and to have children with her (Hosea 1:2-9). There could hardly be a more concrete way to bring the lesson home that God sticks with 'His wife', in spite of her frequent unfaithfulness. However, Gomer (Hosea's wife) keeps on having extramarital affairs, notwithstanding everything Hosea does to convince her of his love. His loves even goes so far that he buys her back from the slave market where she ended up (Hosea 3).

Opinions differ as to the question of whether the story of Hosea and Gomer reflects a historical situation, or should be interpreted as an allegory. Whatever the case, the message is abundantly clear. We humans are often obstinate in our lack of faithfulness towards God. But God does not give up and will spare no effort to restore the tie between Himself and the men and women who have turned their backs on Him. Once in a while we see people like Hosea, who present us with an example of persistent love for others. But such an example – beautiful and impressive though it may be – is but a weak reflection of God's measureless love for us.

My prayer

Merciful God, I confess that, in many things, I am often unfaithful to You. Please, forgive me. And thank You for Your unremitting love towards me.

3 June

Huldah (mole)

Who and when? The wife of Shallum, who was keeper of the king's wardrobe; she was a prophetess during the reign of King Josiah.

Want to know more? Read: 2 Kings 22; 2 Chronicles 34:14-28.

Thoughts for today

In biblical times the men were in charge. This also applied to the religious sphere. But, occasionally, we notice that God intentionally does things differently. Remember women like Deborah, and later the prophetess Anna. There was also Huldah, who spoke out because she was convinced that the Lord wanted to use her as a channel of communication. It would seem that she was fully accepted in that role. When an important scroll (probably part of the book of Deuteronomy) was rediscovered by the high priest Hilkiah and subsequently brought to the king, Huldah was called upon to give advice to him. This was remarkable, to say the least; for, although Huldah was a contemporary of the prophet Jeremiah, it was she who was asked to come, rather than Jeremiah.

No one can deny that in ancient times, as a rule, women played a subservient role. This was true for life in society in general, and also for the religious domain. Unfortunately, even today we hear voices that insist that God does not want to see women perform the same tasks in the church as men. It is argued by some that this is the clear message of the Bible. Admittedly, the society in Bible times was male-dominated; but there were divinely commissioned women who served as counterexamples. The Lord chose both Jeremiah and Huldah to serve as His prophets: and, occasionally, it seems that people listened more closely to a woman like Huldah than to a man.

My prayer

Thank You, gracious Lord, that You want to use both men and women as Your spokespersons.

4 June

Hur

(meaning is unclear)

Who and when? Supported, together with Aaron, the arms of Moses during Israel's battle against the Amalekites. Possibly the husband of Miriam.

Want to know more? Read: Exodus 17:8-13; 24:12-14.

Thoughts for today

Moses ordered Joshua to wage war against the Amalekites, while he positioned himself at a clearly visible spot on the top of a high hill. For a long time the battle remained undecided. 'As long as Moses held up his hands, the Israelites were winning, but whenever he lowered his hands, the Amalekites were winning' (Exodus 17:11). We may have different ideas about the dynamic that was at work. The most common interpretation is that the story underlines the fact that Israel owed its victory to its constant link with heaven.

Moses was an old man, who was physically unable to keep his hands stretched out for a lengthy period of time. Aaron and Hur had come with Moses to the top of the hill and were aware of Moses' physical challenges. They decided to assist him when they saw that 'Moses' hands grew tired' (vs. 12). They found a large stone on which Moses could sit, and – one on one side and one on the other side – they ensured that Moses' hands 'remained steady till sunset'.

Leaders – from ancient Israel to the church today – need strong support, even when they have not yet reached the advanced age of Moses. At times it is physical help, but more often leaders need mental and spiritual support. Leading God's people is not easy. Leaders must deal with numerous problems and, just as in the days of Moses, there are always people who complain. Controversies and conflicts are never far away. A leader will only be able to persevere when there are people who stand around him (or her) and help him/her to maintain uninterrupted contact with heaven.

My prayer

Help me, Lord, to realise that I must support the leaders of the church and that praying for them is the least I can do for them today.

5 June

Ichabod

(the glory has departed)

Who and when? The son of Phinehas and the grandson of the high priest Eli; was born on the day when his mother heard that the ark of the covenant was captured by the Philistines.

Want to know more? Read: 1 Samuel 4:19-22.

Thoughts for today

What brings a mother to give her newborn baby the name Ichabod: *The glory has departed*? It took place in the days of Samuel, the last of the judges. Once again it was a time of crisis. For the umpteenth time Israel had to endure attacks from the Philistines. Extra painful was the fact that the ark of the covenant – the most holy object in God's sanctuary – was seized by the Philistines. In the midst of this national tragedy Phinehas's wife suffered a personal drama. Upon hearing the news that her husband, her brother-in-law and her father-in-law had died as a result of this debacle, the birthing process began. She did not survive the delivery, but did manage to choose a name for her son and to explain her choice. She understood the importance of what had occurred. Under these circumstances Israel could no longer be assured of the presence of God's glory.

The tragic story reminds us of the fact that the presence of God's glory is not a matter of course. God wants to be with us: but there are limits. Individually or collectively we may, as it were, chase God away by creating such a wide gap between our lack of holiness and His glory that the two can no longer co-exist. At such a moment that word, 'Ichabod', fittingly describes that sad reality: the divine glory has departed! We have been warned!

My prayer

We thank You, O God, for coming with Your glory into our lives. May we also today fully appreciate this enormous privilege.

6 June

Isaac

(he laughs)

Who and when? The only son of Abraham and Sarah.

Want to know more? Read: Genesis 17:15-22; 22:1-19; 24; 27:1–28:9.

Thoughts for today

Abraham found it incomprehensible. He was asked to let go of the son he had received through a divine miracle. The Lord told him to sacrifice his son Isaac! One may read the story again and again, but it remains an enigma why God would give such a command to anyone. Isaac himself, however, was utterly co-operative. He trusted his father's assurance that God would, in one way or another, provide 'the lamb for the burnt offering' (Genesis 22:8).

Abraham manifested great faith. But was Isaac's trusting faith not at least as astounding as that of his father? Isaac could easily have escaped from his elderly dad. But he went along and allowed himself to be bound on the altar. According to the historian Josephus, Isaac was about twenty-five years old when it happened. Whether this is correct we do not know, but we do know that he was not a small, powerless child. Would his father end his life, when with the knife in his hand he reached out to 'slay his son'?

Isaac was a prefiguration of Jesus. Isaac surrendered voluntarily. He could have resisted his father. We also know that Jesus went to His death voluntarily. He prayed that it might happen 'not as I will, but as you will' (Matthew 26:39). Isaac did not have to die, since there was a lamb – a symbol of the Lamb of God that would take away the sins of the world. And that also includes all our sins.

My prayer

I thank You, Lord Jesus, for what You did for all people – and thus also for me. Help me to be prepared to fully trust You when You ask me to sacrifice things that are dear to me.

7 June

Isaiah (the Lord saves)

Who and when? Prophet; son of Amos (not the prophet of the book in the Bible with this name); worked for about sixty years in Judah, during the reigns of the kings Uzziah, Jotham, Ahaz and Hezekiah.

Want to know more? Read: 2 Kings 19:2; Isaiah, especially chapter 6.

Thoughts for today

Chapter six of the book of Isaiah provides us with an impressive description of the calling of the prophet. The prophet-elect received an awesome vision of God's majesty. He saw the Lord in His majesty, surrounded by angelic beings. Isaiah thought that he would not survive the experience. ' "Woe to me!" I cried. "I am ruined! For I am a man of unclean lips, and I live among a people of unclean lips, and my eyes have seen the King, the LORD Almighty." Then one of the seraphs flew to me with a live coal in his hand, which he had taken with tongs from the altar. With it he touched my mouth and said; "See, this has touched your lips; your guilt is taken away and your sin atoned for." Then I heard the voice of the Lord saying, "Whom shall I send? And who will go for us?" And I said, "Here I am. Send me!" '
(Isaiah 6:5-8.)

Only a few people have been called by God for a special task in such a dramatic manner. But that does not take away from the fact that all God's children have been called to go into the world with a prophetic message. And, just as was the case with Isaiah's calling, God is asking: 'Whom shall I send? Who is willing to speak to the people on My behalf?' God wants 'prophets' who are willing to communicate His message to the community around us. How do we react? What is our response? Do we spontaneously exclaim: 'Here I am. Send me!'?

My prayer

Lord, help me to respond to Your calling and say: 'Here I am. Send me.'

8 June

Ish-bosheth

(man of shame)

Who and when? The only surviving son of Saul; was proclaimed king after Saul's death by Abner, the commander of the army (ca. 1000 BC).

Want to know more? Read: 2 Samuel 2:8-10; 4:1-12; 1 Chronicles 8:33; 9:39.

Thoughts for today

Ish-bosheth's original name was Esh-baal, meaning 'man of the lord'. He became known, however, as Ish-bosheth, meaning 'man of shame'. As the youngest son of Saul and the brother of Jonathan he was no doubt aware of the fact that God had chosen David as the successor of his father and the next king of Israel. However, when Saul and three of his sons were killed on the battlefield and Ish-bosheth was the only son of Saul who survived the war with the Philistines, he was more than willing to go along with the initiative of the commander, Abner, for him to claim the throne. But not all Israelites agreed. David was proclaimed king by another part of the people. This produced the first (as yet temporary) split of Israel into a southern and a northern part.

Ish-bosheth enjoyed his royal status for only two years. Abner decided to withdraw his support from Ish-bosheth after his royal protégé had (probably without cause) accused Abner of having started a relationship with one of Saul's wives. Thus the role of Ish-bosheth came to an abrupt end. Abner was murdered, and shortly afterwards Ish-bosheth himself suffered a similar fate during his siesta - dying at the hands of two of his trusted servants.

Why did Ish-bosheth ever embark on this adventure? Had he forgotten that not he, but David, had been chosen by God to succeed King Saul? The story once again illustrates that things go from bad to worse when we wilfully go against divine instructions.

My prayer

Father in heaven, please give me the power to arrange my life according to Your plan.

9 June

Ishmael

(God hears)

Who and when? The son of Abraham and Hagar, the servant of Sarah. He became the forebear of a large desert clan.

Want to know more? Read: Genesis 16; 21.

Thoughts for today

Lots of people experience a difficult start in life. They were born and grew up in a dysfunctional family and must, for the rest of their lives, live with the results of a complicated childhood. When they compare their situation with those of others, who seem to have everything going for them, they feel that life is just not fair. Some even conclude that God is very partial.

Ishmael was one of those people who did not have a good start. He was the son of Abraham and Hagar, the servant who was enlisted to provide a son for Abraham when Sarah failed to become pregnant. It looked like a clever plan to achieve God's objective, but it brought nothing but misery. After some time, Sarah miraculously also bore a son (Isaac), but the tension between the two wives became so bad that Hagar and Ishmael were sent away by Abraham.

But that was not the end of the story; for God did not forget Ishmael. He promised Hagar that, like Isaac, Ishmael would also become the father of a great nation. A more precious promise was hardly imaginable in the culture of that time. We may have different values, but the story also speaks to us. It tells us that God does not forget us, even if it appears that life has treated us rather unfairly.

My prayer

Help me, heavenly Father, to trust that You care for me, even though I may have to face difficulties in my life.

10 June

Issachar (there is hire)

Who and when? Issachar was the ninth son of Jacob and the fifth of Leah; he was the progenitor of a large clan, the tribe of Issachar.

Want to know more? Read: Genesis 49:14, 15; 1 Chronicles 12:32.

Thoughts for today

We read in 1 Chronicles 12 about the men from the different tribes who came to enlist in David's army, once it became clear that David's power had been solidly established. There was also a contingent from the tribe of Issachar. We are told that the soldiers that came from these various tribes were 'brave' or 'experienced', and that they were able to handle any kind of weaponry. Surely, these are important qualities if you want to build a strong army.

We read something quite different, however, about the tribe of Issachar. They 'understood the times and knew what Israel should do' (1 Chronicles 12:32). This quality is possibly even more important for a long-term strategy than those other characteristics that are mentioned.

The same applies today for us as God's children who must wage a spiritual battle. Yes, we must be brave and experienced in handling the spiritual weapons the apostle Paul so graphically describes (Ephesians 6:13-17). But understanding the times in which we live and knowing the trends in our society are essential if we want to communicate the message of Jesus in such a way that it will be meaningful for the people who are not yet acquainted with Him.

My prayer

Lord, help me understand what is going on in today's world and what current trends are important, so that I can be relevant when I want to tell people around me about You and what You can do for them.

11 June

Ithamar

(possibly: land of palm trees)

Who and when? Fourth and youngest son of Aaron; became a prominent priest; in his posterity were a number of high priests.

Want to know more? Read: Exodus 6:23; Leviticus 10:12-20.

Thoughts for today

In some countries Ithamar is a rather popular name for boys. Many, apparently, like the sound of the name, even though the meaning of the name is not totally clear. As is the case with many names that we give to our children, Ithamar is a biblical name. He was one of the four sons of Aaron. Two of his brothers (Nadab and Abihu) seriously misbehaved and were killed by God. The two remaining sons, Eleazar and Ithamar, received responsible assignments in the sanctuary service.

Among other things, Ithamar was charged with making an inventory of all the materials that were used in the building of the tabernacle (Exodus 38:21). Later he was given the assignment to supervise two groups of priests, the Gershonites and Merarites (Numbers 4:21-33). In Leviticus 10 we find a list of practical instructions with which Ithamar and his brother were expected to comply. Sometimes we may be inclined to skip the Bible passages that inform us about the details of the sanctuary service. This is not so strange, for some chapters seem rather boring. But it is good to read these parts of the Bible also from time to time. We learn from them how minutely organised everything was, and how detailed the tasks of all the officials at different levels were described.

God is a God or order, and He still expects us to serve Him in an orderly manner, always aware of His infinite holiness.

My prayer

You are a loving but also a holy God. Help me not to forget that today.

12 June

Jabez

(born in pain)

Who and when? A man in Judah; his birth gave his mother much pain. That is why she gave her son this name.

Want to know more? Read: 1 Chronicles 4:9, 10.

Thoughts for today

We find the name of Jabez in one of the genealogies at the beginning of 1 Chronicles, in the midst of a torrent of other names. He was a descendant of Judah. He was special, for 'Jabez was more honourable than his brothers' (1 Chronicles 4:9). Was the reason why he was 'more honourable' simply that he was more talented? Or was he more pious than his siblings? This latter supposition might be true, for his name is accompanied by a statement that is unique in these lists: 'Jabez cried out to the God of Israel, "Oh, that you would bless me and enlarge my territory!" ' God granted him what he asked for.

The text has provided inspiration for many sermons, and 'the prayer of Jabez' is well known. Most of us who pray this prayer do not need a piece of land, but there are lots of other things that are important for us. Jabez realised how dependent he was on God's blessing. Unfortunately, many people today forget to approach God for His blessings. They prefer to trust in their own skills and hard work. They forget to always ask for the protection God is more than willing to give them. Jabez discovered that prayer works. We may enjoy that same experience!

My prayer

Today I simply want to repeat the prayer of Jabez. Lord, give me the things I really need, and, above everything else, protect me against all the evil that surrounds me.

13 June

Jabin

(he understands)

Who and when? The Canaanite king who was defeated by Barak and Deborah; ca. 1200 BC.

Want to know more? Read: Judges 4; Psalm 83:9, 10.

Thoughts for today

During the time of the judges Israel was constantly faced with oppression and violence from the other peoples that still lived in part of Palestine. Among them were the Canaanites who, during the reign of King Jabin, were a power of considerable strength. Jabin reigned from the city of Hazor. At one time this place had been conquered by Israel, but, apparently, after some time Israel had lost the region of Hazor again. For some twenty years Jabin 'cruelly oppressed' Israel. Not only did he have very skilful army commanders, but he also possessed nine hundred iron chariots. The earliest iron chariots date from around 2000 BC, but only a few ancient people groups had these forerunners of the 'tank'. Israel did not appear to possess many iron chariots until much later than the time of Jabin.

Against the military might of Jabin, Israel's sole military strength was some 10,000 infantry. Small wonder that Barak had serious questions about going to war against Jabin. But – as we discover so often in the history of God's people – the strongest army is always the army that has God on its side. Here we see this principle at work as well: for, when things became truly serious, the Lord created panic among the Canaanites and Barak's army was able to destroy the enemy (Judges 4:14-16). It was the biggest victory for Israel since the days of Joshua, at least 166 years earlier. Jabin's hold over Israel had finally been broken. He was pushed back by the Israelites until they destroyed him (vss. 15, 16). However, the victory was due solely to divine intervention!

My prayer

I ask You, Lord, always to stay on my side, so that I can face the problems of everyday life.

14 June

Jacob

(he takes by the heel)

Who and when? One of the sons of Isaac and Rebekah; the father of the twelve sons who would be the forefathers of the twelve tribes of Israel.

Want to know more? Read: Genesis 25-49.

Thoughts for today

Jacob's life was characterised by several dramatic encounters. Think, for instance, of his first encounter with his future father-in-law, Laban: but also of his utter frustration because of his first encounter with Leah as his wife, and his seven years of waiting and working before he could marry Rachel. And, of course, there was - later - the reunion with his brother Esau that had been an occasion of great fear, and again - much later - with his son Joseph, whom he had presumed to be dead. But his most dramatic encounter was, no doubt, with a divine Being near the brook Jabbok.

Jacob was well on his way to meet his brother Esau when, at a shallow place in the brook Jabbok, he made his family, his staff and his possessions cross to the other side, while he stayed behind. In the night that followed 'a man wrestled with him till daybreak' (Genesis 32:23-32). The fight was so intense that Jacob's 'hip was wrenched'. Jacob, however, understood that he was not wrestling with an ordinary human being; and for that reason he did not want to let go of his adversary, finally crying out: 'I will not let you go unless you bless me' (vs. 26).

This wrestling match during this never-to-be-forgotten night became the turning point in Jacob's life. The Person with whom he had fought told him that from then onwards he would no longer be called 'Jacob' but would have a new name: 'Israel'. Jacob understood the significance of what had happened: 'It is because I saw God face to face, and yet my life was spared' (vs. 30). With this experience he was able to meet the great challenge that was before him.

My prayer

God of the patriarchs, will You please also be and remain my God?

15 June

Jael

(mountain goat)

Who and when? The woman who killed Sisera, the commander of the Canaanite army who fled when facing defeat against Barak and Deborah.

Want to know more? Read Judges 4; 5.

Thoughts for today

Was Jael a despicable traitor or a heroine? Jael entered the annals of Israel as the woman who played a crucial role in the war between the army of Jabin, the king of the Canaanites, and the Israelite army under the command of Barak and Deborah. She killed the Canaanite commander in his sleep. Sisera thought he had found a safe house, where he could get some rest. Jael invited him into her tent, and he believed that nothing would happen to him, since Jael was married to the Kenite Heber, who had a friendly relationship with Jabin. Once Sisera was in Jael's tent, and had fallen asleep, she took a hammer and a tent peg. She knew how to handle these tools, for in those days the pitching and striking of the family tents was the work of women. 'She drove the peg through his temple into the ground, and he died' (Judges 4:21). When the job was done, she contacted Barak to give him the news. Apparently, she also had a link to the leader of the Israelite army.

On which side was Jael? According to the 'song of Deborah' (Judges 5), Jael was the 'most blessed of women' (vs. 24). Often it is far from easy to know where your primary loyalty must be. But it is not up to us to judge Jael's motives. We can safely leave that to God.

My prayer

Help me, dear Lord, to know where my loyalties must be when I become involved in a conflict.

16 June

Jair

(he enlightens)

Who and when? One of the leaders in the era of the judges; he fulfilled that role during twenty-two years; ca. 1150 BC.

Want to know more? Read: Judges 10:3-5.

Thoughts for today

For several centuries after the occupation of the 'promised land' Israel had no king. However, in times of crisis there were leaders who provided direction and who became the commanders in the battles with surrounding peoples, such as the Philistines. Jair was one of those judges. We are not told how many wives he had, but the story mentions that he had as many as thirty sons. He gave each of them the control of a small town and a donkey.

What are we to make of this? Is this a blatant example of what we would nowadays call nepotism: making sure that your children get nice jobs? And providing each of his thirty sons with a donkey must have cost Jair a considerable sum. Did Jair pay this from his own pocket or did he use some form of taxation or extortion to fund this? Let us give Jair the benefit of the doubt and assume that he did honour to his name ('he enlightens'). Did he want to teach his sons how to bear responsibilities? Is that the reason why he gave each of them the control of a small town and its surrounding area? And perhaps we should not be quick to conclude that the possession of a donkey was an extravagant luxury. A donkey was not only for personal comfort, but also carried cargo. Was it perhaps Jair's intention to teach his sons that they should be involved in providing things for those for whom they had a special responsibility?

Whatever be the case – we cannot help but think about the One who much later entered Jerusalem on a similar kind of transportation, and who was prepared to carry all our burdens.

My prayer

Dear God, make me prepared to assume responsibilities on behalf of others.

17 June

Jairus

(Greek form of Jair: he enlightens)

Who and when? Leader of a Galilean synagogue; Jesus brought his daughter back to life.

Want to know more? Read: Mark 5:21-43.

Thoughts for today

Jairus's faith was tested to the limit. He came to Jesus and pleaded with Him to come to his house, because his twelve-year-old daughter was on the verge of death. Jesus agreed to go with him but was held up on the way. There was a woman who also needed healing: and this took time. Jesus did not want to ignore her in His efforts to get to Jairus's home a little faster.

This was a bitter experience for Jairus, and what he had feared happened. As they were approaching his home a messenger arrived with the news that it was too late. His daughter had just died. But for Jesus this was no reason to turn back. He said to Jairus: 'Don't be afraid; just believe' (Mark 5:36). And when they arrived at His destination, where in the meantime a wailing crowd had assembled, Jesus addressed the people with these words: 'Why all this commotion and wailing? The child is not dead but asleep.' We might have expected that they would have laughed in His face, and they did: but the miracle happened all the same. In response to the words: 'Little girl, I say to you, get up!' she arose and started to walk around, and then was given something to eat.

The father and the mother of the child and three of Jesus' disciples were present when the girl came back to life. Jairus had not dismissed Jesus when it seemed too late to do something for the girl. Jairus persisted in his faith, and even when everything seemed lost he still trusted that for Jesus nothing is impossible. *Persisting in our faith* is always rewarded.

My prayer

Help us, almighty God, to continue to believe, even when our faith is severely tested.

18 June

James

(derived from the Hebrew name, Jacob)

Who and when? Disciple of Jesus; brother of John and the son of Zebedee; he and John were nicknamed 'sons of thunder'.

Want to know more? Read: Matthew 4:18-22; 17:1-13; 20:20-28; 26:36-46.

Thoughts for today

To begin with, John and James were the two rather impetuous sons of a certain Zebedee. The wife of Zebedee is better known to us than her husband, even though we are not informed of her name. Shortly before Jesus ended His ministry she approached Jesus with a request. She wanted nothing more dearly than that her two sons should each get a prominent position in Jesus' kingdom. We do not know whether this was her own idea or whether her sons had orchestrated her intervention.

It happened about a week before Jesus died on the cross. He had given His disciples clear signals of what was about to take place. By this time John and James should have realised that things would not turn out the way they had hoped they would. While Jesus was preparing Himself for the ultimate humiliation He was to suffer, some of His disciples were mainly thinking of status and honour!

In many ways little has changed. Many people today – even in the church – are obsessed by a desire for status and position. But in John's and James's case it is only one side of the story. The good news is that they were able to overcome this weakness. Instead of becoming a high official in an expanding church, John became a prisoner on the isle of Patmos for the sake of his loyalty to Christ, and James would pay with his life for his faith when he was executed by King Herod (Acts 12:2).

My prayer

Merciful God, help me to keep my desire for status in check at any moment when I am tempted to focus more on myself than on You.

19 June

James

(derived from the Hebrew name, Jacob)

Who and when? A half-brother of Jesus. He rose to an important position in the Jerusalem church; presided over the first synod-like meeting of the church (Acts 15).

Want to know more? Read: Galatians 1:19; Acts 15:1-35.

Thoughts for today

We read in Matthew 12 how Jesus got involved in a discussion with Pharisees and scribes, after He had healed a demon possessed man who could not see or hear anything. While they were still talking, Jesus' 'mother and brothers stood outside' (vs. 46). We know the names of four of them: James, Joseph, Simon and Jude. In addition, Jesus also had some sisters (Matthew 13:55, 56). It may be that we are dealing with children of Joseph from an earlier marriage, or with children Joseph and Mary had after Jesus was born. In several places in the New Testament Jesus' brothers are mentioned. In John 7:5 it is stated in passing that initially Jesus' brothers did not believe in Him. Apparently, this was also true for this James.

To our surprise we discover in the book of Acts that the brothers of Jesus were present when, after the ascension, a small group of Jesus' close disciples were 'together constantly in prayer' (Acts 1:14). James was among them. Later we discover that he was the leader during the important church council that debated whether 'gentile Christians' were obliged to obey all traditional Jewish laws. How do we explain this swift and radical change in the attitude of James and his brothers? Something dramatic must have happened that made them change their mind and abandon their scepticism towards their 'brother' Jesus. The only reason I can think of is Jesus' resurrection and His subsequent appearances (1 Corinthians 15:7). That convinced them: the Lord is truly risen!

My prayer

Thank You, heavenly Father, for the eyewitnesses who can assure us that Your Son is truly risen.

Jannes (full of pleasure)

Who and when? One of the Egyptian magicians who tried to imitate the miraculous signs performed by Moses and Aaron at the court of the pharaoh.

Want to know more? Read: Exodus 7:11, 12, 22; 8:7, 18, 19; 9:11; 2 Timothy 3:8, 9.

Thoughts for today

We do not encounter the names of Jannes and Jambres in the Exodus story, but we find them in the New Testament. The names of these two Egyptian magicians were apparently transmitted through other sources.

Moses and Aaron were commanded by God to convince the pharaoh that he should let Israel go: but the Egyptian king did not want to miss the slave labour the Israelites provided. To change the king's mind God sent a series of terrible plagues that affected the entire Egyptian society. By doing this God wanted to demonstrate who and what He is (Exodus 7:17). Things started with a miracle on a rather limited scale. Aaron was to throw his staff on the ground. It promptly changed into a snake – but Jannes and Jambres and their colleagues were able to do the same. This pattern was repeated a number of times. Jannes and Jambres and the other magicians were able to somehow duplicate the miracles that were performed by Moses and Aaron. However, at a given point they had to give up (8:18, 19).

Occult and paranormal agencies continue to be active in our world, just as they were in the world of Moses and Aaron. The evil one enables people to do inexplicable things; but the power of God is always superior. In the war between the powers of darkness and the Power of Light, the Light will always eventually win.

My prayer

You are the omnipotent God, for whom all powers of evil will eventually have to fade away. Help me, O God, always to avoid the occult and to trust only in You.

21 June

Japheth

(let him make wide)

Who and when? The oldest son of Noah; one of the eight people who survived the Flood in the ark.

Want to know more? Read: Genesis 5:32.

Thoughts for today

Noah and his wife had three sons: Shem, Ham and Japheth. This seems rather straightforward, but we are left with a few awkward questions. Were all three sons of the same age? In other words, did Noah and his wife get triplets, as has sometimes been suggested? One could read that into the words of Genesis 5:32: 'After Noah was five hundred years old, he became the father of Shem, Ham and Japheth.' But other texts seem to indicate that their birth was not simultaneous. They were all born when Noah was about five centuries old. But who came first and who came last? It appears that Japheth was the oldest of the three: and, by the way, it is interesting to note that he was already a centenarian when the Flood engulfed the earth!

The three brothers became the 'fathers' of all human beings who repopulated the earth after the Flood. Genesis 10 informs us which peoples descended from whom. However, we should be careful in drawing any direct conclusions, in particular when linking these to speculations about the origin of different races.

Some have suggested that Japheth was the father of all Caucasian peoples, while dark-skinned people are descendants of Ham. And it has further been stressed by some that Japheth is said to be superior to Canaan, the son of Ham, who is said to be Japheth's 'slave' (Genesis 9:27). Nowhere in the Bible, however, do we find any support for a theory of any racial ranking. This means that we should look for an alternative explanation for this Bible text. The interpretation that became common showed human prejudice, not exegetical skills.

My prayer

Thank You, Lord, that we all are Your children. And that is the only thing that counts.

22 June

Jared

(servant)

Who and when? The father of Enoch.

Want to know more? Read: Genesis 5:18-24.

Thoughts for today

Genesis 5 provides us with the genealogy of Adam's posterity until Noah and his three sons. We read that at age sixty-five a certain Mahalalel became the father of Jared. Considering the extremely high ages of the people at the beginning of this earth's history, Jared had a young father, for Mahalalel lived a respectable 895 years. Jared became the father of Enoch when he was 162 years old. After that he lived another 800 years and thus reached an even greater age than his father.

The genealogy presents us with a fixed pattern. The sons always seem to survive their fathers. We still see that as the normal state of affairs, even though nowadays our lives are a whole lot shorter. When parents lose a child it flies in the face of what we expect; however, it happens all too often. Jared also experienced this. He was still alive when his son Enoch was 'taken away' by God. Enoch was 365 years old when that happened. This means that Jared survived his son by almost six centuries! We have no idea how Jared felt about this. Did he know that God had taken Enoch away? Or did he have to live with the thought that his son went missing and his body was never found? For many parents who go through such an experience it seems even worse than it would be if they knew that their child were dead.

Ever since the Fall the loss of the people we love has been a harsh reality. But we look forward to a future when, together with our loved ones, we will get acquainted with Jared and Enoch . . . and Jesus!

My prayer

Loving Father, I ask You to comfort all those fathers and mothers who have suffered the loss of a child.

23 June

Jason

(Greek equivalent of Joshua or Jesus)

Who and when? Jason lived in Thessalonica; he converted to the Christian faith through Paul's ministry and was dragged to court because of his newfound convictions.

Want to know more? Read: Acts 17:1-9.

Thoughts for today

Paul and Silas were quite successful in their work in Thessalonica. Among their converts were many 'God-fearing Greeks' – Greek people who had come to believe in the Jewish God – and also 'not a few prominent women' (Acts 17:4). This success led to considerable opposition. With the assistance of 'some bad characters' a riot was organised that soon got completely out of hand.

Paul and Silas were obviously the main targets. The crowd wanted to subject them to a kangaroo court. This did not work, for the two preachers were nowhere to be found. Instead, Jason, with some others, was dragged out of his house. He was among those who had accepted Christ. Moreover, he had offered hospitality to Paul and Silas. Eventually he was brought before the city officials and was only set free after he and some others had posted bail.

Today there are still many places in the world where it is dangerous to become a Christian and certainly to assist Christian leaders in one way or another. Sometimes people have to suffer far more than Jason did. We have every reason to be grateful when we live in a country with religious freedom, where being involved in the cause of Christ brings no risk.

My prayer

Heavenly Father, I thank You that in my part of the world we can worship You in freedom and have the liberty to tell others about You. We ask You to be today with all those men and women elsewhere in the world who are persecuted because of their faith.

24 June

Jehoahaz

(the Lord saves)

Who and when? Son of Jehu; king of Israel (819 BC to 804 BC).

Want to know more? Read: 2 Kings 13:1-9.

Thoughts for today

While writing this book of daily devotionals I was struck by the fact of how many biblical names start with the letter J. The reason is that in Bible times many parents wanted to give their child a name in which the Hebrew name of God – YHWH – was incorporated. They wanted to express their gratitude for their newborn baby and hoped that their child would be successful in the power of God. This led to the frequent selection of the consonants *yodh* and *heth* as part of these names: as in, for example, 'YeHoshaphat'. The closest English consonant to the Hebrew *yodh* is the letter J: hence 'Jehoshaphat'.

In the past many children in traditionally Christian countries had biblical names. Many Roman Catholic children – both boys and girls – had Mary as one of their proper names. This is largely a thing of the past, but many children are still named after one of the grandparents or after another relative. Names of famous pop stars, actors or sportsmen and women are more in fashion. However, these names are only popular for a time, until other names become fashionable. Analysing the most popular names, it is, nonetheless, surprising to discover how many have biblical roots.

Not all men and women in Bible times with a name in which part of the name YHWH is incorporated were God-fearing people. That was certainly the case with Jehoahaz. And not all boys and girls who are nowadays growing up with biblical names will go through life with God on their side. But, whatever name we have been given, we may all belong to God's extended family, for YHWH is our Father.

My prayer

Heavenly Father, I thank You that I may bear Your name, since I am one of Your children.

25 June

Jehu

(the Lord is He)

Who and when? The eleventh king of Israel; reigned from ca. 841 BC to ca. 814 BC and established the strongest and longest-reigning dynasty of the Northern Kingdom.

Want to know more? Read: 1 Kings 19:17-19; 2 Kings 9; 10.

Thoughts for today

Jehu did not accidentally become king. He had been chosen by God. The prophet Elijah had been commanded by God to anoint Jehu as the king of Israel. The new king was charged to 'destroy the house of Ahab'. The way in which Jehu acquitted himself of this task and how he dealt with Ahab, together with his wife Jezebel and 'the whole house of Ahab' (2 Kings 9:8), is described in gruesome detail. Jehu also thought of a clever way to kill all the prophets of Baal.

We abhor the way enemies were treated in Old Testament times, but the methods used by Jehu were the rule rather than the exception. Apparently, God accepted what Jehu did as proof of obedience to what He had commanded. Unfortunately, Jehu was not totally consistent in his elimination of the idol worship that was rampant among the people. The golden calves, which since the days of Jeroboam had made Dan and Bethel into 'holy' sites, were left untouched.

God had great plans for Jehu and his posterity, but Jehu remained half-hearted in his religious reforms. He 'was not careful to keep the law of the LORD, the God of Israel, with all his heart' (2 Kings 10:31). This meant – as it always does when God's instructions are only partially followed – that things deteriorated. 'In those days the LORD began to reduce the size of Israel' (vs. 32). It was a clear lesson for all who followed after Jehu.

My prayer

I plead with You, Lord, to give me the strength to be consistent in my service to You and to refuse to make compromises.

26 June

Jemimah

(dove)

Who and when? Oldest daughter of Job, born after the time of his suffering. Job lived in patriarchal times.

Want to know more? Read: Job 42:13-17.

Thoughts for today

The book of Job remains a fascinating story. The main theme of the book of Job is the question that has occupied the minds of humankind throughout the ages: Why do some people have to suffer so terribly? Right at the beginning of the story we are told of a dimension that normally remains hidden to us. Unseen powers play an important role. As we read in the following chapters about the dialogue between Job and his 'friends', it becomes clear that human answers are totally inadequate for solving the mystery of suffering. The final dialogue – between God and Job – gives even more food for thought: namely, that the only possible way for man, with all his limitations, to cope with the problem of suffering is to trust the almighty God unconditionally.

In the final chapter of the book all Job's troubles are over. He is even richer than before, and he gets seven sons and three daughters. He lives 'happily ever after' – that is, for another 140 years. Jemimah is the oldest of the three daughters. The names of the two others are Keziah and Keren-Happuch. Remarkably enough, the names of the three girls are mentioned, while the names of the boys are not. And, against all the rules of patriarchal times, Jemimah and her sisters receive an equal part of the inheritance, just as their brothers. We can only conclude that the fact that this is recorded was intentional. The evil one was defeated, and even the male-female relationship – with the customary inequality and subservience of the women to the men – was (in this instance) restored according to God's original plan.

My prayer

Father of all people, help all Your children today to do their utmost in restoring the original full equality between men and women.

27 June

Jephthah

(he opens)

Who and when? Commander in the battle against the Ammonites in the times of the judges. Ca. 1200 BC.

Want to know more? Read: Judges 11; 12:1-7.

Thoughts for today

Although initially facing some serious disadvantages, Jephthah was eventually accepted as the leader in the war against the Ammonites, who were fierce enemies of Israel. Jephthah first tried to come to an understanding with the Ammonite king through diplomatic means, but when this failed a military solution seemed the only option. He could count on divine support, for 'the Spirit of the LORD came upon Jephthah' (Judges 11:29). At that critical moment, however, Jephthah made a rash promise. He 'made a vow to the LORD: "If you give the Ammonites into my hands, whatever comes out of the door of my house to meet me when I return in triumph from the Ammonites will be the LORD's, and I will sacrifice it as a burnt offering" ' (vss. 30, 31). Jephthah came to regret his promise. When he returned safely from the battlefield, his teenage daughter (his only child) came to meet him. Jephthah was convinced that he could not break his promise and he therefore 'did to her as he had vowed' (vs. 39). Did God really expect Jephthah to sacrifice his daughter? It is hard to imagine, for God has always condemned the practice of human sacrifice that was so prevalent with other nations.

In any case, what we can learn from this tragic story is that we must think twice before we make any promises: and, when we do, we must be sure that we can, in fact, do what we have promised.

My prayer

Protect me, dear God, against rash promises that may land me in major difficulties.

28 June

Jeremiah

(the Lord is exalted)

Who and when? Jeremiah was one of the 'major' prophets of the Old Testament; lived from ca. 645 to ca. 587 BC. His ministry took place during the last phase of the Kingdom of Judah and at the beginning of the Babylonian exile.

Want to know more? Read: Jeremiah, especially 1; 16–21; 32; 36–45.

Thoughts for today

Jeremiah did not have an easy life. The country was in a constant crisis. Under those circumstances Jeremiah was called to a prophetic ministry, but his messages were seldom welcome. On the contrary, his work brought him much personal suffering.

Jeremiah is especially known for the Lamentations that are attributed to him. He 'lamented' his personal circumstances and the fact that his people had been deported to Babylon. He tried to record all the misery that had befallen Judah, but this proved to be exceedingly difficult for him. In his second hymn we read: 'My eyes fail from weeping, I am in torment within, my heart is poured out on the ground' (Lamentations 2:11). Fortunately, Jeremiah did not stay stuck in his sadness, but remained steadfast in his hope that God would intervene: 'Because of the LORD's great love we are not consumed, for his compassions never fail. They are new every morning; great is your faithfulness. I say to myself, "The LORD is my portion; therefore I will wait for him." The LORD is good for those whose hope is in him, to the one who seeks him; it is good to wait quietly for the salvation of the LORD' (Lamentations 3:22-26).

My prayer

Almighty God, You know of the enormous difficulties we must sometimes face. And You also know that we often wonder why there is so much suffering in the world. Help me today, Father, not to forget that there is also another side to the coin. Thank You for Your compassion that we experience anew every day.

29 June

Jeroboam I

(may the people multiply)

Who and when? Jeroboam became king over the ten northern tribes after Solomon's death (930 BC to 909 BC).

Want to know more? Read: 1 Kings 11:26–14:20.

Thoughts for today

We often see that, when facing serious problems, men and women who have become Christians secretly revert to certain practices that they knew from before the time that they were converted – to things that are diametrically opposed to the Christian faith and to what the Bible teaches.

In the case of King Jeroboam I there were other considerations. He knew the true God. He had become king over the northern tribes (after Solomon's death) and decided, from political motives, to introduce a new kind of worship. He did not want his people to go to Jerusalem to worship God, for that would mean they would still have strong ties with the Kingdom of Judah. Jeroboam therefore gave orders to build two new sanctuaries, where he installed new altars and two golden calves. These were the places where his people were to worship from then onwards. 'And this thing became a sin' (1 Kings 12:30).

The prophets tried in vain to convince Jeroboam of his error, but the king persisted in his strategies; but when there was a crisis in his family he panicked and approached the prophet Ahijah. He did not dare to do this openly, so he sent his wife in disguise. If Jeroboam had stayed close to the Lord, his career as a king and his personal life would have been quite different. Jeroboam remains a sad example of what happens when we turn radically away from the true God.

My prayer

Lord, let me learn the lesson from the example of Jeroboam that my only safety is in remaining close to You.

30 June

Jeroboam II

(may the people multiply)

Who and when? Son of King Jehoash; king of Israel for forty-one years (790 BC to 749 BC).

Want to know more? Read: 2 Kings 14:23-29.

Thoughts for today

From a political perspective King Jeroboam II was an important king. 'He was the one who restored the boundaries of Israel' (2 Kings 14:25). He reconquered areas that had once belonged to Solomon's empire. Nonetheless, the author of the second book of Kings did not spend much time on him. The reason is that 'he did evil in the eyes of the LORD'. He did not break away from the evil practices of his namesake (Jeroboam I), who sat on the throne one century earlier and who had 'caused Israel to commit' serious sins (2 Kings 14:24).

However, God did not forsake Israel, in spite of all the wrongs Jeroboam was supporting and that had been followed by large groups in society. 'The LORD had seen how bitterly everyone in Israel, whether slave or free, was suffering' (vs. 26); and, because God had decided 'not [to] blot out the name of Israel from under heaven' (vs. 27), he used Jeroboam, in spite of his idolatrous practices, to deliver his people from their enemies: and God was still prepared to communicate with Jeroboam. Jonah was one of the prophets who brought God's messages to the king (vs. 25). It was not because of any merits of Jeroboam or his subjects that God intervened, but because of His love and His patience. This may, however, never be a reason to continue in our disobedience. The later history of Israel shows how doing so is playing with fire.

My prayer

I thank You, loving Lord, that You also have such great patience with me.

1 July

Jesse

(the Lord exists)

Who and when? David's father and one of Christ's earthly ancestors.

Want to know more? Read: 1 Samuel 16:1-13; 17:12-18

Thoughts for today

Jesse had eight sons and two daughters. At the time of today's story at least three of his sons were old enough to serve in Saul's army, but his son David was still too young to be conscripted. David's daily work was to tend his father's sheep and to run an occasional errand for him. The Bible tells us much more about David than about the lives of his brothers and sisters.

We read in 1 Samuel 16 how Samuel was commanded by God to travel to Bethlehem to anoint one of the sons of Jesse as the successor of King Saul. When Samuel arranged for a festive meal in Bethlehem, Jesse was invited as one of the guests of honour. All Jesse's sons, except David, were also present. It was immediately clear to Samuel that Eliab, the oldest son, was the one to be anointed! However, God indicated to Samuel that Eliab was not His choice. Then Jesse called Abinadab, his second son: but neither was Abinadab the person God wanted. In this manner all Jesse's sons but one were presented to Samuel. In the end Jesse was told to send for his youngest son. When David arrived, God said to Samuel: 'Anoint him; he is the one' (1 Samuel 16:12).

Jesse must have wondered why David was chosen. He had yet to learn that God has His own criteria when electing people for a particular task: 'The Lord does not look at the things man looks at. Man looks at the outward appearance, but the Lord looks at the heart' (1 Samuel 16:7).

My prayer

I thank You, O God, for this lesson that I also need to learn: namely, that our heart is more important than our outward appearance.

2 July

Jethro

(eminent)

Who and when? Father-in-law of Moses, priest in Midian. Also referred to as Reuel. Fifteenth century BC.

Want to know more? Read: Exodus 2:15-22; 3:1; 18.

Thoughts for today

Jethro was a significant person in Moses' life. He was a priest in Midian, a region in the northeastern part of the Arabian peninsula. This is where Moses found refuge after his escape from Egypt, and it is where he met Jethro. Moses married Zipporah, one of the seven daughters of Jethro. He stayed in Midian for forty years, where he watched over the sheep of his father-in-law. Later, after the exodus, Jethro came to visit Moses in the wilderness. Zipporah and Moses' two sons accompanied him. They had stayed behind in Midian during the period of Moses' return to Egypt and the tumultuous events of the exodus that followed.

When Jethro met his son-in-law, Moses, again – not as a shepherd, but as a leader of hundreds of thousands of people – he noticed how exhausted Moses was because of all the administrative issues he had to deal with (Exodus 18:1-27). Often an outsider has a much clearer view of the situation than the people who are in the midst of things. That was also true in this case. Jethro urged Moses not to try to do everything by himself, but to delegate many of his duties to others.

Learning how to delegate is an essential aspect of leadership at all levels. We overestimate ourselves when we think that we can do all things better than others, and that it is risky to let others take care of some of our duties. Moses accepted Jethro's counsel and entrusted part of his work to others. If you are a leader and have not yet learned how to delegate, it is high time to start doing so!

My prayer

Teach me, O God, not to want to do everything myself, and to trust in the capabilities of other people.

3 July

Jezebel (meaning uncertain)

Who and when? Jezebel was a princess from Tyre who married King Ahab (reigned from 872 BC to 852 BC) and introduced the Baal cult to Israel on a large scale.

Want to know more? Read: 1 Kings 16:29-33; 2 Kings 9:30-37; Revelation 2:20.

Thoughts for today

Most Old Testament men and women are not mentioned in the New Testament. Some of them, however, do play an important role in the New Testament. Jezebel has the questionable honour that her name was not forgotten when John was commanded by God to write a letter to the church in Thyatira. This church provided an ample platform to a person who claimed to be a 'prophetess'. This person is referred to as 'that woman Jezebel' (Revelation 2:20). She misled the members of the Thyatira church with her false teachings and encouraged immorality. In the Old Testament sexual immorality is often a metaphor for a relationship with false gods and the promotion of idol worship.

Jezebel was very influential, first as queen and then as queen mother. She used her influence to promote the worship of Baal and Asherah, with success - until the prophet Elijah was able, in the power of God, to turn the tide. The church in the first century also had such a 'successful' Jezebel; and there may well be Jezebels in our day and age. (But don't for a minute think that women are always the culprits!) Today God disapproves just as much as in the past of Jezebels who intentionally mislead their fellow believers and create confusion. John underlines this in his message to Thyatira with these words: 'All the churches will know that I am he who searches hearts and minds, and I will repay each of you according to your deeds' (Revelation 2:23).

My prayer

Lord, open the eyes of all Your children to any Jezebels in their midst.

4 July

Jezrahiah

(the Lord will arise)

Who and when? Leader of the choir at the dedication of the wall of Jerusalem, after part of God's people had returned from the Babylonian exile.

Want to know more? Read: Nehemiah 12:40-43.

Thoughts for today

I remember an event from my childhood days that I found rather strange. Somebody had started a new business in the village where I lived, and the Catholic priest came with his 'holy water' to publicly bless the fledgling enterprise. In the Protestant part of our village this practice was completely unknown. It was only much later that I discovered that among certain immigrant members of my own faith community the dedication of new homes or important objects is quite common.

In the days of Nehemiah (fifth century BC) the practice of dedicating objects also existed. When the wall around Jerusalem had been restored by the exiles who had returned from Babylon, it was dedicated in an impressive ceremony, as is recorded in some detail in Nehemiah 12. It was the occasion for numerous sacrifices, with processions, prayers – and a lot of music and singing. Jezrahiah directed the large choirs that figured prominently in the programme.

Many people in the Western world do not feel the need to link religion to the common things of everyday life. They do not 'dedicate' the ordinary things to God and do not feel the need to link all our common affairs with Him. But maybe we should think again! God is also eager to play a role in our everyday affairs: so why not also dedicate things and events that happen outside the church to our Lord?

My prayer

Also today, dear heavenly Father, I want to dedicate what I do and produce to You and to ask Your blessing over it.

5 July

Joab

(the Lord is Father)

Who and when? Prominent military leader during the reign of King David (ca. 1000 BC).

Want to know more? Read: 2 Samuel 3; 14; 18; 19:1-9; 20.

Thoughts for today

From everything that we read in the Bible about Joab we may safely conclude that he was good at his work. He was a courageous and skilful strategist who won many battles for David. However, Joab was also very keen on protecting his own position. He had an enormous ego, and ruthlessly eliminated everyone who could become a competitor. King David was prepared to pardon men like Abner and Absolom, in spite of their disloyalty, but for Joab such leniency was unthinkable. As far as he was concerned, he always came first. In other words: Joab was driven by unrestrained ambition.

Today, ambition is generally regarded as a positive quality. A person must know what he wants in life and must make sure that he is not taken for granted by others. It is wise to plan your career and always keep your ultimate goal in mind! We often refer to this attitude as being assertive. Any good bookshop has lots of books on this topic.

A Christian should have ambitions, but they must always be embedded in our service to God and to our fellow men. We are on the wrong track if everything is focused on ourselves and our career success. The path for the Christian is not that of hard-nosed ambition as chosen by Joab, but the one of selfless love and service modelled for us by Christ.

My prayer

Help me, heavenly Father, always to make sure that my ambitions are embedded in love for You and my neighbour.

6 July

Joanna

(the Lord is gracious)

Who and when? The wife of Chuza, the manager of Herod's household.

Want to know more? Read: Luke 8:1-3; 23:55, 56; 24:10.

Thoughts for today

The Gospel reaches and changes the hearts of people in all classes of society. It is not primarily, as has been argued by some, a kind of safe haven for 'simple' people – a 'pie-in-the-sky' story that helps poor people face their grinding daily existence. Time and again we see in the New Testament how people from higher social echelons were also touched by the message of Jesus. Joanna, the wife of Chuza (one of the highest officials of King Herod Antipas), was among them. The Bible story does not inform us whether this Chuza was also convinced of Jesus' message, but that may well have been the case.

Joanna had experienced, in a very direct way, what Jesus was able to do. She belonged to a group of women who had been delivered from evil spirits and healed from physical ailments. We do not know what kind of physical or psychological problems Joanna had suffered from, but she must have remembered them well. She had discovered that Jesus was the Messiah, for whom no miracle was too big to perform, and had become one of His disciples and assisted Him in His daily needs. After the death of Jesus, together with a few other women, she cared for His body – later becoming one of the first witnesses to His resurrection.

The Gospel still appeals to people in all layers of society. But let us, in spreading the message of Jesus Christ, not forget the men and women in so-called 'higher circles'. Some of them are also aspirant disciples of Christ!

My prayer

Dear Lord, help me always to remember that You do not care about status or social importance, but that Your only concern is to see people saved through Your Son.

7 July

Joash

(the Lord has given)

Who and when? King of Judah (841 BC to 801 BC).

Want to know more? Read: 2 Kings 11; 12.

Thoughts for today

As a toddler Joash narrowly escaped the massacre his grandmother Athaliah had organised. She succeeded in usurping the throne of Judah, but one of his aunts hid him, together with his wet nurse, in a bedroom. There Joash 'remained hidden with his nurse at the temple of the LORD for six years' (2 Kings 11:3). During those years he was in close contact with the priests and the high priest. That proved to be a very positive influence, and we are told that 'Joash did what was right in the eyes of the LORD all the years Jehoiada the priest instructed him' (2 Kings 12:2).

Joash officially became the king when he was only seven years old. Obviously, for some time others were really in charge of the government. The high priest, Jehoiada, played an important role; but when Joash grew up he ceased to be a marionette in the hands of others. We deduce from 2 Kings 12 that he initiated and promoted numerous religious reforms. No longer did he himself receive instructions, but gradually he was able to lead those who had guided him in his younger years. This is a process we should see more often. It is essential that young people have inspiring role models and benefit from the wisdom of the people around them. But the time comes when they must make their own choices and must themselves become role models for those who are entrusted to their leadership and care.

My prayer

I thank You, Lord, for the people who have been role models for me. Help me also to become an inspiring role model for others.

8 July

Job

(where is my father?)

Who and when? A rich man in patriarchal times, who lost everything but regained his former status after a period of intense suffering.

Want to know more? Read: Job 1; 2; 38-42.

Thoughts for today

The story of Job presents the modern reader with many questions. What do we make of the heavenly discussion between God and Satan about Job's deepest motivations? Is this the way God really works? And how do we reconcile the concept of a loving God with the impression that God had His hand in the suffering that Job endured, including the terrible loss of his children and servants?

Commentators have wrestled with these and many other problems, but reading some of their books has not answered all my questions either. What I have learned, however, as the main lesson from the book of Job is that Job does not turn his back on God, even when things could not get worse. He even ignores the comments of his wife, who urges him to renounce his faith in God when confronted with so much adversity. Neither does Job accept the ideas of his 'friends', who suggest that he carries a big, dark secret with him and that this is why God is punishing him. He summarises his faith in these immortal words: 'Shall we accept good from God, and not trouble?' (Job 2:10) and 'though he slay me, yet will I hope in him' (Job 13:15).

Let us be grateful that the book of Job found its way into the biblical canon. Yes, it leaves us with many perplexing questions, but at the same time it gives us an inspiring example of someone holding on to their faith, even though it is being severely tested.

My prayer

Heavenly Father, I have no idea what troubles I may yet have to face in the future: but help me, whatever happens, never to turn my back on You.

9 July

Jochebed

(the Lord is glory)

Who and when? The wife of Amram and the mother of Aaron, Moses and Miriam.

Want to know more? Read: Exodus 2:1-10; 6:20.

Thoughts for today

We do not know whether Jochebed lived long enough to see her two sons in prominent leadership positions, but we do know of her actions at the beginning of Moses' life. After Jochebed had given birth to Moses, she decided to keep the matter secret, and for good reason. The Egyptian rulers were afraid that the people of Israel would become too numerous and would in the long term present a serious threat to their nation. For that reason they decided to kill all male Hebrew babies (Exodus 1:15-22). Jochebed devised a strategy to save Moses' life. She put him in a papyrus basket and placed it among the reeds along the bank of the Nile. This eventually led to Moses' adoption as a son of one of Pharaoh's daughters. Jochebed provides a clear example of what we would nowadays call civil disobedience.

Another detail is worth mentioning. The midwives who helped the Hebrew women to give birth had their own way of resisting the authorities, and they were able to save many Hebrew boys. They did not yet have Paul's letter to the Romans, where in chapter 13 we are told to obey the powers that are set over us. But they had already understood what the apostle Peter would later say in Acts 5:29 (NKJV): 'We ought to obey God rather than men.'

Christians should be loyal to their rulers; everything would turn to chaos if each of us could individually change the laws of the land and amend the rules of our organisations: but when important moral values are at stake, these should always guide us. In those cases we definitely must obey God rather than men.

My prayer

Help me, Lord, to be loyal to authorities, but give me the insight to know when moral principles must prevail over human rules and regulations.

10 July

Joel

(the Lord is God)

Who and when? A prophet in Israel and/or Judah. There is no consensus as to when he lived or when the book that bears his name was written.

Want to know more? Read: Joel.

Thoughts for today

We know nothing about the person of Joel, except that he was the son of a certain Pethuel. Joel was a common name in Bible times and we can find fourteen Joels in the Bible. The three chapters of the prophetic writing that bears the name of the prophet Joel have the shortest of introductions: 'The word of the LORD that came to Joel son of Pethuel' (Joel 1:1).

Unlike most prophets, Joel does not address any specific enemies of God's people. His message is more general in content. The first part is about the coming judgement, while in the second part the promise of restoration and of the pouring out of the Spirit of God gets most emphasis. Joel was the prophet who predicted Pentecost. The book of Acts refers directly to the prophecy of Joel, when in Jerusalem, shortly after Christ's ascension, miraculous events begin to happen and thousands of people decide to follow Jesus (Acts 2:16-21). We read in verse 16: 'This is what was spoken by the prophet Joel.'

However, what happened then was only a partial fulfilment of Joel's prophecy. Just before the 'day of the LORD' comes – 'great and dreadful' (Joel 2:31) – God 'will pour out [His] Spirit on all people'. The greatest fulfilment of that is still in the future. Will we still be alive when that happens?

My prayer

Your church and every one of Your followers need the 'pouring out' of the Holy Spirit, O God. Giver of all good things, would You please help us to be prepared for this great event?

11 July

Johanan

(the Lord is gracious)

Who and when? Leader of those Israelites who had not been deported to Babylon; contemporary of Jeremiah.

Want to know more? Read: Jeremiah 40-43.

Thoughts for today

A significant part of the people of Israel were *not* deported to Babylon. The Babylonian rulers appointed Gedaliah as the governor of those who had remained behind. Gedaliah believed it was prudent to accept the foreign rule and make the best of it; but some did not agree with this point of view. Ishmael, a more radical leader, led out in a revolt against Gedaliah, in which the latter was killed. This brought Ishmael to power, but not for very long. Johanan, who replaced him, feared that the Babylonians would revenge the murder of Gedaliah, who was their appointee, and decided that fleeing to Egypt was the safest approach. However, the prophet Jeremiah strongly opposed this plan: this was not the Lord's will.

Well, what do *we* do when we are confronted with major difficulties? Do we try to make the best of it? Do we panic and cause further problems? Or do we flee? This last option may seem most attractive, but running away is usually a sign of weakness - especially when it is clear that this will lead to a very uncertain future.

From time to time most of us will face serious problems, possibly for a long period. It may be that we have caused these predicaments ourselves. When this happens, we must honestly evaluate our situation and try to make the best of it; and, when we have faith in God, we know that He is an enormous source of strength: but He never wants us to run away from our problems. With His help we can deal with them.

My prayer

Heavenly Father, help us not to run away from our problems, but to retain our trust that You are a source of inspiration and strength for us, even when everything seems to be going against us.

John

(Greek form of Jochanan or Jehohanan – the Lord is gracious)

Who and when? A disciple of Jesus. He is referred to as 'the disciple whom Jesus loved' (John 13:23).

Want to know more? Read: Matthew 4:18-25; John 19:25-27; 21:1-25.

Thoughts for today

According to the biblical data and early Christian sources, all of the twelve apostles died as martyrs, except John. This does not by any stretch of the imagination mean that life was easy for him. During the reign of Emperor Domitian he was banished to the small Greek island of Patmos, where he received the visions that were the basis for the book of Revelation. We have strong indications that he was set free when the period of persecution ended, and that he spent the rest of his days in the nearby city of Ephesus (on the coast of present-day Turkey). A trustworthy tradition has it that he died in Ephesus and was buried there. A less trustworthy tradition tells us that Mary, the mother of Jesus, could also be found in Ephesus in the final years of her life. Most tourists to Ephesus visit the small chapel that stands on the place where Mary's house is supposed to have been.

Before we totally discredit this tradition, we would do well to remember that John was told by his Master to care for His mother Mary. When Jesus was hanging on the cross He pointed to Mary and said to John: 'Here is your mother.' No doubt John had tried to do what Jesus expected of him. It may be that this is one of the reasons God gave John such a long life. Considering what we know of our loving heavenly Father, this might very well be possible.

My prayer

Thank You, O God, for Your care, which I constantly experience.

13 July

John the Baptist

(the Lord is gracious)

Who and when? Contemporary and cousin of Jesus; announced Jesus' coming and was executed by Herod Antipas.

Want to know more? Read: John 1:19-39; 3:22-36; Matthew 11; 14:1-12.

Thoughts for today

John the Baptist knew his place. He was aware of the remarkable circumstances surrounding his birth and knew that he was predestined for a prophetic role. He was privileged to be the 'precursor' of the promised Messiah. Neverthess, even though large crowds came to listen to him, he had no thought of competing with the Messiah, saying instead: 'A man who comes after me has surpassed me' (John 1:30).

This is an admirable attitude. Most of us have some inborn desire to want to be the first or the best. Even Jesus' disciples were constantly preoccupied with that thought. They argued about who would have the most prominent position in the kingdom they thought Jesus would soon establish.

Many people find it difficult to play second fiddle. They may, for instance, criticise their boss and think that they would, in fact, be much more suited for the top job. We also notice this phenomenon in the church. But if God has given us the role of someone who 'prepares the way', we must be satisfied with this. It only causes frustration and misery if we find it difficult, or even impossible, to have someone 'above' us, who outranks us. We would do well to often repeat the words of John the Baptist: 'He must become greater; I must become less' (John 3:30).

My prayer

Help me, heavenly Father, always to give You the first place in my life.

14 July

Jehoiachin

(the Lord establishes)

Who and when? Was for a short time king of Judah (598 BC to 597 BC), before being deported as an exile to Babylon.

Want to know more? Read: 2 Kings 24:6-16; 25:27-30; Jeremiah 52:31-34.

Thoughts for today

Jehoiachin was the last in a long series of kings who ruled over Judah. Zedekiah was the only one who was yet to follow, but he effectively lost the last vestige of independence and was in all respects a vassal of Babylon. In fact, the reign of Jehoiachin did not have much lustre either. His entire reign is summarised in 2 Chronicles 36 in two verses: 'Jehoiachin was eighteen years old when he became king, and he reigned in Jerusalem three months and ten days. He did evil in the eyes of the LORD. In the spring, King Nebuchadnezzar sent for him, and brought him to Babylon, together with articles of value from the temple of the LORD, and he made Jehoiachin's uncle, Zedekiah, king over Judah and Jerusalem' (verses 9 and 10).

We do not know how long Jehoiachin lived. In any case, he spent a major part of his life in Babylonian imprisonment. After he had been kept under lock and key for thirty-seven years, he was pardoned at the inauguration of a new king. For the rest of his life Jehoiachin lived at the royal court. The new king of Babylon had been told about the fate of this man, whose only 'crime' had been that he, as an eighteen-year-old boy, had been addressed for a few months as 'Your Majesty'.

Today many people are in prison for some, often presumed, political reason. The people and organisations that work on their behalf deserve our full support.

My prayer

Almighty Father in heaven, I ask Your blessing for organisations such as Amnesty International that work on behalf of people who are in prison, often without any valid reason.

15 July

Jehoiada

(the Lord knows)

Who and when? High priest who (in 805 BC) was instrumental in placing Joash on the throne of Judah.

Want to know more? Read: 2 Kings 11; 2 Chronicles 23; 24:1-16.

Thoughts for today

Jehoiada played an important role in the life of the young King Joash. He orchestrated the demise of the apostate Queen Athaliah and the official recognition of the seven-year-old Joash as the king of Judah. The biblical story shows that Jehoiada knew how to take the necessary security measures to protect Joash against assassins and people who, even after her death, remained loyal to Athaliah.

Jehoiada's influence, however, went further than the royal court. He led out in the restoration work of the temple and organised the financial aspect of this project in such a way that corruption was minimised. Once the temple was restored the daily sacrifices could recommence (2 Chronicles 24:14). But, sad to say, the mentality among the people and among the influential men around the king did not change. When Jehoiada died at a ripe old age, the 'officials of Judah' undid much of the good work of Jehoiada. 'They abandoned the temple of the LORD, the God of their fathers, and worshipped Asherah poles and idols' (vs. 18).

A strong leader can play an important role in the processes of change, also in the church. But, if the hearts of the people are not affected, everything reverts to what it was as soon as the leader is no longer there. Reformation always was, and still is, not a matter of power and of submission to the instructions of leaders, but of conversion.

My prayer

Lord, thank You for people like Jehoiada. I pray that their influence may penetrate the hearts of the people.

16 July

Jehoiakim

(the Lord raises up)

Who and when? Jehoiakim succeeded his father as king of Judah and became totally dependent on Egypt. He ruled from 609 BC to 598 BC.

Want to know more? Read: 2 Kings 23:36–24:6.

Thoughts for today

By the time Jehoiakim became king, Judah's role as an independent nation was seriously compromised. Two major powers wanted to extend their sphere of influence in Judah's direction: Egypt and Babylon. Initially it seemed that Egypt was the stronger of the two, but after some time Babylon was destined to gain the upper hand and would bring Judah's independence to an end. Jehoiakim played a role in the final phase of the kingdom of Judah. At first he had to pay a heavy tax to Egypt. This money was to be gathered from the people, which did not exactly enhance Jehoiakim's popularity. And things only got worse when he became a vassal of Babylon.

However, more importantly, Jehoiakim was not popular with God. God was greatly disappointed because 'he did evil in the eyes of the LORD' (2 Kings 23:37). Jeremiah did not have anything positive to say about this king either. He prophesied about Jehoiakim with these words: 'They will not mourn for him' (Jeremiah 22:18). It is indeed a very sad finale for a king when his subjects are not really sorry that he is gone.

Most likely there will be no street or square named after most of us, but we do hope that we will be missed by at least some people! This will, however, to a large extent depend on the way we have lived our lives.

My prayer

Almighty God, help me to stay on the right track, and grant that I may be thus remembered!

17 July

Jehoshaphat

(the Lord has judged)

Who and when? King of Judah; reigned from 870 BC to 845 BC.

Want to know more? Read: 1 Kings 15:24; 22:41-50; 2 Kings 3; 2 Chronicles 17:1-21:1.

Thoughts for today

King Jehoshaphat was one of the good kings of Judah. The author of 2 Chronicles pays a lot of attention to him. 'He walked in the ways [of] his father David' and 'followed [God's] commands rather than the practices of Israel' (2 Chronicles 17:3, 4). This is, by the way, something we see all the time: the deeds of the 'good' kings of Israel and Judah are described in much more detail that those of the 'evil' kings. The reason is the particular perspective of biblical history, where political importance is not the most significant factor.

In passing, 1 Kings 22:48-50 refers to a very special project of Jehoshaphat. After his 'alliance with Ahaziah king of Israel, who was guilty of wickedness' (2 Chronicles 20:35-37), he built a commercial fleet to import gold from Ophir, which failed when the ships were wrecked on their maiden voyage. Was this just a matter of bad luck or poor design, as has happened throughout history – for instance, when in 1628 the new Swedish warship *Vasa* sailed from Stockholm and sank almost immediately? No: Jehoshaphat had received a prophey telling him that 'his works' (his fleet) were to be destroyed by God because of his ties with the godless Ahaziah (2 Chronicles 20:35-37). It was a dark page in the annals of the 'good' King Jehoshaphat.

All too often, people who want to serve God find that there are moments in their lives when they stumble. We do not know what happened to Jehoshaphat in the final period of his life: but we do know that God forgives and is merciful, which would also apply to this 'good' king.

My prayer

Keep me, Lord, from embarking on projects that do not have Your approval. Help me to listen to the voice of Your Spirit.

18 July

Jonah (dove)

Who and when? A prophet in the Northern Kingdom during the early part of the reign of Jeroboam II (792 BC to 753 BC). His ministry is described in the Bible book that has his name, which is found among the 'minor' prophets.

Want to know more? Read: Jonah 1–4.

Thoughts for today

The story of Jonah speaks to our imagination. The incident of the prophet inside 'a great fish' is very popular with children. But today we want to focus for a few moments on how it all began. Jonah was commanded by God to travel to the pagan city of Nineveh to give them the message God had for them. This was not at all what Jonah wanted, so he found a ship that would take him to far-away Tarshish, 'away from the Lord'.

Jonah experienced what countless others after him have also gone through. We may decide to be disobedient when God commands us to do something. We may choose a route for our lives that leads us away from God – but running away from the Lord is simply impossible. That is what the prophet soon discovered. He ran away, but God caught up with him.

Jonah was rather stubborn. God had to intervene more than once to bring Jonah back in line. But God was patient with the prophet. That continues to be a comforting thought for us too. We may have run away from God more than once in our life, but we still have the assurance that God does not easily give up on us.

My prayer

Lord, forgive me if I have sometimes run away from You. Thank You for Your patience and for the fact that You always catch up with me.

19 July

Jonadab

(the Lord is bounteous)

Who and when? Son of Shimeah, the brother of David.

Want to know more? Read: 2 Samuel 13:1-22.

Thoughts for today

Jonadab played a very dubious role in the drama in which Amnon, the oldest son of David, and Tamar were the main characters. Amnon had fallen in love with his half-sister Tamar. He searched for an opportunity to circumvent the rules of the palace, for 'she was a virgin, and it seemed impossible for him to do anything to her' (2 Samuel 13:2). Amnon took his cousin Jonadab into confidence and the latter came up with a plan.

There are remarkable differences in the way the various Bible translations inform us about the special gifts of Jonadab. Some translations tell us that Jonadab was a man 'with much experience', while other Bible versions say that he was 'very crafty' or 'very shrewd'. Apparently, Jonadab had a solution for every knotty problem!

Jonadab's solution did indeed work, for it brought Tamar to Amnon's bedroom. The rest of the story is well known. It provides us with a clear example that not every sort of 'experience' or every kind of clever trick may count on God's approval. Advice that is based on true wisdom is in a very different category!

My prayer

Loving God, You who know everything, please remind me today not to follow my own crafty tricks, but to ask You for true wisdom.

20 July

Jonathan

(the Lord has given)

Who and when? Son of Saul; very successful in combat; becomes close friend of David, even though David is hated by his father.

Want to know more? Read: 1 Samuel 14:24-45; 18:1-3; 31:2.

Thoughts for today

It has been suggested by some that there must have been a homosexual relationship between David and Jonathan. The main basis for this idea is the statement we find in 2 Samuel 1:26, where David is quoted as saying: 'Your love for me was wonderful, more wonderful than that of women.' Homosexuality was well known in ancient times, but everything we know about David gives us no reason whatsoever to assume that he was sexually attracted to men. There was, however, no doubt that there was a very close friendship between him and Jonathan.

True friendship is something very precious. We find many examples of this in the Bible. Jesus had a special relationship with some of His disciples, as, for instance, with Lazarus and John. Unfortunately, in our era of Facebook friends, the concept of 'friendship' has been greatly devalued. Even vague acquaintances are now referred to as 'friends'. Yet, in spite of having scores, or even hundreds, of these so-called 'friends', many people feel extremely lonely.

Loneliness is a plague of our modern times. Real friendship can, however, make a great deal of difference. The problem is that many people – especially men – find it increasingly difficult to build close friendships. One of the most important ingredients for friendship is a shared interest. But it is even more important that we are willing to invest time in our relationships with friends and to always 'be there' for them.

My prayer

Teach me, heavenly Father, how to build true friendships and how I can 'be there' for my friends under all circumstances.

21 July

Joram

(the Lord is exalted)

Who and when? King of Israel (851 BC to 841 BC); contemporary of the prophet Elisha.

Want to know more? Read: 2 Kings 3; 5.

Thoughts for today

King Joram had to deal with Naaman, the Syrian army commander, who was suffering from a serious skin disease and had been told by his physicians that there was no hope for him. He had heard about the prophet Elisha and about the miracles this prophet performed. He therefore set off to Israel with a large entourage. Protocol required that he should first visit the king of Israel with the letter that his own king had provided him with. The content of the letter caused a serious misunderstanding. The Syrian king asked Joram in his letter to ensure that Naaman would be healed. It did not mention any involvement of the prophet Elisha. Joram suspected a conspiracy. Was his Syrian counterpart looking for an excuse to start a war? Did he really expect Joram to heal the patient? 'Am I God? Can I kill and bring back to life?' King Joram exclaimed in his desperation (2 Kings 5:7). As was the custom in those days, King Joram 'tore his robes' to express how dark the whole situation seemed to him.

Joram was, however, wise enough to see his own limitations. The story goes on to tell us that the prophet Elisha heard about what had happened and let it be known that Naaman should come to him. He sent a message: 'Make the man come to me and he will know that there is a prophet in Israel.' Thereupon Naaman went to see Elisha and was cured. It brought Naaman to the recognition that the God of Israel was far superior to all Syrian gods. Unfortunately, we do not read that Joram put aside the idols he worshipped. If that had happened the outcome of the story would have been even better.

My prayer

All-powerful God, please lead our lives in such a way that we see Your love and power and will set aside all things that hinder us in our focus on You.

22 July

Joram

(the Lord is exalted)

Who and when? King of Judah; reigned from 848 BC to 841 BC

Want to know more? Read: 2 Kings 8:16-24; 2 Chronicles 21:5-20.

Thoughts for today

When comparing the kings of the Northern Kingdom (Israel) with their colleagues in the kingdom of the two tribes, Judah, we discover that, on average, the kings of Judah receive a more positive press in the Bible. Beginning with King Jeroboam I, the ten tribes followed their own rebellious ways. Jerusalem was no longer the focus of their religious life, but this was now concentrated on two sanctuaries - one in Bethel and one in Dan - where golden calves were worshipped. Reading about the history of those times, we repeatedly hear the names of the pagan gods, Asherah and Baal. But, sad to say, this was not just happening in the Northern Kingdom, as there was also a considerable amount of cross-pollination between Israel and Judah. We detect this during the reign of King Joram (not to be confused with the king of Israel with the same name who lived at almost the same time).

Joram of Judah was married to a woman who was a relative of King Ahab - the notorious king in the time of Elijah. Second Kings 8 explicitly mentions that Joram went astray, 'for he married a daughter of Ahab' (vs. 18). It is a telling example of how spouses may influence each other. Partners have a great responsibility towards each other - not only in the affairs of everyday life, but also in the spiritual domain. They can support each other, and together strengthen their relationship with God, or pull each other away from God and together experience a steady spiritual decline.

My prayer

Loving God, let us always realise that we bear a great spiritual responsibility for our partners and for others who are close to us.

23 July

Joseph

(may He add)

Who and when? Son of Jacob and Rachel; became the vice-ruler of Egypt.

Want to know more? Read: Genesis 35:24; 37; 39–50.

Thoughts for today

Today's story speaks to our imagination. The young dreamer is thrown into a deep well by his brothers, before being sold as a slave bound for Egypt. Some time later Joseph finds himself in an Egyptian prison, but at a given moment his services as an interpreter of dreams are required at the court of the pharaoh. This is the beginning of a meteoric career that makes him the second most powerful man in Egypt.

Why did Joseph become a prisoner? As a slave of Potiphar he had won his master's trust and received many privileges. Moreover, he was a young and attractive man. Potiphar's wife was interested in having a fling with him and did everything possible to seduce him. Joseph was a man of flesh and blood. He must often have felt lonely: and, lo and behold, he was offered the opportunity to hold a woman in his arms. It required a lot of inner strength to resist this enormous temptation, but in God's strength Joseph was able to resist. He did not want to deceive his master Potiphar; but he also saw another dimension of the temptation: 'How then could I do such a wicked thing and sin against God?' (Genesis 39:9.)

Potiphar's wife claimed that Joseph had taken the initiative and, as a result, he was immediately imprisoned. Was that how God rewarded Joseph for sticking to his principles? When we follow the story further we soon discover that God did not abandon Joseph, even though he had to go through a very difficult period. Joseph's experience shows that loyalty towards God is the only safe path into the future.

My prayer

Dear heavenly Father, my prayer is also for today: lead me not into temptation!

24 July

Joseph

(may He add)

Who and when? Husband of Mary, Jesus' mother.

Want to know more? Read: Matthew 1:18-25; 2:13-23.

Thoughts for today

Often Joseph's role in the story of Jesus' birth is underrated, which is unfortunate. Joseph had to show an enormous amount of faith. He was engaged to Mary, when all of a sudden she told him she was pregnant. He was certain that it could not be his child and he, therefore, considered breaking off their relationship. However, in a dream God informed Joseph that Mary had not had some secret affair, but that she had become pregnant through the Holy Spirit. It cannot have been easy for Joseph to accept that explanation! Nonetheless, he decided to provide all the support Mary needed on their journey to Bethlehem.

As soon as the child was born a new crisis dawned. King Herod wanted to eliminate all possible competition, and this meant a direct threat to the life of the newborn 'King'. Joseph was now told by God to take Mary and her child and flee to Egypt. That was no small matter in those days: but once again Joseph's faith was strong enough, and the same was true after their return from Egypt, when he received further instructions through a dream.

It would be proper to place more emphasis on Joseph's faith than we often do. He did what God asked him to do, under very challenging circumstances. Perhaps we should add his name to the gallery of 'heroes of the faith' recorded in Hebrews 11: or, maybe, we should just remind ourselves from time to time of his example when our faith is challenged in an extraordinary manner.

My prayer

I ask You, Lord, to give me a strong enough faith to follow Your instructions whatever the circumstances may be.

25 July

Joseph of Arimathea

(may He add; originated from Arimathea)

Who and when? Member of the Sanhedrin; follower of Jesus.

Want to know more? Read: Matthew 27:57-61; Luke 23:50-56.

Thoughts for today

Joseph of Arimathea is the patron saint of the undertakers. This is the result of Joseph's courageous initiative after Jesus had died on the cross. He approached Pontius Pilate and asked for permission to take the body of Jesus and to bury it in the new rock-hewn tomb that he had prepared for himself.

This act would undermine his standing among his colleagues in the Jewish council. It was, without any doubt, a difficult decision for this prominent man who was from Arimathea, a village at about thirteen kilometres from Jerusalem. Mark 15:43 tells us, nonetheless, that 'he went boldly' to Pilate. At this crucial moment he openly confessed by his actions that he had chosen to follow Jesus. Luke summarises it in just a few words: He was 'a good and upright man, who had not consented to their decision and action [of the council] . . . and he was waiting for the kingdom of God' (Luke 23:50, 51).

Thus, in the midst of this tragedy, there is suddenly a piece of good news. When push came to shove the disciples were nowhere to be seen: but from an unexpected corner came someone who was no longer afraid to stick out his neck – who made it clear that, in spite of all that had happened, he had not lost his faith in Jesus. In addition, there were also some women who, together with Joseph from Arimathea, wanted to prepare the Lord's body for burial. When this took place it was still Friday – the day on which everything seemed to have gone horribly wrong. But the tomb of Joseph of Arimathea would not be needed for long. . . .

My prayer

Thank You, Lord, for people like this Joseph, who in critical circumstances openly make their choice for You. Give me this courage too.

26 July

Joshua

(the Lord is deliverance)

Who and when? Assistant of Moses, and later his successor.

Want to know more? Read: Joshua.

Thoughts for today

Joshua led the people of Israel as they took possession of the 'promised land', and in the allocation of the different regions after the people had wandered through the wilderness for forty long years. Now the job was finished. 'The LORD had given Israel rest from all their enemies around them' (Joshua 23:1). By now Joshua was old and he knew that his death was imminent. He therefore called the people together near Shechem and gave an impressive speech. He reminded them of the sad fact that in the past they had time and again given in to the temptation to serve the gods of the nations they had been in contact with, rather than the Lord. Joshua knew that this temptation would reoccur. Therefore he called on them to make a final choice: worship either the true God or the idols of the nations around them! *If you really do not want to serve the true God, then decide which other gods will have your allegiance. But I want you to know that I have already made that choice and will always stick to it. Whatever may happen, 'as for me and my household, we will serve the LORD'* (Joshua 24:15).

Joshua made that choice for his family, presumably since he knew that they had also made that decision for themselves. God gave all of us the privilege of free choice. We cannot avoid it: we must choose God or the gods of this world (all those other things that may get the highest priority in our lives). We cannot postpone that choice forever and must remind others of the fact that they must also choose. However, we can only be credible in urging others to choose God if we do not waver in our own choice for Him.

My prayer

Lord, I want to be on Your side. Help me never to waver in my choice for You.

27 July

Josiah

(the Lord heals)

Who and when? King of Judah (639 BC to 609 BC); restored the worship of the Lord.

Want to know more? Read: 2 Kings 22; 23; 2 Chronicles 34; 35.

Thoughts for today

Josiah was very young when he became king. For some time he was king only in name: but, when he was old enough to take charge of the affairs of his kingdom, he soon proved to be cut from the right kind of cloth for the task. From the age of sixteen, we discover in 2 Chronicles 34:3, 'he began to seek the God of his father David.' Four years later, when he was about twenty years old, 'he began to purge Judah and Jerusalem of high places, Asherah poles, carved idols and cast images.' Josiah was quite systematic in his reforms. Six years later the temple could be restored. This was the moment when an important event took place in this process of reform. During the construction work in the temple the high priest Hilkiah found a scroll of the book of Deuteronomy (or a part thereof) – the scroll in which the law of God was repeated in every detail (the word *Deuteronomion* in Greek literally means 'second law').

Josiah did not immediately put the scroll away in some safe place, so that it would not once again be lost. He studied it and arranged for a reading of the 'Book of the Covenant' (2 Chronicles 34:30) before the people. From then onwards the temple services were held as prescribed by the Word of God, and two years later the people celebrated Passover for the first time after a long period of neglect. Josiah understood that all kinds of measures were needed to give a new focus to his people, but also that a real reformation must be based on loyalty to the Word of God.

My prayer

I realise, Lord, that there is a constant need for reformation, also in my own life. May Your Word always be the basis for such reforms.

28 July

Jubal

(ram's horn or trumpet)

Who and when? Son of Lamech and grandson of Methushael; the first musician.

Want to know more? Read: Genesis 4:21.

Thoughts for today

Jubal became 'the father of all who play the harp and flute' (Genesis 4:21). Experts do not always agree about the various musical instruments that were used in ancient times. The New International Version (1984 edition) of our text refers to the 'harp and flute', while other translations speak of the cither and the flute, and other translators again decided to use 'organs and harps'. It remains a very complex problem, for we have no detailed descriptions or video images that would enable us to identify the musical instruments of Bible times and to compare them with the instruments of today.

This much, however, is abundantly clear: music did not emerge only at a later stage in the history of humankind. Just a few generations after Adam we meet a man who made musical instruments and presumably taught others how to use them. It is hardly important to know exactly what these instruments looked like. Or is it?

Generations of 'conservative' Christians (in the past and today) have insisted that some instruments (in particular percussion instruments) are not suitable for worship. They maintain that other instruments, for instance the organ, are more 'sacred' than others. There is nothing in the Bible that would support that suggestion. Whether or not music is 'sacred' does not depend on the instrument that is chosen, but on the way in which it is used and the intentions of the person who plays that particular instrument.

My prayer

Thank You, Lord, for the great variety of musical instruments and for the possibilities to enjoy all kinds of music and to use them to Your honour and glory.

29 July

Judah

(let him be praised)

Who and when? Fourth son of Jacob and Leah; ancestor of Jesus.

Want to know more? Read: Genesis 29:35; 38; 44:14-34; 49:8-12.

Thoughts for today

At the end of his long and eventful life Jacob blessed his sons. We find in Genesis 49 a mix of the knowledge that Jacob had acquired of the character of his sons and the prophetic insight that God gave him. For Judah, the last son he had with Leah, Jacob had only positive words. This is remarkable, since Judah had done some things that were very wrong. The episode that is recorded in Genesis 38 shows the dark side of Judah. In that chapter we find the story about Judah's daughter-in-law Tamar, who was prepared to do anything to get a son. She was even ready to prostitute herself to that end. And who was her 'customer'? Her father-in-law, Judah!

However, in Genesis 44 we see another picture of Judah. There he is in the palace of Joseph, who had become the viceroy of Egypt. Judah shows true remorse about his role in the sale of Joseph into Egyptian slavery. He is even prepared to serve Joseph as a slave, if that would help to set his youngest brother Benjamin free.

When blessing Judah, Jacob says: 'Judah, your brothers will praise you' (Genesis 49:8). He is depicted as a lion! It is also mentioned that 'The sceptre will not depart from Judah' (vs. 10). And, indeed, he became an ancestor of 'the lion of Judah', the Messiah. The lives of many of us resemble that of Judah. We may have done some very positive things, and we may also have made some serious mistakes; but, if we repent of the sins we have committed, God can, in the end, also richly bless us – as Jacob blessed Judah.

My prayer

Lord, I realise that, like Judah, I often fall short of what You expect from me. But I thank You for Your forgiveness and the assurance that in the end I may also receive Your blessing.

30 July

Judas

(Greek form of Judah: let him be praised; Iscariot: man from Kerioth)

Who and when? The disciple who betrayed Jesus; he committed suicide.

Want to know more? Read: Matthew 10:2-4; 26:20-56; 27:1-10.

Thoughts for today

Jesus was betrayed by two of His disciples. When Peter was asked whether he had ties with the Man who was being accused of inciting rebellion against the authorities and of blasphemy, he denied this vehemently. Fortunately, Peter recognised what he had done and repented. Soon afterwards his relationship with Jesus was restored.

Judas Iscariot was the other disciple who betrayed Jesus. Was his act of betrayal worse than that of Peter? We may tend to think that way, because it leaves a foul taste in our mouth when we hear that someone was paid by a third party to betray an innocent person; and it seems even worse when we realise that thirty pieces of silver was the amount that was usually paid for a slave in those days. Apparently this was the value that was put on the Son of God.

Could Judas have been forgiven for his horrible deed? Yes; and we note that he tried, in fact, to seek forgiveness: but he went to the wrong address. He approached the religious leaders, because 'he was seized with remorse' (Matthew 27:3). He should have gone to God. No sin is so big that it cannot be forgiven – even a terrible deed of the worst kind of betrayal – but Judas did not turn in remorse to God, and saw no other way out than to take his own life, thereby jeopardising all prospect of life eternal. A more powerful warning cannot be found in the Bible.

My prayer

Lord, I know that I too have sometimes betrayed You by my behaviour and by not making clear that I belong to You. Forgive me and help me, so that this will not happen again.

31 July

Jude

(or Judas – Ioudas – the Greek
form of Judah: let him be praised)

Who and when? One of Jesus' half-brothers; brother of, among others, James. Possibly a son of Joseph from an earlier marriage.

Want to know more? Read: Matthew 13:55; Jude.

Thoughts for today

One of the half-brothers of Jesus was named Jude. Most likely he was the author of the short New Testament epistle that bears his name. Anyone who is somewhat acquainted with biblical history knows that the name Jude evokes a negative reaction, since Jesus was betrayed by someone with that name. We know very little about the Jude who wrote the few pages that come immediately before the Revelation of John. The only thing we know for certain is that at first he did not believe in Jesus, but that after the resurrection and ascension of Jesus he belonged to the group of believers. Jude does not advertise his family ties with Jesus in the first verse of his letter, but in all modesty identifies himself as 'a brother of James'. In addition he calls himself 'a servant of Jesus Christ'.

Through the ages many people have been proud of their pedigree. Often people are quite keen to tell others about the important men and women among their ancestors: and they usually do not keep it a secret for very long when they have a relative with an important position. It seems as if part of the prestige and importance of that person, or those persons, reflects on them. It is often used to underline one's authority, something along the lines of: 'Listen to me, I am not just anybody. . . .' Jude knew that he had no claim to anything special. He had failed to offer support when his half-brother Jesus went from place to place to bring His message of the coming kingdom and to help people. But – God be praised – he was now a servant of Jesus: and that is what the people should know.

My prayer

Dear God, help me to be modest in the way I present myself and always to be Your loyal servant.

1 August

Junia

(belonging to Juno)

Who and when? A man or woman of Jewish descent; member of the church in Rome when Paul wrote his letter 'to the Romans'.

Want to know more? Read: Romans 16:7.

Thoughts for today

Junia (or Junias) was one of the people who received Paul's greetings at the end of his letter to the Romans. It remains uncertain whether we are dealing with the name of a man or a woman here, but this becomes important in the discussion about the role of women in the church, since Junia(s) is referred to as 'outstanding among the apostles' (Romans 16:7). If Junia was a woman, we may then conclude that women qualified for the office of apostle in the early church.

There is considerable evidence that this Junia was indeed a woman. For many centuries the majority of biblical exegetes were of that opinion. It was not until the woman-unfriendly atmosphere of the Middle Ages that this idea was rejected. It is a striking example of how our way of reading the Bible is almost inevitably affected by the time in which we live and the culture in which we share.

It is important to realise that we always read the Bible through our own spectacles, according to the particular colour of our glasses, and that we must therefore make a concerted effort to recognise our own prejudices and assumptions so that we do not read with the underlying (often unconscious) desire of seeing our own ideas confirmed, but honestly try to discover what the Word of God wants to tell us.

My prayer

Heavenly Father, I thank You for Your Word. Please help me in my reading always to be aware of my own preconceived ideas, and correct these when and where needed.

2 August

Kedorlaomer

(servant of the god Lagamer)

Who and when? Local ruler over Elam; was defeated by Abraham.

Want to know more? Read: Genesis 14.

Thoughts for today

In Genesis 14 we meet nine local rulers, who controlled an area mainly consisting of the region of the Jordan valley and the area more to the East (towards Mesopotamia). One of them, Kedorlaomer (who controlled Elam, an area in the southwest of modern Iran), had ambitions to extend his rule over a much larger area, and at a given moment a group of 'kings' decided to stop him. This led to fierce fighting between a coalition of five of these 'kings' against four others.

There have been thousands of wars in ancient times and ever since. Why is this struggle between Kedorlaomer and a number of local rulers, in part of what we today call the Middle East, mentioned in the Bible? It is because Sodom was one of the parties in the conflict: and Sodom was the place where Lot, the nephew of Abraham, lived. With his entire family and all his possessions, Lot was abducted by the confederation of Kedorlaomer. He owed it to the courageous intervention of his uncle Abraham that he survived the ordeal, together with his extended family. Abraham could marshal 318 armed men, and as the result of a number of strategic decisions he was able to decisively defeat Kedorlaomer.

All Kedorlaomers must know that, however powerful they may think they are, they will always suffer defeat when God enters the equation and ensures that those who resist evil will be victorious.

My prayer

Let me, dear God, experience Your ability to save me in tough situations.

3 August

Keren-happuch

(horn of black eye paint)

Who and when? Youngest daughter of Job; born after his misery had ended.

Want to know more? Read: Job 1:2; 42:14.

Thoughts for today

Job had seven sons and three daughters before one disaster after another struck him. His ten children died when the house in which they were partying collapsed on them. When Job's misery ended God returned his former prosperity to him. The number of sheep, oxen, camels and donkeys was now even double what he had in former times; and once again he had ten children: seven sons and three daughters. One of the daughters was called Keren-happuch. Perhaps Job noticed after she was born that she had beautiful eyes, and for that reason chose a name that had to do with eye make-up.

Some Bible commentators stress that the story of Keren-happuch and her seven brothers and two sisters shows that God will always compensate us for what we lose during our lives. Sometimes – as in the case of Job – this happens during our lifetime. But we may also have to wait until we are with God for such restitution to happen. Such an explanation is meant as comfort: but does it really provide any solace? In any case, it does not miraculously dry our tears or make us suddenly grasp why we had to suffer. We can be sure that Job did not understand all that had happened to him when he once again had seven sons and three girls, even after the delight of looking into the eyes of Keren-happuch. However much we may continue to speculate or philosophise, suffering remains a mystery that we must live with as long as we are in this world. But we may find consolation in God's promise that one day our lives will be lived in perfect and eternal bliss.

My prayer

Let us, Lord, in the midst of all the puzzles and riddles of life, never forget that You will, either in this life or the next, compensate us generously.

4 August

Keturah

(perfumed)

Who and when? Third wife of Abraham, after Sarah, who had died, and Hagar, who was banished.

Want to know more? Read: Genesis 25:1; 1 Chronicles 1:32.

Thoughts for today

'Abraham took another wife.' This happened most likely after Sarah had died. By now Abraham was an old man. Keturah was much younger, as we can conclude from the fact that she could give Abraham six more sons. This means that Abraham had another six male descendants besides Isaac, who had a special position, and Ishmael, who had been brought into the world by Hagar, the servant of Sarah. At least two of these boys became the forefathers of separate clans (Genesis 25:2-4; 1 Chronicles 1:32, 33). Abraham must have felt that Keturah played an important role in the fulfilment of God's promise that he would became the father of *many* nations.

Why did Abraham take Keturah as his wife? There is no indication that there was a romantic relationship; and neither does it seem that Abraham was lonely. The reason was, no doubt, that Abraham was keen to have more sons. That was a normal wish in Bible times: but was this according to God's plans for Abraham? Interestingly, four of Keturah's sons disappear completely from the record of Scripture. Why? God had promised Abraham that he would have numerous descendants, but did Abraham not fully trust in God, and was he here relying at least in part on his own initiative?

Keturah seems to play only an insignificant role in Abraham's story: but let us not forget that many women who certainly deserved to be mentioned are never given any credit in the annals of history. This also applies to Keturah, for caring for an elderly husband, giving birth to six children and raising them was no mean feat.

My prayer

Lord, help us not to overlook the role of women like Keturah, who may remain unknown but have a great track record!

5 August

Kilion

(wasting)

Who and when? Son of Elimelech and Naomi; husband of Orpah the Moabite.

Want to know more? Read: Ruth 1:1-5; 4:9.

Thoughts for today

How wise was it for Elimelech and Naomi to move to Moab, together with their sons Mahlon and Kilion, when a famine broke out in the region (near Bethlehem) where they lived? Did they not know that the Moabites were idol worshippers of the worst kind? And had they forgotten God's repeated instructions that His people must stay away from places where other gods were worshipped, often with the most degrading immoral practices? What's more, did Elimelech and Naomi not foresee the risks they would have to face with their boys? The idols of Moab might have been of wood and stone, but Mahlon and Kilion were not. It was bound to happen: the two boys found Moabite girls that took their fancy.

Was the misery they had to face after a number of years a divine punishment for their unwise decision to move to Moab, in spite of all the temptations and spiritual dangers they would meet? Undoubtedly some people in their home country thought so when they heard that all that was left of this family were the three widows. I read some sermons on the internet about the fate of Naomi and her family that are full of condemnation. After all, God's judgement was surely to be expected after Elimelech's decision to live among the Moabites. However, nowhere in the book of Ruth do we find even a hint of such condemnation: and, if there were anything to be condemned, that would be something we can safely leave to God.

My prayer

I thank You, Lord, that You are the One who judges people. Grant me the insight always to leave the judgement over other people to You.

6 August

Kish

(gift)

Who and when? Father of King Saul; ca. 1050 BC.

Want to know more? Read: 1 Samuel 9.

Thoughts for today

The Benjamite Kish was a wealthy man (1 Samuel 9:1) who lived just over a thousand years before Christ. In those days wealth was not expressed in dollars or euros, and not even primarily in gold or silver; wealth was mostly a matter of livestock: but being rich brought a lot of worries. Bandits could steal their herds, which also had to be protected against wild animals. Moreover, there were no large-scale, barbed-wire fences and cattle grids to ensure that their livestock would not run away.

One day the donkeys of Kish were nowhere to be found. These donkeys probably represented a substantial amount of capital, and he dispatched his son Saul, with a servant, to start a search for them. They went to one district after another, but the donkeys were nowhere to be found. Eventually, the donkeys were discovered by someone else (vs. 20), but Saul was not aware of this, and he could not continue his search indefinitely. The food that he had taken along was about to run out. Moreover, Saul knew his father. After a few days he said to his servant that they should be heading home, for 'my father will stop thinking about the donkeys and start worrying about us' (vs. 5).

Kish was a rich man, but Saul knew that his possessions were not all-important to him. People mattered more to him than material wealth. Unfortunately, not all wealthy people operate on that principle.

My prayer

Heavenly Father, please remind me, whenever I need it, that people are more important than material possessions.

Kohath

(assembly)

Who and when? Kohath was a son of Levi. Later his descendants, the Kohathites, were an important clan in the tribe of Levi.

Want to know more? Read: Genesis 46:11; Numbers 3:27-32.

Thoughts for today

It is well known that the men of the tribe of Levi had a special role. God had appointed them as the group that was to care for the sanctuary and all its sacrificial services. During their wilderness wandering they lived together on the southern side of the tabernacle. Later, when Israel had settled in the 'promised land', a number of cities were reserved for them.

Aaron and his posterity belonged to the clan of the Kohathites. They were priests, but most other descendants of Kohath had another role. They were to look after the furniture and all the sacred objects that were used in the sanctuary services. One might say that they formed an in-house service team. Most Kohathites thus remained somewhat in the shadow. Their task was mostly to provide support.

Today we see many who volunteer their services in the church without ever being in the forefront. They make their contributions without becoming very visible. At times people may become discontented with their background roles. They must, however, realise that they are the present-day Kohathites and that the entire system would come to a standstill without their contribution. The person who cleans the church or prepares the weekly bulletin is just as important as the person in the pulpit, while the 'greeter' at the door is just as essential as the elder.

My prayer

O Lord, let me be content with the task that You have given me – even if it has low visibility.

8 August

Korah

(bald)

Who and when? With Dathan, Abiram and some 250 others, Korah rebelled against the authority of Moses and Aaron.

Want to know more? Read: Numbers 16.

Thoughts for today

The story of the rebellion against Moses and Aaron under the leadership of Korah, Dathan and Abiram is quite depressing. The core of the problem was that these men aspired to be priests, but had not been chosen for that task. They were Levites who were appointed to perform a variety of tasks in the sanctuary, but were not allowed to do the work of priests. They were especially jealous of Moses and Aaron. After all, who had given them the right to boss everybody around?

There was a clear answer to that question: God had given them that right. And Korah and his associates knew this. For Moses had been the person who had met with God on Mount Sinai, and it had become abundantly clear that God had chosen Aaron to serve in a special capacity as Moses' spokesperson.

Jealousy is a deadly evil that poses a threat to all relationships. It may lead to open conflict and may well ruin everything. It is especially catastrophic when it occurs in the church. God's measures against Korah and his followers show how serious this is in His eyes. It is essential that we be willing to accept the fact that others, rather than we ourselves, have been called to perform certain important tasks; and that there is always enough opportunity for all of us to commit our talents and skills to the cause of God.

My prayer

Dear God, may we be content with the assignment that You have given us and respect those whom You have appointed as leaders.

9 August

Laban

(white)

Who and when? Brother of Rebekah, father-in-law of Jacob, and father of Leah and Rachel.

Want to know more? Read: Genesis 29:1–32:1.

Thoughts for today

The history of Jacob and Laban can be summarised in just three words: *the deceiver deceived!* After Jacob had fled his parental home, he found a place to stay with Laban, the brother of his mother Rebekah, who decided to employ him. After a month Laban agreed that Jacob would not have to work for free. Since Jacob had fallen in love with Rachel, the youngest daughter of Laban, the moment he first saw her, it was agreed that he would work for seven years for Laban and would then be permitted to marry Rachel. Well, we know what happened. When the great moment had arrived, and he woke up after his first night as a married man, Jacob did not find Rachel at his side, but Leah!

Laban also proved to be highly untrustworthy on other occasions. He kept changing Jacob's wages after he had given his two daughters to him. Tired of this, Jacob decided that enough was enough and that he would leave in secret, with his family, his servants and his livestock. Laban pursued him and then, after an intense confrontation with Jacob, Laban 'kissed his grandchildren and his daughters and blessed them' (Genesis 31:55), and they separated for good.

Many families are torn apart by relational problems, and many promises are not kept. Fortunately, in many cases the problems are eventually resolved. Let us always do what we can to help people resolve their relational difficulties and reach peace!

My prayer

Dear God, help me never to deceive others, even when the deception would be advantageous for me.

10 August

Lamech

(warrior)

Who and when? One was a descendant of Cain; the other, the father of Noah.

Want to know more? Read: Genesis 4:18-24; 5:28-31.

Thoughts for today

According to Genesis 4 Lamech is the son of Methushael and a descendant of Cain, but in Genesis 5 Lamech appears to be the son of Methuselah, which makes him one of the forefathers of Jesus. We must conclude that there were two Lamechs. The first has a number of sons, but there is no mention of a Noah. We are told about the second Lamech that he became the father of Noah when he was 182. But the differences between these two men called Lamech are not limited to their genealogy. The second Lamech shows that he believes in God. This is apparent from the name he chooses for his son: Noah, for 'he will comfort us in the labour and painful toil of our hands caused by the ground the LORD has cursed' (Genesis 5:29).

The first Lamech is a different kind of person. We see how Cain's character is reflected in him. The short description that is given of him shows a number of negative characteristics. He is arrogant and has no respect for the life of other human beings. This is crystal clear from what he says to his two wives: 'I have killed a man for wounding me, a young man for injuring me' (Genesis 4:24).

A name does not tell the full story – and sometimes it tells us very little or nothing. The two biblical characters called Lamech may have shared the same name but they were totally different people. We must remember not to judge people by their names (or their titles), but by how they live. This, after all, is what God does!

My prayer

Lord, we are sometimes inclined to judge other people by their names or their titles. Help us first of all to look at their character and their manner of life.

11 August

Lazarus

(Greek form of the Hebrew Eleazar: God has helped)

Who and when? A brother of Martha and Mary and a friend of Jesus. They lived in Bethany. Lazarus was resurrected by Jesus.

Want to know more? Read: John 11:1-44.

Thoughts for today

'Jesus wept' (John 11:35). This is the shortest Bible verse, but possibly also one of the most touching. Jesus loved (and loves) all people, but He regarded some as His special friends. Lazarus was one of those people. No wonder, then, that Jesus wept at the grave of Lazarus.

But some will argue: why did Jesus weep? He knew that He would call Lazarus back to life. He even said that Lazarus's death was not irreversible: 'Our friend Lazarus has fallen asleep; but I am going there to wake him up' (11:11). And this is what happened after four days, by which time the body of Lazarus had already started to decompose.

What, then, is the significance of Jesus' tears? Was it in reality just a piece of theatre? No, absolutely not. This is one of the clearest indications that Jesus had indeed become fully human – He experienced human emotions. At times He was hungry or thirsty. He knew moments of joy and happiness, but also of sorrow and pain; and, even though He had come to conquer death, the reality of death horrified Him when He was among us. The story of Lazarus underlines, in a striking way, how the eternal, almighty Son of God became a human being to save us. It may be beyond our comprehension, but we can still be immensely grateful for this fact.

My prayer

Thank You, Lord, that You were willing to cry, with the ultimate intention that all tears will one day be forever swept away.

12 August

Leah

(cow)

Who and when? The oldest daughter of Laban; as the result of deception by Laban she became Jacob's first wife. She gave birth to six sons and one daughter.

Want to know more? Read: Genesis 29; 30.

Thoughts for today

Jacob was in love with Rachel, but was tricked into a marriage with her older sister, Leah, before they could marry. It is one of the many illustrations that the ideal of marital bliss has an optimal chance of success within the relationship of one man and one woman, both of whom love each other and want to stay with each other until death 'do them part'.

The trickery to which Jacob fell victim was simply wrong, and nothing good can be said about the role of Laban in the whole affair. To what extent Leah helped her father in deceiving Jacob is not clear. However, there is no doubt that Jacob continued to prefer Rachel over Leah, who always played second fiddle to her sister. Rachel was 'lovely in form, and beautiful', but Leah was much less attractive. 'Leah had weak eyes,' we are told (Genesis 29:17). However, the Bible story clearly indicates that Leah also loved her husband. We are not told about Rachel's feelings, even though she was Jacob's favourite.

Rachel and Leah lived in an atmosphere of continuous competition. This had, in the first place, to do with the number of sons they were able to give to their husband. In those days fertility was of prime importance, and in this respect Leah was the clear winner. Was it a matter of sheer luck? Or was God involved in this? From the names that Leah chose for her sons it would appear that she believed that God had blessed her. When her first son was born, she called him Reuben – 'she said, "It is because the LORD has seen my misery" ' (vs. 32). No doubt, Leah took this as a special encouragement in the midst of her problems.

My prayer

Thank You, Lord, that You are always aware of the problems I have to face.

13 August

Levi

(attached)

Who and when? The third son of Jacob and Leah.

Want to know more? Read: Genesis 29:34; 46:11; 49:5-7; Numbers 8:5-26; 18:23-32.

Thoughts for today

Jacob did not have much that was positive to say about Levi when, just before his death, he blessed his sons. Was it due to the abominable behaviour of Levi when – together with his brother Simeon – he killed all male inhabitants of Shechem in revenge for the rape of their sister Dinah? When he blessed them, Jacob commented: 'Simeon and Levi are brothers – their swords are weapons of violence. . . . I will scatter them in Jacob and disperse them in Israel' (Genesis 49:5-7).

These final words of Jacob about Levi being scattered were fulfilled, but in a way that differed from what he had in mind. When, after the exodus of Israel from Egypt, God gave instructions for the building of the tabernacle and its services, the descendants of Levi – the Levites – were chosen to care for the sanctuary and all the activities connected with it. They did not get a part of the land of Canaan, like the other tribes, but were dispersed over the entire country. Their existence, however, was not in danger, for God stipulated that the other tribes were to give ten percent of their income to the Levites.

That Levi was prone to violent behaviour was no reason for God to keep blaming his posterity for what their forefather had done. Ancestry does not determine whether or not people will be called to serve in the cause of God. On the contrary: in Jesus' genealogy we find men and women of very dubious reputation. The question of whether God can use us depends only on who we are and want to be, and not on who our ancestors were.

My prayer

Thank You, Lord, that You are interested in my heart, and not in my pedigree.

14 August

Lois

(maternal)

Who and when? The grandmother of Timothy.

Want to know more? Read: 2 Timothy 1:5.

Thoughts for today

Timothy was a third-generation Christian. Both his mother, Eunice, and his grandmother, Lois, were women of 'sincere faith' (2 Timothy 1:5). We do not know whether Timothy later had any children and grandchildren who would continue in the same vein. But even though we sometimes see faith (or unbelief) spanning several generations, it is not something like blue eyes or blonde hair and other hereditary characteristics.

How, then, is faith transmitted from one generation to the next? It is essential that the story of the Bible is told and re-told in an attractive way, and that faith is talked about in the home. But even more important within the family are role models who 'live' their faith: for faith must, most of all, be seen.

Parents have a key role in the passing on and the modelling of their faith. However, this also applies to all those who are involved in the education of our children, including those in the homes where they frequently spend time. Grandparents also have a substantial role to play in the early years of the children – increasingly so in our Western world, as grandparents will often take care of the kids of their working sons and daughters on weekdays. Of course, as with any carer, grandparents should take care that the ideas they share with these little ones are balanced, biblical and Christ-centred at all times. Lois remains a good example for us, even for those of us who are not (or not yet) grandparents.

My prayer

Heavenly Father, help me today to model my faith for others in an attractive manner.

15 August

Lot

(meaning uncertain)

Who and when? Nephew of Abraham; accompanied Abraham from Mesopotamia; chose to live in the area around Sodom.

Want to know more? Read: Genesis 12:1-9; 13; 18:16-33; 19.

Thoughts for today

Lot had an eventful life. Together with his uncle Abraham he migrated to another country. Both became so rich that they needed a large area for their livestock. When Abraham gave Lot the choice of where he wanted to settle, Lot opted for the fertile Jordan valley, in the vicinity of Sodom. There a dramatic incident occurred when two strangers were in search of a place where they could stay for the night, and the men of Sodom got very upset when Lot invited them into his home. It led to the destruction of Sodom, which also claimed the death of Lot's wife. The story of Lot ended with the episode of his drunken stupor, when, oblivious to what he was doing, he committed incest with his daughters.

We cannot help but wonder whether things could have gone in a totally different way. Lot knew that he was going to live in a region that had a very bad moral reputation. 'The men of Sodom were wicked and were sinning greatly against the LORD' (Genesis 13:13). Did Lot think that he and his family were strong enough not to be affected? Admittedly, it was attractive in many ways to choose the area around Sodom. 'The whole plain of the Jordan was well watered, like the garden of the LORD, like the land of Egypt, towards Zoar' (vs. 10).

Often our material and our spiritual interests clash with each other. When that happens, it is essential to make the right choices. Let us not, like Lot, allow ourselves to be enticed by the material advantages we see.

My prayer

Help us, O God, to take wise long-term decisions, while always prioritising our spiritual well-being.

16 August

Lucifer

(brilliant one)

Who and when? Isaiah used the term 'morning star' for the king of Babylon, who reflected the work and character of Satan. In this connection the Latin name Lucifer is frequently used.

Want to know more? Read: Isaiah 14:12.

Thoughts for today

One might well ask whether the name Lucifer should have a place in a book with devotional messages that is based on biblical names, for, strictly speaking, this name does not occur in the Bible. It is, however, used six times in the Vulgate, the Latin Bible translation that for many centuries was highly respected in the Roman Catholic Church. In Protestant circles it has also become quite common to refer to the devil as Lucifer.

The information that we can find when we look at several statements in the Bible is that an important angelic being – a 'morning star' and 'son of the dawn' (Isaiah 14:12) – was forced to leave his heavenly home after having rebelled against the Most High. Ever since that fateful moment, Lucifer has tried to export his rebellion elsewhere: for instance, to the earth, where he has brought death and destruction and still 'prowls around like a roaring lion' (1 Peter 5:8).

The power of the devil should never be underestimated. His fate, however, has been sealed. In one of his visions the apostle John saw how the devil will ultimately be 'thrown into the lake of burning sulphur' (Revelation 20:10). That is the 'end of the story' for Lucifer – and it must be added that all who have chosen Lucifer as their leader will meet the same terrible end. In sharp contrast, all who have chosen to follow Jesus as their Light are fully outside the danger zone. Their future is the bliss of eternal life!

My prayer

Lord in heaven, I realise that the devil constantly tries to pull me away from You. But I know that You are much more powerful than Lucifer. I thank You for that comforting knowledge.

17 August

Lucius of Cyrene

(Latin form of Luke: light-giving)

Who and when? Christian in Antioch, belonging to Paul's network.

Want to know more? Read: Acts 13:1; Romans 16:21.

Thoughts for today

The church in Antioch (in modern Turkey) must have been a diverse and interesting group. It was one of the first Christian churches, and it was here that the name 'Christians' was coined for the followers of Jesus (Acts 11:26). Together with Barnabas, Paul was commissioned by this church to undertake his first missionary journey. It would seem that there was a very positive spirit in this church.

The brief description in Acts 13:1 indicates that the church in Antioch was also quite diverse: Barnabas was originally from Cyprus (Acts 4:36); Lucius had come from Cyrene (now in the eastern part of Libya); and then there was a 'Simeon who was called Niger'. This description would seem to indicate that this Simeon was dark-skinned and had come from 'black' Africa. The members of the church had different social backgrounds. Cyrene boasted a medical school, and Lucius (just as Luke) may well have been a medical doctor. We do know, however, that he was among a group in Antioch who were counted among the 'prophets and teachers'. A certain Manaen had, before becoming a Christian, 'been brought up with Herod the tetrarch'.

From the very beginning local Christian churches saw an influx of migrants, as for instance Lucius, who had come from elsewhere. The composition of the Antioch church showed that in all their diversity people can be one in Christ.

My prayer

I thank You that You are the Father of all of us, however different we may be.

18 August

Luke

(Greek form of a Latin name, Lucanus: light-giving)

Who and when? Co-worker with Paul. He was a medical doctor of non-Jewish descent and the author of one of the gospels and of the book of Acts.

Want to know more? Read: Colossians 4:10-14; 2 Timothy 4:11.

Thoughts for today

There is a well-nigh universal consensus that Luke wrote the gospel that bears his name as well as the book of Acts. His background is rather vague, though. We know that he was medically trained, for Paul refers to him as 'the doctor' (Colossians 4:14). We also know that when writing these two books of the Bible he approached his work rather systematically. The prologue of his gospel is very instructive: 'Many have undertaken to draw up an account of the things that have been fulfilled among us, just as they were handed down to us by those who from the first were eye-witnesses and servants of the word. Therefore, since I myself have carefully investigated everything from the beginning, it seemed good to me to write an orderly account for you, most excellent Theophilus, so that you may know the certainty of the things you have been taught' (Luke 1:1-4).

The Bible is God's inspired Word, but that does not mean that everything was, word for word, dictated to the Bible writers. Luke based his account primarily on the reports of eyewitnesses. He did further research, and then organised his material accordingly. His intention was to convince a certain Theophilus of the truth of the Christian message. One day Luke will discover how many people, besides Theophilus, have been strengthened in their faith through his work.

My prayer

I thank You, O God, that You are the source of all truth and that You have used people like Luke to communicate Your truth in a form that humans can understand.

19 August

Lydia

(the one from the country of Lydia)

Who and when? Woman in Thyatira (Lydia); she made her living in Philippi.

Want to know more? Read: Acts 16:11-15.

Thoughts for today

Soon after Paul had seen the vision of 'a man from Macedonia' who urged him to 'come over to Macedonia', he 'put to sea' and travelled to Philippi, which was an important city in modern Greece. As always, Paul wanted to meet on Sabbath with the Jewish citizens, with whom he could share the good news about Jesus Christ. Apparently there was no synagogue, but there was 'a place of prayer' near the river. That is where Paul met a group of women who had assembled on the Sabbath.

Modern tourists who visit Philippi are shown, just outside of the city, near the Krenides river, a chapel that has been built by Greek-Orthodox Christians to mark the spot where Paul baptised the first European Christians. Tradition informs us that this was also the spot where Paul met that group of women during his first Sabbath on European soil. One of these ladies was Lydia, a businesswoman, who had established a trading business in purple cloth. According to the Bible story she was 'a worshipper of God' – common ground upon which Paul could build – but it took more than the words of Paul to convince her. We are told, 'The Lord opened her heart to respond to Paul's message.' Lydia and her household were then baptised, and her home became the base for Paul's Gospel work in Philippi.

We would do well to take some time to analyse what happened – what methods Paul used and what factors played an important role in this first evangelistic outreach in Europe. Could we perhaps have greater success if we paid more attention to some of these elements?

My prayer

Help me, Lord, to identify people like Lydia in my environment whom I might tell about You.

20 August

Lysias

(providing a solution)

Who and when? Full name: Claudius Lysias; in charge of the Roman garrison in Jerusalem in the time of Paul.

Want to know more? Read: Acts 23:26-30.

Thoughts for today

Claudius Lysias was of Greek nationality (as the name indicates), but was able to buy his Roman citizenship (Acts 22:28). Perhaps this was also the occasion when he adopted the name Claudius. Paul could also claim to be a Roman citizen, but he was Roman by birth. He appealed to his civil status when he was faced with problems in Jerusalem, having been accused by the Jewish religious leaders of having desecrated the temple. This had an immediate effect. It ensured that he was no longer in danger of being lynched by a Jewish mob, but was subject to the Roman legal process. Lysias heard about a Jewish conspiracy to kill Paul and decided that the apostle was to be transported under heavy guard to Caesarea, where he would be interrogated by Felix, the Roman governor of Judah.

Paul was prepared to face difficulties because of his faith and his apostolic mission: but, whenever possible, he made use of his legal rights. Fortunately, in Lysias he met someone who was well versed in Roman law and tried to apply this in an honest way. Paul left a useful example for the followers of Christ who, through the ages, have faced persecution because of their faith. True enough: a disciple of Christ may have to suffer a lot of trouble, but that does not mean that he/she should not use all available legal possibilities.

My prayer

Dear God, help me always to be loyal to You, whatever the cost: but also show me the legal and other opportunities to avoid major difficulties, so that I can continue my service for You.

21 August

Malachi

(my messenger)

Who and when? A prophet in the fifth century BC; author of the last book of the Old Testament, which bears his name.

Want to know more? Read: Malachi.

Thoughts for today

The prophet Malachi wanted to focus on the spiritual problems of the people, many of whom had returned from exile in Babylon. This included the corruption of the priests, and the way in which the services in the temple were conducted, as well as the sins of individuals. Malachi does not mince words. For example, in Malachi 3:8 he accuses the people of robbing God. They answered with this question: 'How do we rob [God]?' On behalf of God, Malachi replies that they are robbing Him by withholding what is owed to Him and by using that for themselves. He is, in particular, speaking of the tithes and offerings they had not given to the people who were to care for the temple and its services.

Malachi's appeal echoes through the ages and has not lost any of its relevance. ' "Test me in this," says the LORD Almighty, "and see if I will not throw open the floodgates of heaven and pour out so much blessing that you will not have room enough for it" ' (3:10). Ever since the days of Malachi people everywhere have experienced that God keeps His promises. They have discovered that God indeed is willing to open the floodgates of heaven to release His blessings. Have you been faithful in giving your tithes and other gifts? If not, it is not too late to start, remembering that God also speaks to you when He says: 'Test Me and see.'

My prayer

Help me, Lord, to be faithful in giving my tithes and offerings, so that I can experience Your bountiful blessings.

22 August

Malchus

(king)

Who and when? Servant of Caiaphas, the high priest. Peter cut off Malchus's ear when Jesus was arrested.

Want to know more? Read: Matthew 26:48-56; Luke 22:51; John 18:1-11.

Thoughts for today

A remarkable incident took place when Jesus was being arrested. As soon as Judas had betrayed his Master with a kiss, Peter became so angry that he withdrew his sword (which, to the surprise of many of us, he appears to have had with him), and sliced off an ear from the head of the servant of the high priest. Fortunately, Jesus was quick to intervene, criticising Peter's rash actions and performing His last healing miracle. The ear of the servant was not packed in ice and taken to a doctor so that it could be sewn back. Even under these bizarre circumstances, Jesus gave, with a simple touch, a powerful manifestation of His power and of His love.

Malchus is not mentioned elsewhere in the New Testament. We only know his name because John in passing mentions it in his record of Jesus' arrest. However, I would not be surprised if we were to meet this Malchus again in God's new world. What he experienced in the Garden of Gethsemane must have remained with him for the rest of his life. He was there when Jesus was arrested – the Jesus who hours later was crucified, but of whom it was widely reported that He came back to life. He felt the sharp pain when he was hit by the sword of one of Jesus' close friends. But this same Jesus made sure that he would not be handicapped for the rest of his life. It is unthinkable that this experience did not forever change his life.

My prayer

Reading the story of Malchus, I realise, O Lord, the immensity of Your love. Thank You, Lord, that Your love also touches me when I have to deal with unexpected setbacks.

23 August

Manasseh

(making to forget)

Who and when? The oldest son of Joseph and his Egyptian wife.

Want to know more? Read: Genesis 41:50-52; 48:1-20.

Thoughts for today

Joseph was about thirty years old when he received a high position at the court of the Egyptian pharaoh. In the preceding years he had experienced more trouble than most people have to face in their entire lives. We might think that being sold as a slave to a foreign country, as well as the ugly incident in the home of Potiphar, would have marked him for life: not to mention that, after he had interpreted the dream of the pharaoh and been elevated to a position of enormous responsibility, he was still a foreigner without any family. His father and his brothers were far away and he was unlikely ever to see them again.

Joseph, however, did not dwell on these negative aspects of his life. He gladly accepted the offer of the Egyptian king to marry Asenath, a woman from a prominent Egyptian family, and was delighted to have two sons with her. 'Joseph named his firstborn Manasseh and said: "It is because God has made me forget all my trouble and all my father's household." '

That Joseph chose the name Manasseh for his son testified to the fact that he was able to turn the corner in his life. The birth of Manasseh enabled Joseph to forget that so much in his life had gone wrong. It was not because his memory was faulty, but because he had learned to leave the past in the past, and to focus on the future. If you can do this, you are a privileged person!

My prayer

You are the God of the past, the present and the future. You know that we are often focused on the past. Help us to live, first of all, in the present, while looking with full confidence towards the future.

24 August

Manoah

(rest)

Who and when? The father of Samson, one of the judges. Ca. 1200 BC.

Want to know more? Read: Judges 13; 14.

Thoughts for today

Samson's birth was preceded by an unusual incident. Manoah's wife was visited by an unknown person who told her she would bear a son. That was great news, because so far she had not been able to fall pregnant. She told Manoah about this 'man of God' who had brought her this glad tiding and who had also said that her son would be charged with a very special task. For that reason he should be raised as a Nazirite. Manoah was not sure what to think about the story his wife told him; so he prayed to God and asked whether the 'man of God' could come once more, this time with him present. And this happened.

Manoah listened as the 'man of God' repeated what he had already told his wife. He then invited his visitor to stay for a meal, but the stranger declined the offer. However, he did suggest that Manoah sacrifice a 'burnt offering' to God; and then we read: 'Manoah did not realise that it was the angel of the LORD' (Judges 13:16). This fact finally dawned on him when 'the angel of the LORD ascended in the flame' (13:20).

When God communicates with us, it may often take quite some time before we, like Manoah, realise that God is trying to get in touch with us and has a message for us: but God is patient with us – hoping that we will ultimately listen to what He wants to tell us.

My prayer

I thank You, Lord, that You also want to get in touch with me. Help me to recognise Your voice and to listen to the message You have for me.

25 August

Mark

(meaning is unclear)

Who and when? A cousin of Barnabas. Accompanied Paul and Barnabas during their missionary journey. After a fierce disagreement with Paul, Barnabas and John Mark teamed up together, while Paul was joined by Silas.

Want to know more? Read: Acts 12:12; 15:36-41.

Thoughts for today

John Mark had joined Paul and Barnabas on their first missionary journey: but halfway, somewhere in the southern part of Asia Minor, John Mark was unable to continue and quit. Some two years later, when Paul and Barnabas were about to depart on their second missionary journey, a strong disagreement arose. Paul absolutely refused to accept Barnabas's proposal to take John Mark along once again.

The biblical data tell us how through the years John Mark demonstrated that he was not as weak as Paul had assumed. He became a successful partner of Barnabas, after Paul and Barnabas had each chosen their own project. It appears that John Mark also had close ties with the apostle Peter, and it is thought that he functioned for some time as the apostle's personal scribe and translator. The knowledge about Jesus' life he gained during that time was the basis for the gospel he subsequently wrote. Several letters of Paul also indicate that there was no lasting rift between John Mark and Paul.

It may happen that we have to go through a rough spot in our lives. Hopefully, people will, when that happens, not immediately write us off: and, when given a second chance, it is important to seize that opportunity with both hands.

My prayer

Thank You, Lord, for the new chances You continually give me. Help me to make good use of them.

26 August

Martha

(Aramaic: lady; mistress)

Who and when? Lived with Mary and Lazarus in Bethany; friend of Jesus.

Want to know more? Read: Luke 10:38-42; John 11:1-54; 12:1, 2.

Thoughts for today

For whom do we have more sympathy, for Martha or for Mary? Perhaps our first choice is Martha. She cares for her guests, makes sure the house is in order and that meals are served on time – especially when their Friend Jesus has come to visit them. Mary appears to be the more social type. She sits down near Jesus and listens to all He has to say. Martha shows her irritation. Why must she always do all the work? Why does Mary not help her a bit more? Martha voices her frustration and asks Jesus what He thinks of the attitude of her sister. We are possibly a little surprised about Jesus' reply. He suggests that 'Mary has chosen what is better' (Luke 10:42), and that Martha should be more relaxed about the situation.

In John 11 and 12, Martha once again plays a more active role than Mary. When Lazarus has died, Martha sets out to fetch Jesus; and when, shortly after this, a meal is arranged, it is once again Martha who takes the initiative. Should we perhaps conclude that Martha and Mary simply differed in character? They were both dedicated to their Lord, but they each showed this in their own special way. Yes, people are different – then and now. However, this does not take away from the fact that there is more to life than work and that we should also focus on other things that are at least as important.

My prayer

Thank You, Lord, for the Marthas and Marys around me, and give me the insight into how I can combine the good qualities of each of them in my life.

27 August

Mary

(Greek form of the Hebrew name Miriam; meaning is unclear)

Who and when? The mother of Jesus; engaged to Joseph at the time of Jesus' birth.

Want to know more? Read: Matthew 1:18-25; Luke 2:1-21; Matthew 13:55.

Thoughts for today

Apocryphal stories and legends about Mary abound. As the centuries passed Mary became the most important 'saint' for many Christians. Roman Catholics would eventually state that she had been 'immaculately conceived'. They also believe that Mary ascended to heaven, and some even refer to her as 'co-redemptrix'. The Bible gives no support whatsoever for either of those ideas, but she certainly was a very remarkable woman who deserves our deepest affection and respect. Mary accepted her unique assignment to become the earthly mother of the Son of God. Much of what she experienced while her Son was growing up she did not fully understand, but she still 'treasured all these things in her heart' (Luke 2:51).

Our faith experience is radically different from that of Mary, who played such a unique role in the life of Jesus: but, like Mary, we find there are many things that we do not understand. In our Bible reading we meet numerous things we may find very difficult to understand and accept; and most of us go through life with many questions about our faith. Mary 'treasured' the things she did not understand 'in her heart'. She believed that, as time went by, she would get more answers and would better perceive how different elements were connected. We should apply this same strategy when we are struggling with difficult questions. We should 'treasure' them in our hearts and wait patiently until we have experiences that help us understand what may thus far have remained dark to us.

My prayer

Almighty God, I have many questions, but I know that You have all the answers. Teach me how to be patient and to wait until many of the things that now seem puzzling to me will become clear.

28 August

Mary

(Greek form of the Hebrew name Miriam; meaning is unclear)

Who and when? The sister of Lazarus and Martha, who were friends of Jesus; lived in Bethany, not far from Jerusalem.

Want to know more? Read: Luke 10:38-42; John 11; 12:1-8.

Thoughts for today

Apart from the mother of Jesus, this Mary from Bethany is perhaps the best-known of the different Marys that we meet in the Bible. We know her as the woman who did not want to miss a word of what Jesus said. While her sister Martha was busy with the household chores, Mary sat at the feet of the Master and listened attentively to what He wanted to tell her. We also meet Mary as the mourning sister, who, together with her sister Martha, was deeply distressed when her brother Lazarus died. In addition, there is the well-known story of how, just a few days before Easter, Mary anointed Jesus' feet, moved by an enormous sense of gratitude.

This Bible story makes clear that Mary was unafraid to openly witness about her conviction that Jesus was her Redeemer. In John 11:45 we read: 'Many of the Jews who had come to visit Mary, and had seen what Jesus did [resurrect Lazarus], put their faith in him.' It would seem likely to me that all that time she had spent listening attentively to Christ's teaching put her in a position to help others wanting to know more about Jesus.

What a wonderful encouragement she is to the rest of us as we seek to help others find faith in Jesus through our words and deeds.

My prayer

Show me today, Lord, the possibilities that come my way to tell people about You, and give me the joy to see how others 'put their faith' in You.

Mary Magdalene

(Mary, coming from Magdala)

Who and when? One of the women present at Jesus' crucifixion and at His resurrection.

Want to know more? Read: Luke 8:2; Mark 16:9.

Thoughts for today

Millions of people heard of Mary Magdalene for the first time after reading Dan Brown's bestseller *The Da Vinci Code*. The book suggests that Jesus had an intimate relationship with this Mary and might even have been married to her. Many readers conveniently forget that Brown's book is a work of pure fiction, in which no attempt is made at historical accuracy. Most of this speculation about Mary Magdalene comes from non-biblical sources, and it remains an open question as to how much of this – if any – actually has some historical basis.

There has been much debate about the precise identity of Mary Magdalene. Some have suggested that she is the sinful woman who anointed Jesus' feet (Luke 7:36-50), and artists have often portrayed her as such. There are others who don't share that view and reject the 'fallen woman' label. The biblical information about Mary Magdalene is rather scant, but we do know that, after Jesus had delivered her from seven evil spirits (Luke 8:2), she moved around in the company of Jesus, the disciples and a number of other women. Later she was the very first person to meet the risen Christ (John 20:1).

We must be content with this information, little though it is. But it gives enough of a basis to discover a touching illustration of the redeeming love of the Saviour, whereby a demon-possessed woman with a bleak future was saved from her terrible predicament and could start a new life. This is what Jesus can still do for people today.

My prayer

I thank You, Lord, for Your willingness to help people, whatever their problems are.

30 August

Matthew

(from the Aramaic: gift of the Lord)

Who and when? Tax collector from Capernaum, called by Jesus to be one of His disciples. Also known as Levi.

Want to know more? Read: Matthew 9:9-13; Acts 1:13.

Thoughts for today

Once again we meet a man who underwent a remarkable change when Jesus entered his life. Before Matthew (also known under his Jewish name, Levi) was called by Jesus, he worked as a tax collector in Capernaum. That was the reason why he was despised by most, if not all, of the Jewish people. He not only worked for the Romans, but he belonged to a group of people who were notorious for their crookedness. However, when Jesus called him, he immediately left his office and followed Jesus. That is, in fact, all we know about Matthew: except that he later wrote one of the four gospels. When writing his book about the life of Jesus he kept his main target audience in mind: the new Christians with a Jewish background.

The Bible - the New Testament in particular - presents us with many men and women who underwent an enormous change in their lives. Matthew is a very remarkable example. His gospel became a gripping testimony of who Jesus was and what He did. But he refrains from drawing attention to himself. He could have gone into great detail in telling in a dramatic way about his own experience: but he did not. Such a change is only possible when a person has been overwhelmed by the Person and message of Jesus. That enables one to speak and write without seeking the spotlight for oneself. And that gives the inner power to live the new life that Christ provides.

My prayer

Thank You, Lord, for inspiring examples such as that of Matthew.

31 August

Matthias

(abbreviated form of Mattathias: gift of the Lord)

Who and when? Was chosen by the apostles to replace Judas.

Want to know more? Read: Acts 1:23-26.

Thoughts for today

Jesus chose twelve disciples. After the betrayal by Judas, their number had decreased to eleven. The eleven disciples decided to make their group complete once again by selecting a twelfth disciple. They found two suitable candidates and drew lots to make their final selection. This sounds a little strange to our ears, as we would prefer other methods when we want to choose a person for a church office.

But perhaps it is not as strange as it may appear: for the disciples also did something else before they cast lots. 'They prayed: "Lord, you know everyone's heart. Show us which of these two you have chosen" ' (Acts 1:24). Surely, this is the most important element when someone must be found to fill a particular vacant church office. Today we usually select a nominating committee, which, often after an intense and lengthy meeting, proposes a candidate. This, we think, is a much safer method than using lots. However, our approach may often be a lot less objective than we think, and can easily be subject to personal opinions and prejudices. Therefore, the method used is not the most important factor, but it is rather the willingness to bow our heads in prayer, to ask God to make clear to us (through, or sometimes in spite of, the method we use) which man or woman is most suitable for the post we need to fill.

My prayer

Dear God, may we also rely on Your guidance when we are involved with church elections.

1 September

Melchizedek

(my king is righteous)

Who and when? King of Salem and priest of 'God Most High'; he met Abraham and blessed him.

Want to know more? Read: Genesis 14:17-24; Hebrews 6:20–7:21.

Thoughts for today

Lots of different theories have been proposed about the identity of this mysterious Melchizedek. In many cases we can consult the biblical genealogies to find some particulars about the origin of important Bible characters. However, in Melchizedek's case we can only guess. In Hebrews 7:3 we read that Melchizedek was 'without father or mother, without genealogy, without beginning of days or end of life'.

Abraham did not doubt for a moment that he was dealing with a unique person. Receiving Melchizedek's blessing must have been a very special experience. He spontaneously gave this priest-king ten percent of the loot he had taken during the expedition to free his cousin Lot from the leaders of the clans in the area where Lot lived.

Melchizedek was a 'type' – a foreshadowing – of another Priest-King: Jesus Christ. The author of the 'epistle' to the Hebrews states that Melchizedek was 'a priest for ever', and that he was 'like the Son of God'. Like Melchizedek, Christ did not owe His priestly status to human lineage, and He was, therefore, far superior to the priests who served in the Old Testament sanctuary.

As we continue our reading of the book of Hebrews we are assured that we always have access to Christ, our High Priest, who is 'a priest for ever, in the order of Melchizedek' (Psalm 110:4). What else would we choose to do than to spontaneously offer Him our gifts and ask for His blessing?

My prayer

I thank You, heavenly Father, that I have unlimited access to You and can ask You daily for the strength I need in order to live in accordance with Your will.

2 September

Mephibosheth

(he who scatters shame)

Who and when? Son of Jonathan and grandson of King Saul; ca. 1000 BC.

Want to know more? Read: 2 Samuel 4:4; 9:1-13; 16:1-4; 19:24-30; 21:1-7.

Thoughts for today

Mephibosheth was only five years old when he lost not only his grandfather Saul, but also his father Jonathan. Both men died in a battle near the mountain of Gilboa. When the sad news reached the place where Mephibosheth lived, another tragedy occurred. The woman who cared for Mephibosheth got such a shock that she dropped the child, with the result that he was crippled for the rest of his life. The life of the handicapped prince did not, therefore, start well. He did survive the massacre that ended the lives of seven of his cousins (2 Samuel 21:1-9), but as the grandson of a king who had died in defeat on the battlefield he did not face a very promising future.

Mephibosheth, however, was in for a surprise. David had his faults, but he was not resentful. He knew that at a given moment in the past God had chosen Saul to be Israel's king. He himself had tried to show loyalty towards Saul, and he had become a trusted friend of Jonathan - Saul's son and the father of Mephibosheth. That was reason enough for David to order a search for the crippled Mephibosheth and to welcome him to his palace.

Mephibosheth found that, fortunately, there are people who attach great value to old friendships and to earlier promises. It is wonderful if we can also experience this. In any case, David's example provides us with a signal that we should honour old friendships and the promises we have made.

My prayer

Dear God, give us the experience that Mephibosheth had, that there are always people who treasure old friendships.

3 September

Merodach-Baladan (Marduk has given a son)

Who and when? Assyrian king; reigned from ca. 721 BC to 709 BC.

Want to know more? Read: 2 Kings 20:12-19; 2 Chronicles 32:31; Isaiah 39:1-8.

Thoughts for today

The Babylonian king, Merodach-Baladan, tried to entice King Hezekiah to make an alliance with him. This was shortly after Hezekiah had been very ill and had been told by his doctors that his problem would be fatal. However, after he had pleaded with God for recovery, he was given an extra fifteen years of life (Isaiah 38:5).

This is how the story proceeds: 'At that time Merodach-Baladan son of Baladan king of Babylon sent Hezekiah letters and a gift, because he had heard of his illness and recovery. Hezekiah received the envoys gladly and showed them what was in his storehouses – the silver, the gold, the spices, the fine oil, his entire armoury and everything found among his treasures. There was nothing in his palace or in all his kingdom that Hezekiah did not show them' (Isaiah 39:1, 2). This brought heavy criticism from the prophet Isaiah. Hezekiah had just received the promise that he would live for another fifteen years, and as a sign that God's words could be trusted the sunlight went back 'on the stairway of Ahaz' (38:8). But was this miracle what still filled Hezekiah's heart when the envoys arrived? No, his first thought was that he should impress the foreign guests with his material prosperity.

God was deeply disappointed with Hezekiah: and we may expect Him to react in the very same way when we are primarily focused on the things we possess and on what we have achieved, rather than on the blessings we have received from Him. It was a missed opportunity to tell Merodach-Baladan, through his envoys, about the God he served, instead of bragging about himself.

My prayer

Lord, forgive me when, just like Hezekiah, I am focused on myself rather than on telling other people about the blessings You have given me.

4 September

Meshach

(Babylonian; possibly: who is the lunar god Aku?)

Who and when? He was an exile at the Babylonian court; one of the three young men who, together with Daniel, were deported to Babylon.

Want to know more? Read: Daniel 1:7–3:30

Thoughts for today

The story of the three men in the fiery furnace is full of superlatives. King Nebuchadnezzar was not just a little angry when the three men – Meshach, Shadrach and Abednego – refused to kneel before the enormous golden image that he had ordered to be made. No, he was 'furious with rage' (Daniel 3:13, 19) as he was told about the non-compliance of the three friends. He therefore ordered that the furnace in which they were to be executed should 'be heated seven times hotter than usual' (vs. 19). The men who had dared to disobey the ruler of the great Babylonian Empire were tied up by 'some of the strongest soldiers in his army' (vs. 20) and then thrown into the flames.

Suddenly, however, the king got the fright of his life. Rather than seeing with satisfaction how the *three* men were consumed by the fire, he saw *four* men walking in the midst of the sea of flames instead. He saw that the fourth looked 'like a son of the gods' (vs. 25). All the high officials who had seats of honour saw how a supernatural being rescued Meshach and his friends, and how the three men stepped unscathed from the furnace, without even a singed hair on their heads.

Nebuchadnezzar was one of the most powerful rulers of ancient times: but he was completely powerless when faced with the God of Meshach, Shadrach and Abednego. May we never forget that the God who rescued these three men is still more powerful than all earthly rulers put together.

My prayer

I thank You, Almighty God, that I may entrust myself to You, knowing that I am totally safe with You.

5 September

Methuselah

(man of the javelin)

Who and when? The oldest person who ever lived; he died when he was 969 years old.

Want to know more? Read: Genesis 5:21-27.

Thoughts for today

I cannot imagine what it would be like to live for 150 years, let alone that I would come anywhere near the 969 years of Methuselah – the highest age any human person has ever reached. Some years ago a French woman who had lived for a verified 122 years and 164 days died. Her name was Jeanne Louise Calment. There have been other claims about people elsewhere in the world that have reached an even higher age than this French lady, but in each of these cases supporting documentary evidence is missing.

Was Methuselah happy to live so long? Of course, he could experience a lot of things. If the genealogies in Genesis can be taken at face value, Methuselah must have known Adam, and he died in the year that the Flood occurred. These days we hear of many men and women who reach a high age – according to current life expectancy rates – but who do not actually enjoy it. They become so old that they outlive most of their family and friends – and often even their own children. Also, old age tends to impose considerable physical and mental limitations on most of us. Many therefore – rightly – conclude that the quality of life is more important than its duration.

Nonetheless, we say that people have reached a 'blessed' age. We appreciate the fact that on average we live longer than generations before us. And, as believers, we have the assurance that we have a very long life ahead of us – even longer than that of Methuselah – without any age-related restrictions. The time will come when the elements of *quality* and *duration* will never again be in tension.

My prayer

Lord, I pray for a long life, in good health, but most of all I thank You for the privilege that in the world to come I will enjoy everlasting life.

6 September

Micah

(who is like the Lord?)

Who and when? A wealthy man in the time of the judges who built a private sanctuary and employed a Levite as his priest.

Want to know more? Read: Judges 17 and 18.

Thoughts for today

When hearing the name, 'Micah', most of us will think first of all of the prophet Micah. However, among the Micahs of the Bible there is another man on whom I want to focus today. This Micah's mother, who lived in the mountainous area of Ephraim, decided to have a silversmith make her an idol, covered with silver. She put it in Micah's house, where he established his own shrine, and housed it along with some other idols. He made some priestly garments and, initially, he employed his own son as priest for his sanctuary. However, he replaced his son when he met a young Levite who accepted his offer of work. Micah thought that the Lord would be pleased. He said: 'Now I know that the LORD will be good to me, since this Levite has become my priest' (Judges 17:13).

Micah's religion mixed elements that were inspired by the official sanctuary service together with his own ideas. The author of the book of Judges comments: 'In those days . . . everyone did as he saw fit' (Judges 17:6).

If there ever was a time in which Micah's example was followed, it is today. For many the church may have become a relic of the past, but there continues to be a huge interest in spirituality. All too often, however, we see a mix of authentic Christian elements and ideas that have been borrowed from various other sources. But the fact that people may be satisfied with this does not automatically mean that it also pleases God.

My prayer

Lord, please keep on reminding me how You want to be served.

7 September

Micah

(who is like the Lord?)

Who and when? Prophet during the period of Jotham, Ahaz and Hezekiah (mid-eighth century BC).

Want to know more? Read: Micah.

Thoughts for today

The prophet Micah has a message of judgement, but also of comfort and delivery. God's grace provides the tune to which the Bible book that bears the name of this prophet is set. God's judgement is not the end of the story. 'In the last days the mountain of the LORD's temple will be established' (Micah 4:1).

The prophet Micah looked beyond his days to the greatest event in all human history: 'But you, Bethlehem Ephrathah . . . out of you will come for me one who will be ruler over Israel' (Micah 5:2). It is clear to us, who live after this prophecy has been fulfilled, that these words pointed to the birth of the Messiah - the One who would be the eternal and ultimate Comforter and Saviour.

When Micah had come to the end of his prophecies he posed a question to which he knew the answer: 'Who is a God like you, who pardons sin and forgives the transgression of the remnant of his inheritance?' (7:18.) In these words the hope for God's people in the days of Micah was anchored. God forgives and He 'delight[s] to show mercy' (vs. 18). The reason is not that sin does not trouble God, but that He is a God of compassion and grace.

This also is the basis for the hope of all of us today. We stand before God just as guilty as the people of Israel in the time of Micah. They constantly strayed from the right path: but there was always the opportunity for forgiveness and delivery, and that is also true for us.

My prayer

Merciful God, I realise that I stand guilty before You: but I also know that You are a God of mercy. I thank You for this from the bottom of my heart.

8 September

Michael

(who is like God?)

Who and when? A prominent heavenly being.

Want to know more? Read: Daniel 10:1–12:4; Jude 9.

Thoughts for today

The Bible mentions about ten people with the name of Michael. The best known of these is a 'person' of a totally different order. In Jude, vs. 9, we read about the archangel Michael, who wanted to resurrect Moses and take him to heaven, but the devil disagreed and is described as 'disputing' with him about the body of Moses.

Those who believe in the Bible must also believe in the existence of angels, even though their existence and their activities raise many unanswered questions. We get the distinct impression from various statements that there are different ranks in God's heavenly army. It seems that Michael belonged at the top. In some places so much power and influence is ascribed to him that many have concluded that Michael is, in fact, none other than Jesus Christ Himself.

Michael is also mentioned towards the end of the book of Daniel, where he is very active in the political events of Daniel's world. Much of Daniel, chapter 10, may not be immediately clear to us, but it underlines one very significant truth: much more is happening between heaven and earth than our human senses can perceive. God is incessantly active in our individual lives, and in those of His people, but also in the events that happen in the larger world. He makes use of human beings to execute His plans, but also involves other created beings, of whom Michael is one of the most prominent. One day we will have a better understanding of how God rules the universe. Until then we must be content with this assurance: angels are 'ministering spirits' who also constantly 'serve' us (Hebrews 1:14).

My prayer

Lord, in Your glory and majesty You are surrounded by an enormous army of angels. I thank You that these angels also surround me.

9 September

Michal

(abbreviated form of Michael: who is like God?)

Who and when? Daughter of Saul and wife of David; ca. 1000 BC.

Want to know more? Read: 1 Samuel 18:20-28; 19:11-17; 25:44; 2 Samuel 3:13-16; 6:16-23.

Thoughts for today

Michal was not David's only wife, but she occupied a very special place in his life. When King Saul suggested that David should marry his youngest daughter, he asked for a very unusual dowry. He wanted one hundred Philistine foreskins. This was a trick and he hoped that David would get killed in his attempts to assemble this dowry. However, David returned safely from his expedition and brought Saul twice as many as he had asked for. This is how Michal became David's wife. When her father did everything he could to pursue and kill David, she did not side with him, but with David. On another occasion she arranged for David's (narrow) escape from Saul's men: but then Saul took Michal away from David and married her off to someone else. David protested and she was returned to him.

We also read about a peculiar incident between Michal and David some time later when David escorts the ark of the covenant back to Jerusalem. He is so exuberant in his joyfulness that he dances at the head of the procession. Seeing this, Michal despises her husband. How can the king behave like this? She clearly has no idea of how important this event is for David and why he identifies with his people in this manner. This is probably because she does not appreciate that the ark is a symbol of Israel's national identity, and she has no empathy for David's feelings. At this moment it seems that she is mostly interested in status, decorum and self-interest. It is sad when these things become most important in someone's life.

My prayer

Lord, may status never be the most important thing in my life. Help me to show my joy openly when things are happening that are of great significance for people around me.

10 September

Miriam

(Egyptian: the beloved one)

Who and when? The sister of Moses and Aaron.

Want to know more? Read: Exodus 2:1-10; 15:20, 21; Numbers 12.

Thoughts for today

Prejudice is something as old as the world that occurs among all segments of society. It was not unknown in ancient times. Take Miriam, for example. She had watched over baby Moses. She had left Egypt when her people were delivered under the leadership of her brother. On that occasion she was touched by God's Spirit and sang a hymn in honour of the Almighty, and 'all the women followed her, with tambourines and dancing' (Exodus 15:20).

But we also discover other things about Miriam. While in the wilderness, the Israelites started complaining about their circumstances. Sadly, Aaron and Miriam, the brother and sister of Moses, were also infected by the virus of discontent. They became jealous of their brother and thought that things would go much better if Moses shared more of his authority with them. One reason for their rebellious attitude is singled out. They made some demeaning remarks about the fact that Moses had married a foreign woman. This 'Cushite wife' (Numbers 12:1) was probably Zipporah, who married Moses during his stay in Midian. Most likely she was dark-skinned.

Fortunately, there are many happy marriages between people of different ethnicities. There are other differences between partners that pose a much greater threat to their relationship than skin colour! Nonetheless, skin colour remains a reason why people are frequently discriminated against, even by family members. This is absolutely wrong, and we learn from this episode in Miriam's life that God does not want anyone to display this kind of prejudice.

My prayer

O God of all people, give me the determination and the courage to combat all forms of racial prejudice.

11 September

Mordecai

(Babylonian: servant of Merodach)

Who and when? Uncle of Esther; employed at the court of the Persian king; ca. 475 BC.

Want to know more? Read: Esther 2-10.

Thoughts for today

Mordecai was a Jewish exile who through a series of remarkable events became an important functionary at the Persian court. It would not have been easy to serve as a Jew in such a pagan environment. How do you remain faithful to your religious convictions and, at the same time, manifest loyalty to a regime that operates with radically different principles? Such situations may result in an acute crisis, when you are faced with the choice: obedience to the authorities or to your conscience. Perhaps it is advisable not to strive for such a high position: unless you have, like Mordecai, the strength to abide by your principles, trusting God, whether He helps you avoid the consequences or not.

Not all of us will experience such a dramatic situation as Mordecai, when he put his life at risk by his refusal to kneel before Haman (Esther 3:2). Haman was just an ordinary human being, and, being a Jew, Mordecai would only bow down before the God he served. But, like Mordecai, we too will, from time to time, experience the tension between our faith and our daily life and work. We also live in a society where the norms of God's kingdom are often ignored. This means that our loyalty may also be put to the test. How consistent are we when this happens? Are we prepared, if need be, to accept disadvantages in our daily lives, so that we can remain true to our faith - even if that would be damaging to our career or harm our social network? And do we have the trust that somehow God will lead the way if we are faced with a serious impasse?

My prayer

Lord, I ask You for the inner strength to remain loyal to You under all circumstances.

12 September

Moses

(drawn out)

Who and when? The leader of the Israelites when they were delivered from their Egyptian slavery and during the years of their sojourn though the Sinai desert. Ca. 1450 BC.

Want to know more? Read: relevant chapters in the Bible books of Exodus, Leviticus, Numbers and Deuteronomy.

Thoughts for today

Moses' name is mentioned in the Bible no less than 867 times. We meet him, of course, constantly in the first section of the Bible that is commonly referred to as 'the Books of Moses'. However, he is also mentioned many times in the New Testament. For example, he appeared on the Mount of Transfiguration with Elijah (Matthew 17:1-8). But we find one of the best-known New Testament references to this great man of God in the Letter to the Hebrews: 'By faith Moses, when he had grown up, refused to be known as the son of Pharaoh's daughter. He chose to be ill-treated along with the people of God rather than to enjoy the pleasures of sin for a short time. He regarded disgrace for the sake of Christ as of greater value than the treasures of Egypt' (Hebrews 11:24-26).

Moses was faced with a dramatic choice. Circumstances he could not have foreseen brought him to the court of the pharaoh. He literally lived like a prince and he enjoyed all the luxuries that were part of this kind of life. Nonetheless, he chose a totally different destiny that would bring him a lot of stress and deprivation. Moses was able to make the right choice by comparing temporary pleasures with eternal happiness. There were indeed the fleeting advantages of prosperity and status, but Moses looked towards the ultimate reward that far exceeded all the Egyptian treasures. He never regretted his decision. What choice do we make? Do we also choose what will remain rather than some temporary advantages?

My prayer

Heavenly Father, help me to choose the eternal heavenly reward rather than the fleeting pleasures that do not give any lasting satisfaction.

13 September

Naaman

(pleasant)

Who and when? Military leader from Aram who was healed by Elisha from a deadly disease (ca. 850 BC).

Want to know more? Read: 2 Kings 5.

Thoughts for today

Naaman was prepared to do anything – if only he could be healed from the disease that threatened to take his life. Following the advice of the servant of his wife, he had travelled to Israel and had arrived at the doorstep of the house of the prophet Elisha. This prophet was reputed to be a man of God who was often instrumental in healing people. Naaman had expected that he would have to follow some complicated procedures: but that was not what he was asked to do. He was told simply to go to the River Jordan and immerse himself seven times. Initially, Naaman refused to follow these simple instructions. Surely, it could not be that easy! At that point he did not yet grasp that his healing was a divine gift. The only thing he was expected to do was to accept that gift humbly, with both hands.

Naaman's skin disease is a fitting illustration of our sin problem and how we can be rescued from it. Many people (lifelong Christians included) think it is difficult to be saved for eternity. They believe salvation entails a lot of complicated requirements they have to comply with. Others, however, tell them: 'It is, in fact, very simple. The only thing you are expected to do is to believe that God has forgiven you and has adopted you as His child. You must only accept that Jesus also gave His life on your behalf.' Many object to this and say: 'It cannot be that simple!' But it is. Getting rid of your guilt and having a right relationship with God is offered to us as a totally free gift. The only thing God expects from us is to show that we are prepared to bow our stubborn heads before Him.

My prayer

I thank You, O God, that You have thrown me and all other people a lifebuoy. Help us to grab it and never to let go.

14 September

Nabal

(foolish)

Who and when? Nabal lived in the time of David; he refused to show appreciation for the protection he had received from David and his men. Ca. 1000 BC.

Want to know more? Read: 1 Samuel 25.

Thoughts for today

Nabal was extremely rich (1 Samuel 25:2). He possessed three thousand sheep and a thousand goats, but he was not a pleasant person. He 'was surly and mean in his dealings' (vs. 3). This became clear on the occasion that David sent ten men to Nabal, when he and his household celebrated the annual shearing of his sheep.

David had assembled a small army around him, as he tried to avoid being killed by Saul's soldiers. For an entire season David and his men had protected the flocks of Nabal. Nabal knew about this, but it went against his nature to show any gratitude – especially if it cost him something. We often notice this attitude with rich people. They want to amass even more than they already have and hate to share their riches with others – even when they have provided an important service. Fortunately, Abigail, Nabal's wife, had a different attitude and succeeded in calming David down; but the end of the story was that Nabal, upon hearing what David had intended to do with him, suffered a heart attack from which he died ten days later.

Nabal was not only egocentric and greedy, but he was also a fool. Abigail knew this better than anyone. She said: 'His name is Fool, and folly goes with him' (25:25). Prosperity and wealth should be accompanied by generosity and wisdom. Nabal lacked these two qualities, especially the latter one. Let us, when things are going well for us in material respects, never forget that we must be wise stewards of what we possess and must always be prepared to assist those who need help and to share some of our abundance with them.

My prayer

I thank You, Lord, for the material blessings I experience. Help me to be a wise steward of what You have given me.

15 September

Nadab

(generous)

Who and when? Son of Aaron; did not follow God's instructions in dealing with the offerings of the people.

Want to know more? Read: Exodus 6:23; 24:9-11; Leviticus 10:1-3.

Thoughts for today

Nadab and Abihu, the sons of Aaron who also served as priests, were killed when they 'offered unauthorised fire before the LORD' (Leviticus 10:1). We are not told exactly what they did, but it is clear that they categorically refused to follow the instructions that God had given (Leviticus 10:3). They acted 'contrary to God's commands', and the consequences were severe: 'Fire came out from the presence of the LORD and consumed them, and they died *before the LORD*' (vs. 2, emphasis supplied).

Nadab and his brother had been 'before the Lord' on an earlier occasion. We read about this in Exodus 24:9-11. Moses had gone up the mountain, together with 'Aaron, Nadab and Abihu, and the seventy elders of Israel. . . . Under his [God's] feet was something like a pavement made of sapphire, clear as the sky itself. But God did not raise his hand against these leaders of the Israelites; they saw God, and they ate and drank.'

Being in God's presence brings blessing. It means that you begin to know more about God; that you 'see' God – just as Nadab and Abihu did. However, if you subsequently forget what you have seen and do not follow His instructions, things can go very wrong: for you always remain in God's presence. When you intentionally ignore Him and His wishes, you will reap the consequences.

My prayer

Lord, I want to be in Your presence and see Your glory: and help me never to forget what I have seen.

16 September

Nahum

(consolation)

Who and when? One of the 'minor' prophets who gave his name to the Bible book with this name (seventh century BC).

Want to know more? Read: Nahum.

Thoughts for today

The three chapters of the book of Nahum do not make for very pleasant reading. About a century and a half after the city of Nineveh had turned to God as a result of Jonah's preaching, it had once again become a centre of wickedness and cruelty, where neither God nor His commandments had any influence. Nahum predicted the total destruction of this 'city of blood' (Nahum 3:1). About one hundred years later his prophecy was fulfilled. When, on his expedition to the East, Alexander the Great passed the place where Nineveh had once stood, he was not even aware of it, so thoroughly had Nineveh been wiped from the map.

Nahum's prophecy is crystal clear. God's patience has been exhausted. 'The LORD is slow to anger and great in power,' but He 'will not leave the guilty unpunished' (1:3). Nahum depicts Israel's God as One who 'takes vengeance and is filled with wrath' (1:2). No one, Nahum emphatically states, 'can endure his fierce anger' (1:6).

But the prophet has more to say. He immediately adds: 'The LORD is good, a refuge in times of trouble. He cares for those who trust in him' (1:7). These words illustrate God's uniqueness and tell us that wherever His justice is applied, His goodness, love and forgiveness are only a sincere prayer away.

My prayer

Almighty God, may we always realise that You are good and full of love, and that whatever You do is always for our ultimate good.

17 September

Naomi

(my pleasantness)

Who and when? An Israelite woman who, with her husband and two sons, went to Moab in order to escape a famine; mother-in-law of Ruth.

Want to know more? Read: Ruth.

Thoughts for today

Some people experience more than an average amount of misery. Naomi falls into that category. A famine forced her and her family to flee from her home and her country. Then, after some time, she became a widow. And, as if that were not tragic enough, her two sons also died. One of her daughters-in-law decided to remain in Moab when the famine had passed, and Naomi decided to return home. When she arrived back home the news rapidly spread. 'The women [who had known her before her departure to Moab] exclaimed: "Can this be Naomi?" ' (Ruth 1:19.) Yes, Noami replied, indeed, it is me: but ' "don't call me Naomi," she told them. "Call me Mara, because the Almighty has made my life very bitter" ' (vs. 20). Naomi felt very sorry for herself. 'I went away full, but the LORD has brought me back empty' (vs. 21). Naomi was totally disillusioned. Why did she have to suffer so much?

We may not have been through quite as much misfortune as Naomi, but many of us also tend to bemoan our situation and keep asking: 'Why? Why me?' Yet the story of Ruth tells us that a new perspective emerges when we get a grip on ourselves and look for new opportunities. This is what Naomi did, with the support of her daughter-in-law Ruth. Who knows what new opportunities we may discover after life has for some time been tough for us? And who knows from what direction these new chances might come?

My prayer

Merciful God, give us the courage and the strength, and open our eyes, to see new opportunities after we have gone through a difficult phase in our lives.

18 September

Naphtali

(my wrestling)

Who and when? The sixth son of Jacob; his second child with Bilhah.

Want to know more? Read: Genesis 30:8; 49:21; Joshua 19:32-39.

Thoughts for today

Naphtali was one of the nation of Israel's forefathers. Some of his brothers, however, are much better known to us. In fact, we know little more about Naphtali than a few tiny bits of information about the area that the families belonging to the tribe of Naphtali received when the 'promised land' was divided among the tribes.

However, the name of Naphtali is intriguing. He did not get that name from his biological mother, but from a woman called Rachel, who directed things in the background. Rachel had for a long time remained childless, and that made her decide to give her servant Bilhah to Jacob, hoping she would give birth to some children who could then be counted as hers. Bilhah's firstborn was Dan, with Naphtali coming next. Why did Rachel select the name 'Naphtali' for Bilhah's son? Here's her explanation: 'I have had a great struggle with my sister, and I have won' (Genesis 30:8). Rachel's relationship with her sister Leah was one of unrelenting jealousy. Leah gave birth to one son after the other, while Rachel, Jacob's preferred wife, remained childless during a major part of her life. Rachel had never been able to deal with that fact.

That there would be problems between the two sisters was to be foreseen, considering how Jacob was first tricked into marrying Leah and then had to wait another week before Rachel too could become his wife. It is tragic when families cannot resolve a conflict and make peace, even after years have passed. Rachel and Leah provide a sad example of a situation that often occurs today.

My prayer

I realise, gracious God, how destructive jealousy is. Help me in conquering feelings of jealousy whenever I fall victim to them.

19 September

Nathan

(he that God has given)

Who and when? A prophet in the time of King David (ca. 1000 BC).

Want to know more? Read: 2 Samuel 7; 12:1-15; 2 Chronicles 9:29; Psalm 51.

Thoughts for today

Most of us would not have wanted to be in Nathan's shoes: not, in any case, when God told him to go to David and tell him what God thought about his ploy to get Bathsheba as his wife. David did not immediately realise what Nathan would have to say, when he was told of the prophet's wish to come and see him. Not until Nathan had told a story about the rich man, who in a devious way had succeeded in taking the one sheep away from a poor man, did the penny drop. Only then did the king understand the evil he had done. Shortly after Nathan's visit David wrote about his remorse in a deeply moving hymn that we know as Psalm 51.

Nathan did what God had commanded him to do. To prophesy means to faithfully communicate the message you have received from God. A prophet who refuses to do so thereby negates his calling.

All those who believe that we live in a time in which prophetic messages - such as we find in the Bible - should be communicated to the people around us must, like Nathan, go with courage to the people for whom the message is intended, even if they have reason to think that this message will not be welcome. At the same time the approach of Nathan provides an excellent example of how such a difficult message may be communicated. Nathan showed that we must 'package' what we have to say in such a way that the penny will drop.

My prayer

Please help me, Lord, always to 'package' Your prophetic message for this time in such a way that it will resonate with the people I want to reach.

20 September

Nathanael

(God has given)

Who and when? One of the men Jesus called to be His disciples; probably identical with Bartholomew.

Want to know more? Read: John 1:43-51; 21:2.

Thoughts for today

Earlier in this book we already met Bartholomew and indicated that he most probably is also referred to in the Bible as Nathanael. The calling of this disciple has a few aspects that are worth stressing. Nathanael's calling was not the result of coincidence. Jesus already thought of him before He met him. He knew that Nathanael was the kind of person He wanted to have with Him. He said: 'Here is a true Israelite, in whom there is nothing false' (John 1:47).

When Nathanael asked Jesus how He knew him, Jesus replied: 'I saw you under the fig tree.' How reassuring is the certainty that Jesus already sees us before we even know Him. But Jesus did not directly go to the spot where He knew He could find Nathanael. After Philip had encountered Jesus, he went straight away to his friend Nathanael to tell him about Jesus. This is how Jesus worked, and He still uses the same method today. He still uses people to spread the news about Him.

There is a good chance that you, who read today's short devotional, have also been introduced to Jesus by someone else – perhaps by your parents, a teacher, a colleague, or a friend – but this realisation immediately raises the question: have *you* recently introduced someone to Jesus?

My prayer

Lord Jesus, open my eyes so that I may see the chances that present themselves for introducing someone to You.

21 September

Nebuchadnezzar

(may Nabu protect the king)

Who and when? Ruler of the Babylonian Empire (605 BC to 562 BC); deported large numbers of Judeans to Babylon.

Want to know more? Read: Daniel 1-4.

Thoughts for today

We know the great King Nebuchadnezzar best from the stories about his dream and its explanation by Daniel, and about the fiery furnace from which Daniel's three friends were rescued by a heavenly being. But most Bible readers are also acquainted with the story of the king's seven-year mental illness. Nebuchadnezzar had been warned that his hubris could easily seal his fate in a dramatic way. Indeed, when, a year later, the king walked on the roof of his magnificent palace, he looked with great pride over the big city and spoke the arrogant words: 'Is not this the great Babylon I have built as the royal residence, by my mighty power and for the glory of my majesty?' (Daniel 4:27) – at that very moment the king lost his mind and was in the grip of a rare mental disorder. But after seven years his mental health was restored by God, just as suddenly as he had lost it.

Nebuchadnezzar was fully restored to his royal position. More importantly, he had learned his lesson. He now realised that not *he* but the God of Israel is the centre of the universe: 'All the peoples of the earth are regarded as nothing. He [God] does as he pleases with the powers of heaven and the peoples of the earth. No one can hold back his hand. . . . I, Nebuchadnezzar, praise and exalt and glorify the King of heaven' (4:35-37).

Through the centuries there have been men and women who believed they were the masters of their own destiny: but, happily, there have also always been men and women who discovered that they do not have the final word, but God.

My prayer

Lord, I pray that I will not need such a painful lesson as Nebuchadnezzar received to make me realise that You are the Almighty.

22 September

Nehemiah

(the Lord has comforted)

Who and when? Butler at the court of the Persian king Artaxerxes; was allowed to go to Jerusalem and assist in the rebuilding of the city. Governor of Judah (445 BC to 433 BC).

Want to know more? Read: Nehemiah 1:1-2:20; 12:31-43; 13:6-31.

Thoughts for today

The book of Nehemiah tells us about the restoration of the wall around the city of Jerusalem, and about the new start of the services in the temple. Nehemiah comes across as a good leader and an efficient administrator. When he felt that he had completed his work, he returned to Babylon once again to resume his 'normal' tasks. However, after some time he returned to Jerusalem, where it soon became obvious that his influence was badly needed.

The Judeans who had returned to their land were struggling to keep safe among the hostile neighbouring peoples. Moreover, they were constantly subject to influences that undermined their religious status. Their identity as a special people of God was under continuous attack. They had given shelter (in the temple, of all places!) to someone who absolutely should not have been there (Nehemiah 13:7-9), but there were also numerous other abuses. Nehemiah also noticed how many of the Judeans had taken foreign wives. These women had not accepted the Judean way of life, did not speak the language of Judah, and in many ways presented a risk for the religious identity of God's people. We would today, no doubt, opt for other measures than Nehemiah did, but remaining alert with regard to our religious identity remains as urgent as ever.

My prayer

Lord, I want to be Your child and to be part of a faith community that is loyal to You. Help me in staying true to my religious identity as a child of You.

23 September

Nicodemus

(Greek: victor over the people)

Who and when? A Pharisee who had a conversation with Jesus during the night and later decided to follow Him.

Want to know more? Read: John 3:1-21; 7:50-52; 19:38-42.

Thoughts for today

Nicodemus wanted to know more about Jesus and His message; but as a Jewish leader he could hardly show his interest openly. That would have put his reputation and status in serious jeopardy. Jesus understood this. He was prepared to talk with Nicodemus, even if that would have to happen during the night. Jesus did not tell him: 'Come back tomorrow at a more reasonable hour.' He saw that Nicodemus had a real interest. He replied to his questions and gave him much to think about: but he also granted him enough time. Gradually Nicodemus had the courage to more openly express his opinion about Jesus, and, when the Pharisees later debated among themselves what to do with Him, Nicodemus warned them not to condemn Him before they had all the facts. Then, when Jesus had died, he offered to help arrange for His burial.

Often a definitive choice for Jesus, as in the case of Nicodemus, is preceded by a long process of thoughtful questioning. Postmodern people often need even more time to make a final commitment to Christ than was usual for people in the past. Jesus accepted that Nicodemus needed time, and He also accepts it when people today go through a long process. However, this does not take away from the fact that there must be a moment when a choice is made; and the message Jesus had for Nicodemus has not changed: only after becoming a new person can one enter the kingdom of God (John 3:1-7).

My prayer

Thank You, eternal God, that You allow me enough time: but help me not to defer my decision to the point that I lose the intention of following You.

24 September

Nicolaus

(Greek: conqueror of the people)

Who and when? Man from Antioch who converted to Judaism and later became a Christian. He was chosen as one of the seven 'deacons' in Jerusalem.

Want to know more? Read: Acts 6:1-7.

Thoughts for today

The church in Jerusalem grew exponentially, and after some time the apostles were beginning to lose their grip on its activities. They were so busy preaching the Gospel and performing all kinds of administrative duties that some important things remained undone. At least, that is how some groups in the church experienced it. The Greek-speaking Jews 'complained against the Hebraic Jews because their widows were being overlooked in the daily distribution of food (Acts 6:1). Whether this was actually true or just a perception we will never know, but perceptions usually create just as many problems. The apostles, therefore, decided that they should delegate the social welfare aspects of their ministry to a special group of leaders: namely, Nicolaus and six other men.

The choice of the apostles was not only inspired by the social and organisational skills of Nicolaus and his six colleagues. They were looking for men who were 'full of . . . wisdom' and had a solid reputation, and who were clearly led by the Holy Spirit. On the surface their job may have seemed mostly of a practical and organisational nature, but the apostles saw it as a spiritual work – just as much as their own. For that reason there was a ceremony to dedicate these men for their task. It is also true for men and women today, who, like Nicolaus, deal with all kinds of practical matters in the church. Theirs is also a *spiritual* work – something they and the other church members should always remember.

My prayer

Good God, let me never forget that all work in the church is of a spiritual nature.

25 September

Niger

(Latin: black)

Who and when? Nickname of Simeon, one of the leaders of the church in Antioch.

Want to know more? Read: Acts 13:1.

Thoughts for today

'Simeon' was a Jewish name, while 'Niger' probably points to a pagan influence. Whatever be the case, this Simeon Niger was no doubt someone we would in our Western world refer to as an 'immigrant'. In many countries a black person tends to be regarded as a 'foreigner'. Well, this 'foreigner' had become a Christian and was now part of the leadership team of the church in Antioch. He is mentioned among the 'prophets and teachers' and played a role in the commissioning of Paul and Barnabas at the start of their first missionary journey.

From these few details about this Simeon, 'called Niger', we may conclude that the members of the Antioch church were well aware of the colour of Simeon's skin: but, apparently, this was a non-issue for them; and that is how it should be, because we all belong to one and the same human family. Moreover, we are one in Christ, regardless of our ethnic or cultural background, economic status or gender. Sadly, the church in ages past has often neglected this fundamental principle, and all too often groups of Christians have discriminated against other Christian groups on this basis: and even today this evil (for that is what it is) has not been fully rejected in many places in the world.

Are there people in the congregation to which you belong like 'Simeon, called Niger'? If there are, it is your duty to do what you can to ensure that every trace of discrimination – if that should be found – is totally eradicated.

My prayer

Thank You, Lord, that we all are sons and daughters of You, our heavenly Father.

26 September

Nimrod

(rebel)

Who and when? The son of Cush. One of the key figures in the period between Noah and Abraham.

Want to know more? Read: Genesis 10:7-12.

Thoughts for today

Nimrod was 'a mighty hunter before the Lord'. It is not clear how exactly we should interpret these words, but we may safely assume that he did not just hunt rabbits and hares. The text suggests that people were talking about him and that he was widely admired.

Nimrod was a man with considerable clout, who initiated the building of several cities in Mesopotamia. We hear about his 'kingdom' and about names like Akkad, Babylon and Nineveh. The next story in Genesis tells us about the tower of Babel (Genesis 11). We do not know whether Nimrod was also involved with this adventure. It might well be, as there is a link between him and Babel.

People who accomplish many things, and who are admired by lots of people, can easily fall for the temptation to think only of their own fame and interests. One might say that this kind of arrogance will, sooner rather than later, lead to a Babylonian mentality, in which God is no longer part of the equation. That is the picture whenever the name of Babylon is mentioned in the Bible. As always, the tendency to emphasise only what *we* have accomplished, and to rely on *our own* influence and power, can bring us to the point where we become like Nimrod and eventually feel very much at home in modern 'Babylon'.

My prayer

I thank You, God, for the talents that I have received and for the fact that I am good at certain things: but help me never to think that these skills are the most important things in my life.

27 September

Noah

(rest)

Who and when? Builder of a big ship in which he and seven other people survived the Flood.

Want to know more? Read: Genesis 6:9-10:32.

Thoughts for today

Many books and sermons about Noah emphasise that Noah spent one hundred and twenty years building a large vessel that was to rescue eight people and a large number of animals from destruction: yet it is impossible to verify from the biblical data that the construction took exactly that many years. We may be sure, however, that it was an immense undertaking. To construct his ship Noah probably employed not just his sons, but also other workers. There is no doubt that this was a long-term project that required a lot of manpower!

What enabled Noah not only to start this gigantic job, but also to keep at it, and finish it? We all know how difficult it often is - even with very popular projects that seem to make good progress - not to lose our courage and our focus when other things are clamouring for our attention. But Noah was able to persevere.

In Hebrews 11:7 we find the key to Noah's perseverance: 'By faith Noah, when warned about things not yet seen, in holy fear built an ark to save his family.' 'By faith' remains the key to keep going, also for those who live at the end of time and have been given the task of preparing others for that event.

My prayer

Heavenly Father, You know that it is at times difficult to persevere in the things that You ask from us. Thank You for the inspiring example of Noah.

28 September

Obadiah

(servant of the Lord)

Who and when? A prophet in Judah, the Southern Kingdom, at the end of the sixth century BC; author of the shortest book in the Old Testament.

Want to know more? Read: Obadiah.

Thoughts for today

The Old Testament mentions at least eleven men with the name of Obadiah. Among them the prophet Obadiah, who was roughly a contemporary of the prophet Jeremiah, is no doubt best-known. His words are addressed to the people of Edom, Israel's brother-nation, who were descendants of Esau. Obadiah does not mince words when he addresses the Edomites.

Obadiah's criticism regarding Edom is perhaps best summarised by the word 'arrogance'. 'The pride of your heart has deceived you, you who live in the clefts of the rocks . . . you who say to yourself, "Who can bring me down to the ground?" ' (Vs. 3.) But the prophet says to the arrogant Edomites: ' "Though you soar like the eagle and make your nest among the stars, from there I will bring you down," declares the LORD' (vs. 4).

Through the ages arrogance has sealed the destiny of many people groups and nations; and countless individuals have also experienced that pride often leads to a lot of trouble. It is not without reason that in the past the church pointed to pride as one of the 'deadly sins'. The New Testament church of Laodicea was also characterised by a regrettable dose of arrogance, and ever since many other church organisations have displayed these Laodicean characteristics. Do you detect some traces of such overconfidence in yourself? Read the words of Obadiah and ask God for the strength and determination to get rid of all traces of arrogance.

My prayer

Lord Jesus, teach me to follow Your example of humility.

29 September

Obed

(servant)

Who and when? Son of Boaz and Ruth; forefather of Jesus.

Want to know more? Read: Ruth 4:13-17, 21; 1 Chronicles 2:12; Matthew 1:1-17.

Thoughts for today

Ruth could never have dreamed that everything would turn out so well in the end. She returned as a widow, penniless, with her mother-in-law Naomi, to the area of Bethlehem. Naomi had spent a considerable time in Moab while a famine raged in her own country. When she was ready to return, one of her daughters-in-law persisted in her decision to accompany her. She wanted to remain close to Naomi, but had also decided to serve Naomi's God. After a series of remarkable events she married Boaz, a rich landowner. A little later she gave birth to a son, who was named Obed. We conclude from the story that Naomi continued to be closely involved with the new family of Boaz and Ruth, and that the neighbours also showed their joy about the happiness Ruth and Naomi had found.

We know very little about this Obed; however, it is inspiring to take a close look at the genealogies in which Obed is mentioned. He produces a son (Jesse), who himself is blessed with sons – David being one of them. That makes Obed a link in the chain of Christ's human ancestry – the Son of God and the Son of David.

Ruth could never have imagined that she – a Moabite woman – would, with her son, become part of the human pedigree of the Saviour. Her loyalty to the God of Naomi was indeed richly rewarded.

My prayer

My great God, I realise that I am not part of the human genealogy of Your Son: but I thank You that, because of the work of Your Son, I may nevertheless belong to Your extended family.

30 September

Oholah

(her tent; she has pitched her tent)

Who and when? Name of a prostitute whom the prophet Ezekiel pointed to as a symbol of Israel.

Want to know more? Read: Ezekiel 23.

Thoughts for today

Oholah and Oholibah are the chief characters in a parable that Ezekiel was to tell the people on behalf of God. What we read about these two women needs very little further explanation. Ezekiel 23 is perhaps the most sexually explicit chapter in the Bible, and it portrays Oholah and Oholibah as totally immoral women who were not very particular about the persons they slept with. They were, the prophet Ezekiel explains, types (illustrations) of what the citizens of the Northern Kingdom (ten tribes) and the Southern Kingdom (two tribes) had become. They had apostatised on a large scale and committed spiritual adultery with the neighbouring peoples, just as Oholah and Oholibah had committed physical adultery.

Our first impression might be that the story is rather sexist. Why would the prophet use the image of two immoral women? What about the men who are more than willing to use their services? However, the imagery flows from a symbolism we find time and again in the Bible: God as the caring Husband, and the people who belong to Him - both Israel and the church - as His beloved wife or bride.

There was never any problem with God's care for His people; but there was often a huge problem with the love and faithfulness of the people with whom He had entered into a covenant relationship. The question for us is: 'Can God count on our unconditional loyalty towards Him today?'

My prayer

Lord, forgive us if we have ever turned away from You and been unfaithful to You. We thank You, however, for the fact that we may always return to You and that You continue to love us.

1 October

Oholiab

(the father's tent)

Who and when? One of the craftsmen employed in the building of the tabernacle.

Want to know more? Read: Exodus 31:6; 35:30-35; 36:1-7; 38:21-30.

Thoughts for today

The tabernacle – the portable sanctuary that was carried along as Israel journeyed in the wilderness – was of modest proportions. The length of this construction (including the holy and the holy of holies), which could be easily disassembled, was about fifteen metres and its width was about five metres. Therefore, it may surprise us when we discover the details of what went into its construction. Bezalel and Oholiab had permission to hire as many other craftsmen as they deemed necessary and they could order the best wood, in addition to large quantities of gold, silver and bronze, and the finest cloth.

The description the Bible gives of the tabernacle allows us to imagine the result of the work of Oholiab. He and his fellow artisan were not only expected to make something that would be functional, but also something that was exquisitely beautiful. We deduce from God's instructions for the construction of the tabernacle – and later for the temple – that God loves beauty. Perhaps the builders of the medieval cathedrals understood this better than we often do today as we construct our meeting places.

It is an aspect we nowadays often largely ignore. We emphasise the functionality of what we design. When we build a new church, the building itself and its furniture must preferably be multifunctional. The thought of costs and efficiency is predominant in our minds. These things are certainly important, but let us never forget that God also loves beauty.

My prayer

Dear Lord, You have created countless beautiful things. Help me never to forget that You love things of beauty.

2 October

Omri

(the Lord is my part)

Who and when? One of the most important kings of the Northern Kingdom consisting of the ten tribes (884 BC to 873 BC); father of Ahab.

Want to know more? Read: 1 Kings 16:23-28.

Thoughts for today

The Bible does not give a great deal of attention to King Omri, for he 'did evil in the eyes of the LORD' (1 Kings 16:25). That is the most important thing about Omri as far as the writer of Kings is concerned. He does, however, also mention that Omri wanted to have a new capital city for his kingdom (Samaria), just as King David had built Jerusalem as his capital. From a political perspective this was a smart move. Extra-biblical sources inform us that Omri ruled over an extended area. Archaeologists have identified a stele (memorial stone) that confirms the obligation of the king of Moab to pay tribute to Omri. The marriage of his son Ahab with the daughter of the king of Tyre indicates that Omri had a good relationship with the Phoenicians.

We would be inclined to think that one of the essential qualities for a ruler is to be a skilled politician. That was also true in the ancient world, even though in those days it was also very important to be a courageous military leader with keen strategic insight. Nowadays the word 'politics' gives many of us a bad taste in our mouths, especially when it concerns the church – locally and at the 'higher' levels – and, indeed, we can learn from the chronicle of Omri's achievements that God operates according to other norms. A person may be a clever politician or strategist, but the most important thing remains that he/she 'does what is good in the eyes of the Lord'.

My prayer

My Father in heaven, help me today to do what is 'good in Your eyes'.

3 October

Onan

(strong)

Who and when? Second son of Judah. He was reluctant to accept all the responsibilities of a levirate marriage with the widow of his brother Er.

Want to know more? Read: Genesis 38:6-11; Numbers 26:19.

Thoughts for today

In the eighteenth century Onan's name was used to describe a form of birth control (*coitus interruptus*), which became known as onanism. In recent times, however, the term has also been used to describe masturbation. Since Onan was so severely punished by God, many have concluded that this kind of sexual activity is one of the most serious sins that a human being can commit. In the past it was often thought that it would result in terrible diseases and deformity. However, if we read Onan's story carefully, we soon understand that it is about something else.

Why did Onan get such a bad reputation? The problem was that he did not want to conform to the practice of his times that required him to make sure that his deceased brother would have descendants. He refused to provide his sister-in-law with at least one child, for fear of reducing the inheritance of his 'real' children. It was this egocentric, materialistic attitude that God resented so strongly.

The incident of Onan is a good illustration of the problems that arise when we read the Bible without duly taking into account the circumstances and customs of the times in which the biblical story is situated. If we read with our own presuppositions, without recognising what things meant in their original historical and cultural context, we arrive at faulty conclusions.

My prayer

Thank You, O God, for Your Word. Help us to do our best to understand the background of what we read!

4 October

Onesimus

(useful; profitable)

Who and when? A slave who had run away from his master and come into contact with Paul.

Want to know more? Read: Colossians 4:9; Philemon 10-20.

Thoughts for today

In the world of the New Testament slavery was a common phenomenon. Onesimus is one of the few slaves we know by name. He was owned by Philemon, a Christian who probably lived in Colosse. Onesimus had fled and stayed for some time near a place where Paul was held as a prisoner, and he had come to know Onesimus well. We do not know where this was, as during his ministry Paul was a prisoner in various places. When writing to Philemon from his prison cell he refers to Onesimus as 'my son' (Philemon 10). Paul's main intention with this letter was that he was anxious to see that Onesimus, upon his return to his master – now as 'a dear brother' (vs. 16) – would not meet too many problems.

It is difficult for us to imagine Onesimus's situation. He had become a Christian. He had tasted freedom for a short time, but now the apostle urged him to return to his master – his 'dear brother' in Christ, but nonetheless still his owner. We can only speculate about the relationship between Philemon and Onesimus from that moment on. Hopefully, Paul's intervention did help to ensure that there was no longer only a master-slave relationship but also a brotherly bond.

Today, relationships may also be intertwined in challenging ways. Another Christian may be the owner of the house you rent, or run a business that competes with yours. The person who is your boss at work may sit next to you in church. It can be a challenge to combine the 'brotherly' and 'sisterly' with other relational aspects; but we must do so, for we are first and foremost brothers and sisters in Christ.

My prayer

We thank You, Lord, that You are the Father of all of us. Help us always to realise what it means to be a 'brother' or 'sister' of our fellow believers.

5 October

Orpah

(stubborn)

Who and when? Sister-in-law of Ruth; stayed in Moab when her mother-in-law (Naomi) left for home with her sister-in-law Ruth.

Want to know more? Read: Ruth 1:1-18.

Thoughts for today

People with the same background often make very different choices. We see an example of this in the decisions made by Ruth and Orpah. Each of these two Moabite women was married to a son of Naomi and Elimelech. After being married for about ten years they had both lost their husbands. Both of them had come into contact with the God of their husbands and of their in-laws. But after the famine was over, and Naomi decided to return to her own country, they went their separate ways. Ruth decided to accompany Naomi. Her reaction to Naomi was: 'Your people will be my people, and your God my God' (Ruth 1:16). But Orpah 'kissed her mother-in-law good-bye' (vs. 14), as she preferred to stay with her own people and to continue worshipping the gods of the Moabites.

Naomi had to accept that Orpah had made her own choice. She had done what she could to tell both Orpah and Ruth about the true God. Ruth decided that she wanted to serve the God she had become acquainted with, while Orpah went in another direction. What Naomi experienced is what many parents and parents-in-law also experience. They do what they can to lead their children and their spouses on the path of faith, but ultimately the choice is not theirs. We also see this during evangelistic meetings. Some react like Ruth; others, like Orpah. It must have been sad for Naomi to see Orpah depart, but God alone saw Orpah's heart and knew what brought her to her decision. And the final outcome of Orpah's choice is a matter for God to decide and not for us to speculate about.

My prayer

Lord, I pray that I will never lose my determination to follow You.

6 October

Othniel

(my strength is in God)

Who and when? The first judge in Israel; some time after Joshua's death; fourteenth century BC.

Want to know more? Read: Joshua 15:17; Judges 1:12-15; 3:7-11.

Thoughts for today

Othniel was the first in a series of 'judges' – leaders who, over a period of about 350 years, brought deliverance to the Israelites when they had to face enemies, and were also involved in giving advice and resolving conflicts. There was no question of a dynasty, nor of any democratic election process. God was the Ruler of His people, but in His care and mercy for His people He arranged from time to time, at crucial moments, for someone to emerge who could deliver His people.

With Othniel we see the start of a pattern that would be repeated over a number of centuries. 'The Israelites did evil in the eyes of the LORD and served the Baals. . . . They forsook [God] and served Baal and the Ashtoreths' (Judges 2:11-13). However, when the situation became critical, they would call upon God for help and the Lord, in His love, would send them a deliverer. After that things would go well for a limited time.

Othniel was the first man who was sent by God as 'judge'. He was the son of Caleb's brother and he undoubtedly knew about the courage of his uncle, one of the 'spies' who had been sent to explore the 'promised land'. Othniel had remained faithful to the God of Israel; and, when God called him to become a 'judge', he was ready for his assignment. 'The Spirit of the LORD came upon him' (Judges 3:10) and enabled him to do what was expected from him. He dealt decisively with the enemy, and 'the land had peace for forty years' (3:11). Othniel experienced what humans can do when they are guided by the Spirit.

My prayer

Dear God, please keep on reminding me that I can only be truly successful in the projects that I work on if I am guided by Your Spirit.

7 October

Pashhur

(multiplies liberty)

Who and when? A priest who resisted the prophecies of Jeremiah and locked the prophet up for a night.

Want to know more? Read: Jeremiah 20:1-6.

Thoughts for today

In the story of Jeremiah we meet three persons named Pashhur. One was a strong political opponent of the prophet Jeremiah (Jeremiah 21:1). Later we encounter another Pashhur who also was an enemy of Jeremiah (Jeremiah 38:1). Then in chapter 20 we meet a priest named Pashhur whom Jeremiah's prophecy about 'every disaster' that the Lord was 'going to bring on' Jerusalem 'and the villages around it' (Jeremiah 19:15) made angry. He was the chief supervisor of the temple, which made him an important person. He was extremely irritated with this obnoxious Jeremiah, who created so much unrest and undermined the authority of the spiritual leaders. Therefore, he wanted to scare the prophet so effectively that he would stop his activities. He had him beaten up and locked away for a night: but this did not deter Jeremiah at all, and the next day he boldly predicted that Pashhur and his associates would be punished.

Jeremiah could not be scared away by people like Pashhur. He experienced what lots of people of all ages have found. Faithfulness towards God and telling others about what God is asking from them often meets strong opposition; but we may be sure that God does not forsake His people and still has the power to silence all 'Pashhurs'.

My prayer

My faithful God, I need courage and faith to continue my witness for You, even when those in my environment do not appreciate this.

8 October

Paul (small)

Who and when? Paul, who was originally named Saul, came from Tarsus, studied under Gamaliel, persecuted Christians and was converted on the road to Damascus. He became a prominent apostle and the author of many portions of the New Testament.

Want to know more? Read: Acts 9:1-31; 13:1–28:31; 2 Corinthians 11:21-33; Philippians 3:5-7.

Thoughts for today

When Saul became an apostle his name was changed to Paul. From that moment his life would be dedicated to the preaching of the Gospel message. Facing numerous dangers he travelled through Asia Minor, Greece and Italy, without worrying about his own comfort, to tell people about the living Lord, whom he had personally encountered. He demonstrated enormous flexibility: when meeting with Jews he adapted to their customs and traditions, but when he was with 'Gentiles' he did what he could to be accepted by them.

In 1 Corinthians 9:22 Paul wrote: 'To the weak I became weak, to win the weak. I have become all things to all men so that by all possible means I might save some.' Was Paul simply an opportunist or a pragmatist? No: his approach was rooted in a deep love and concern for the people he came into contact with. Jesus came to this world and became one of us, and Paul wanted to follow that supreme example and get into the skin of the men and women he tried to reach. This fundamental attitude is required if we are to have success in our mission.

My prayer

We ask You, heavenly Father, to give us the willingness to enter into the world of other people, so that we can most effectively reach them with the message in their circumstances.

9 October

Peninnah

(one with rich hair)

Who and when? One of the two wives of Elkanah. The other wife was Hannah, the mother of Samuel.

Want to know more? Read: 1 Samuel 1.

Thoughts for today

When reading the story of Peninnah for the first time we might be inclined to pity her. As was the custom in those days, Elkanah had more than one wife. Besides Hannah there was Peninnah; and, as was the case with many plural marriages, this resulted in a home poisoned by jealousy. It was clear that Elkanah preferred Hannah over Peninnah. This was, for instance, apparent when the family went to the sanctuary in Shiloh to bring their annual sacrifices. Hannah would get twice as much meat from the sacrifice as Elkanah gave to Peninnah, which tempts us to wonder how Elkanah could be so insensitive.

What complicated matters further was the fact that Peninnah gave birth to several children, while Hannah was not able to conceive – that is, until a miracle put an end to her misery. Peninnah used her motherhood as an excuse to continuously taunt her rival. In 1 Samuel 1:7 we are told that she 'provoked' Hannah. Hannah, in turn, felt she had good reason to be envious, since God 'had closed her womb' (vs. 5). Peninnah, on the other hand, could not accept that she had to be content with the second place in Elkanah's heart.

The story of Elkanah and his two wives is one of the many illustrations of the fact that forgetting the ideal of Eden (one man and one woman) is an endless source of trouble. It also illustrates how people who live closely together can make life well-nigh impossible for each other; and it shows how difficult it can be to accept the fact that things in life do not always turn out as we had hoped. What is clear is that jealousy can only make everything worse.

My prayer

Heavenly Father, help me to banish all feelings of jealousy from my life and to accept that things are often just what they are!

Peter (cf. Aramaic *Kefas*: rock)

Who and when? One of the twelve disciples who were with Jesus; he became one of the pillars of the early church.

Want to know more? Read: Matthew 4:18-25; 8:14, 15; 14:22-34; 16:13-20; 26:36-56; John 21:1-23.

Thoughts for today

Peter knew the answer when Jesus asked His disciples who the people thought He was: 'Who do people say the Son of Man is?' The disciples reported that they had heard different responses. According to them, some thought that He was John the Baptist; others said He was Elijah who had returned, or Jeremiah or some other prophet. This was the launching pad for another, more crucial, question of Jesus: 'But what about you? . . . Who do you say I am?' (Matthew 16:13-15.) In other words: 'You have been with Me now for a considerable time. Do you also think that I am one of the prophets, who has come back to life?' Peter was the first one to reply: 'You are the Christ, the Son of the living God.' Peter had grasped the secret of Jesus' true identity (vs. 16).

The question about Jesus' identity is just as relevant today as it was two thousand years ago. All kinds of answers are given to the question of who Jesus is. For many He is no more than a historical figure. They find His story inspiring and see Him as a good human being, who is a perfect role model for us. Unfortunately, there are countless people who do not know the right answer. The truth is that Jesus is far more than just a good man. He is the God-man, who came to us in order to solve the problem of sin – and thus also of death – once and for all. He is our Saviour, the Redeemer of mankind. He is our Lord, to whom we owe unconditional loyalty.

My prayer

Thank You, Lord, that I know who You are: but teach me about all its implications, and help me to know how to support people as they wrestle with this question for themselves.

11 October

Philemon

(loving)

Who and when? A Christian in Colosse. Paul wrote to him about his slave, Onesimus, who had escaped.

Want to know more? Read: Philemon.

Thoughts for today

There are, hopefully, very few Christians who will argue that slavery is not a grave moral problem. With that in mind, however, the reader of Paul's letter to Philemon may think they have found one! Paul had come into contact with a certain Onesimus: a man who was the property of Philemon, a member of the Christian church in Colosse. He had run away, and since his escape Onesimus had converted to Christianity. Today we would, with our background, assume that Onesimus ought to remain a free man. We would probably say that Paul should have made it clear to Philemon that a Christian should not own slaves, let alone Christian slaves. That, however, is not what we read in this letter. Instead, Paul urged Onesimus to return to his master and admonished Philemon to treat his slave Onesimus in a brotherly manner in the future.

The short epistle to Philemon is a clear illustration of how to interpret situations that occurred in Bible times. Slavery is a great evil: but it was part and parcel of ancient society and could not suddenly be done away with. This does not, however, in any way mean that it can be justified in later times. The Bible is always to be read against the background of the time in which its messages were written. As we read these messages today we must search for the underlying principles and apply these as conscientiously as we can.

My prayer

Heavenly Father, help me in my Bible reading to discover the fundamental principles that I must apply in my own life today.

12 October

Philetus

(loving)

Who and when? A member of the church who denied the reality of the resurrection to come; Paul warns against his activities in his second letter to Timothy.

Want to know more? Read: 2 Timothy 2:14-21.

Thoughts for today

The emergence of false teachers was one of the challenges Paul had to face in the churches he founded. He advised his younger colleague, Timothy, 'against quarrelling about words' and not to get involved in 'godless chatter' (2 Timothy 2:14, 16); and he added: 'Don't have anything to do with foolish and stupid arguments, because you know they produce quarrels' (vs. 23). In fact, what he wrote to Timothy Paul also said to Titus: 'But avoid foolish controversies and genealogies and arguments and quarrels about the law, because these are unprofitable and useless' (Titus 3:9).

There may be, however, situations that demand a more forceful reaction. The message of some false teachers 'spread like gangrene' (2 Timothy 2:17). Of these false teachers two are mentioned by name: Philetus and Hymenaeus. They argued that the resurrection had already occurred. According to them the resurrection was a spiritual event that takes place in our hearts. They denied that there would be a literal resurrection of the dead at the end of time, with all the things related to it. Such teachings destroy the core of the Christian faith.

Christians may have different opinions about many topics. However, there are also some important points that must always be affirmed. Among these is the reality of Jesus' resurrection and our resurrection at the end of time. If we deny these truths, we have lost the right to call ourselves Christians. That was true for Philetus and for all those who followed him.

My prayer

Risen Lord, may I never doubt the good news of our future resurrection from the dead.

13 October

Philip

(fond of horses)

Who and when? One of the twelve disciples of Jesus; came from Bethsaida.

Want to know more? Read: Matthew 10:2-4; John 1:43-46; 6:5-7; 12:20-26.

Thoughts for today

Jesus went to Galilee the day after He had added Andrew and Simon Peter to His circle of disciples. There He met Philip. We know precious little about him and we can only guess why his name was associated with horses. He should not be confused with the 'deacon' with the same name who explained the Gospel to a high Ethiopian official (Acts 8:26-40).

However, the little we know about this Philip gives us food for thought. As soon as he is called by Jesus, Philip tells others about it. He meets Nathanael and cannot remain quiet: 'We have found the one Moses wrote about in the Law, and about whom the prophets also wrote – Jesus of Nazareth, the son of Joseph' (John 1:45). We discover a short but meaningful chain of events: Jesus finds Philip. Philip does not wait until Jesus has found all the others He wants to have around Him as His disciples. He makes no secret of what he has experienced and immediately makes contact with Nathanael.

When Jesus has found us, we must not silently wait until He has also found other people in our wider network. It must be a logical consequence that we will do all we can to communicate to others that Jesus has entered our lives. Like Nathanael, others may at first be sceptical, but we must always be open to the possibility that, after some hesitation, they will also respond to Jesus' call and decide to follow the Man of Nazareth.

My prayer

Thank You, Lord, that You have called me. Give me the courage to tell others about this, whenever I see a good opportunity.

14 October

Philip

(fond of horses)

Who and when? One of the seven 'deacons' who were appointed in the Jerusalem church.

Want to know more? Read: Acts 6:1-7; 8:5-13, 26-40; 21:7-9.

Thoughts for today

Philip was a multifaceted and committed man. The early church in Jerusalem grew so fast that the apostles could no longer care spiritually for the church and also do justice to its practical needs. Therefore it was decided to recruit seven men who would assist the apostles. They are usually referred to as the seven 'deacons'.

Today most people would see this as a logical strategy. They feel strongly that pastors and other people with a spiritual ministry should do their work in the spiritual realm and leave other aspects of church work to people like Philip. For Philip, however, such a rigid division of labour was unacceptable. He was so full of the Gospel that he could not remain silent about his faith, and, as a result, we see that he spent at least part of his time preaching. He had considerable success in Samaria, where his preaching was accompanied by miracles, and many men and women were converted (Acts 8:4-8). Philip also explained the Gospel message to the Ethiopian official whom he met on his way home from Jerusalem in his carriage. He was reading a scroll of Isaiah and did not understand its meaning.

There was also another side to Philip. He lived with his family in Caesarea. At home he had four unmarried daughters, who possessed the gift of prophecy: a very special family, indeed! No wonder that Paul was eager to visit them (Acts 21:8). Philip was an inspiring example for his children. Of course, we cannot decide for our children whether they will believe in Christ or not. Sadly, some children choose not to follow their Christian parents; but, like Philip, we can all spread the Gospel in addition to our 'normal' tasks!

My prayer

Lord, help me always to ensure that I have time to witness for You.

15 October

Philologus

(fond of learning)

Who and when? Member of the church in Rome.

Want to know more? Read: Romans 16:15.

Thoughts for today

Philologus is one of the more than thirty persons who receive greetings from the apostle Paul at the end of his letter to the church in Rome. It is remarkable to note how many people Paul knew in a church where, until then, he had never been. As we go through the list of names we also note that he knows men and women from all layers of society.

The church in Rome consisted of a number of house churches. It has been suggested that there may have been at least five house groups when Paul wrote his letter to the Romans. One of these groups met in the home of Philologus. We learn this from the statement in Romans 16:15: 'Greet Philologus, Julia [his wife? his sister?], Nereus and his sister, and Olympas *and all the saints with them.*' Philologus may well have been an educated person (as his name suggests), and he may have had a big enough house to facilitate church meetings for a sizeable group of believers.

In the recent past many denominations have promoted small-group ministries and the house-church model as methods for church growth. This has proved to be successful in many places, but it has also caused resistance. Many prefer a large or at least a reasonably-sized congregation, with a wide range of activities, a well-planned worship service and beautiful music. However, in this discussion we do well to remember that the 'house church' actually has the best credentials. It is the oldest Christian congregational model we can find.

My prayer

Dear God, help us to be open for change and experiments, and to choose models of being church that are both biblical and fit the needs of the time in which we live.

16 October

Phoebe

(pure, radiant)

Who and when? A deaconess in the church of Cenchrea, near Corinth. She carried Paul's letter to the church in Rome.

Want to know more? Read: Romans 16:1.

Thoughts for today

Phoebe was an enterprising woman who could be trusted with a mission. She travelled from the port city near Corinth to Rome, to deliver the letter Paul had written 'to the Romans'. In those days this required considerable nerve. Most likely she did not travel on her own, but nonetheless it was an adventurous and risky job that calls for our admiration.

This sister Phoebe was, so we read, 'a *servant* of the church in Cenchrea' (Romans 16:1). The Greek term that lies beneath this translation may indeed be used in this general sense of 'servant': but other translations suggest that she was a 'leader' of the local church, whereas still other translations, such as in the *New Living Translation*, are definitely also possible. There we read that Phoebe was 'a *deacon*'.

In any case, Phoebe was an important person in the church in Cenchrea. Sometimes it is suggested that Paul did not have such a high regard for women: but a careful reading of the last chapter of the letter to the Romans points us in a completely different direction. In that chapter Paul mentions a number of women who were highly respected by Paul in their leadership roles. In current debates about the role of women in the church, this is an important point to note.

My prayer

I thank You, loving Father, for women such as Phoebe, who have provided strong leadership in the church and continue to serve as role models for women in ministry.

17 October

Pilate

(Latin: armed with a dart)

Who and when? Roman prefect over Judea from AD 26; committed suicide in AD 41.

Want to know more? Read: Matthew 27:1-26; Luke 23:1-25.

Thoughts for today

Pilate knew in his heart that 'the king of the Jews', who stood before him, was innocent. His wife had a dream in which she was told that Jesus ought to be set free. She sent a warning to her husband not to get involved with 'that innocent man' (Matthew 27:19). Pilate knew what he should do, and that is why he thought up a clever strategy. He would propose to the crowd that they could have a choice. He could pardon another Jesus – Jesus Barabbas, who was a notorious rioter – or the Jesus 'who is called Christ' (Matthew 27:22). He was certain that the people would have enough sense to ensure that Jesus Barabbas would remain in prison. That proved to be a tragic miscalculation. Incited by the Jewish leaders, they were prepared to accept any proposal, as long as the Jesus who had been arrested would be eliminated.

Pilate could have demonstrated that he did have principles: but he washed his hands as a token of his innocence and told the Jewish leaders to sort out the problem with Jesus themselves. Jesus Barabbas walked away a free man, and to further gratify the mob Pilate had Jesus flogged before the Jewish leaders. And so Pilate entered history as the man who, at a critical moment, silenced his conscience and knowingly chose to do the evil thing. How different it might have been if he had listened to his conscience . . .

My prayer

Almighty God, help us to listen to our conscience when making difficult decisions.

18 October

Potiphar

(the one whom the sun-god Ra has given)

Who and when? Commander of the bodyguard of the Egyptian pharaoh; bought Joseph as a slave from the Midianites.

Want to know more? Read: Genesis 37:36; 39:1-20.

Thoughts for today

It was a case of what we today would call 'sexual harassment'. The wife of Potiphar, Joseph's master, wanted to have sex with Joseph. The temptation was far from subtle. She was the wife of Potiphar and the mistress of the household, and she was used to getting her way. It was quite risky for Joseph to refuse what she wanted. But he did, for he wanted to be true to his principles. It stands to reason that Potiphar was enraged when his wife told him that 'that Hebrew slave you brought us' had tried to rape her (Genesis 39:17); and it was perhaps not so strange that he believed his wife's version of what had happened.

Or should Potiphar have reacted differently? Should he have immediately locked Joseph up 'in prison, the place where the king's prisoners were confined' (vs. 20)? Had Potiphar not noticed how special this slave was? 'The LORD was with Joseph and he prospered' (vs. 2). That was why Potiphar made Joseph 'his attendant . . . [and] put him in charge of his household, and he entrusted to his care everything he owned. From the time he put him in charge of his household and of all that he owned, the LORD blessed the household of the Egyptian because of Joseph. The blessing of the LORD was on everything Potiphar had, both in the house and in the field' (vss. 4, 5). Should that not have been sufficient reason for Potiphar to give Joseph the benefit of the doubt and also to listen to Joseph's version of the story?

My prayer

Please, help me, Lord, not to have my judgement ready before I have listened to the various versions of whatever has happened.

19 October

Puah

(splendour/brightness)

Who and when? One of the midwives serving the Hebrew women in Egypt; she was disobedient to the pharaoh.

Want to know more? Read: Exodus 1:15-22.

Thoughts for today

Life continued as usual in the Goshen area, where the descendants of Jacob worked as slaves. Children were born. The women were assisted by two midwives when they gave birth. These midwives were very courageous women. They were determined to frustrate the strategy of the pharaoh, who wanted to prevent a further increase of the Hebrew population. They wanted to make sure that the Jewish boys would not die on the day they were born! This demanded an enormous amount of nerve, because their ploy did not remain unnoticed. Their approach was especially daring and could quite easily have cost them their lives (see Exodus 1:17, 18).

Instead of going against the will of the pharaoh, Puah and her colleague could have followed a different kind of reasoning, such as: 'We do not like doing this, but we have no option but to obey the authorities. If we don't, we may well lose our own lives.' This is, for example, how many people reasoned during World War II. Of course, they did not want to tell the Germans about the Jews that were in hiding, but what choice did they have? Puah and Shiphrah felt, however, that they *did* have a choice. They followed their conscience. They thought of a pretext to explain to the king that it was not their fault that the Jewish boys stayed alive! They always arrived, they said, when the Hebrew women had already given birth! God rewarded their courage. Their lives were spared and God blessed them with their own children – something that was highly prized in their time.

My prayer

Loving God! You were willing to take an enormous risk in sending Your Son to our hostile world. Please prepare us to show courage and take risks for You, when that is necessary.

20 October

Publius

(Latin: belonging to the people)

Who and when? Roman official on the island of Malta at the time when Paul was shipwrecked there and stayed on the island for some time.

Want to know more? Read: Acts 27:13–28:10.

Thoughts for today

The story of how Paul was transported as a prisoner from Palestine to Rome is fascinating. When the ship on which he was sailing was shipwrecked near Malta, he almost drowned: but Paul and those who were with him safely reached the shore of the island. There the local population gave them a cordial reception. The people lit a fire so that the men who had made it to safety could warm themselves. Soon, however, a new terror threatened. The heat forced a snake that was hiding in the firewood to escape from the fire. Paul was bitten on the hand, but, to the utter amazement of those around him, suffered no nasty consequences.

Hearing what had happened, Publius, the Roman official, invited Paul and his entourage to visit him. This group seems to have included Luke, who later recorded the story in these words: 'He welcomed us to his home and for three days entertained us hospitably' (Acts 28:7). They stayed three days in the residence of Publius as his guests, which was not how prisoners were usually treated! However, Publius not only heard about the miracle with the snake, but also experienced how his father was healed from his sickness by Paul. No doubt Paul also witnessed of his faith in Jesus Christ, but Publius seems not to have been converted. If that had been the case, Luke would certainly have included that in his story. But this fascinating story is an illustration of how God can in a surprising way change events that, at first sight, may seem rather hopeless. We can have the assurance that this can still happen today!

My prayer

Almighty God, it is great to know that You can change the shipwrecks of our lives into very positive experiences.

21 October

Quirinius

(unknown; may be derived from the Sabine word *quiris,* or 'spear'.)

Who and when? Roman governor of the province of Syria at the time of Jesus' birth.

Want to know more? Read: Luke 2:2.

Thoughts for today

The Bible mentions only two persons with names beginning with a Q. In Romans 16 Paul sends greetings to a substantial number of people, among whom a certain Quartus is listed. Apart from him there is only Quirinius. Many people have heard of him, since he is mentioned in the story of Christ's birth. A census was held in the Roman Empire during the reign of Augustus. Quirinius was to organise this in Syria, of which Judea was a part. Luke informs us that this 'census . . . took place while Quirinius was governor of Syria' (Luke 2:1).

The reference to Quirinius has led to much discussion and controversy among biblical scholars. We know from Roman sources that this Publius Sulpicius Quirinius ruled over Syria from AD 6 to AD 9, and that he arranged for a census during this time. Many experts have argued that Luke must have been confused when he dated Quirinius's role in Syria as much earlier. Others, however, have argued convincingly that Quirinius may have ruled more than once for a few years over Syria on behalf of the emperor.

Should we get excited about the historical uncertainty that surrounds Quirinius? There are many instances when there have been serious doubts about the historical veracity of a Bible story, but where later discoveries confirmed the biblical record. In any case, Luke 2 is not about Quirinius, but about Jesus Christ, who was born in Bethlehem as our Saviour. Everything else is only of marginal importance.

My prayer

Help me, heavenly Father, always to distinguish between what is essential and what is only of marginal importance, and to remember what is most important of all: the fact that Your Son came to this world – to save me too.

22 October

Rachel

(ewe)

Who and when? The youngest daughter of Laban; married to Jacob; she became the mother of Joseph and Benjamin.

Want to know more? Read: Genesis 29–35.

Thoughts for today

The story of Rachel is a combination of romance and tragedy. Days after his arrival at the home of his future father-in-law, Jacob knew he wanted to have Laban's youngest daughter Rachel as his wife. But Laban was shrewd. He manipulated things in such a way that Jacob ended up having to work fourteen long years for Rachel. After seven years he was tricked into marrying Leah, the older sister of Rachel, who, according to Laban, was first in line to get married. It was the start of a problematic marriage and a complicated family life for Jacob as well as for his wives – especially when the servants of both Leah and Rachel also began to play an important role.

Leah was blessed with several sons, whereas Rachel had to wait many years for hers, and she would eventually die after giving birth to Benjamin; but, whatever else may be said about this dysfunctional family, there was a deep love between Jacob and Rachel. The long waiting period before Rachel became Jacob's wife seemed 'like only a few days to him because of his love for her' (Genesis 29:20).

This story contains several traditions that we today might consider strange, but apparently God understood that Abraham, Isaac and Jacob would often follow the long-established customs of their day. At the same time this story also provides us with a clear warning that ignoring the divine ideal for family life (one man and one woman, who are committed to each other in a lifelong, exclusive relationship) can result in countless problems and a lot of misery.

My prayer

Lord, it often seems difficult to stick to the original model of a lifelong relationship between a man and a woman. I pray that we may not lose sight of that ideal.

23 October

Rahab

(broad)

Who and when? Prostitute in Jericho, who hid the 'spies' who had come to explore the 'promised land'.

Want to know more? Read: Joshua 2; Matthew 1:5.

Thoughts for today

In the genealogy of Jesus, at the beginning of the Gospel of Matthew, we discover the name of Rahab. This may come as rather a surprise, because Joshua 2:1 calls her a 'prostitute'; but this is not all we know about Rahab. In his letter the apostle James states: 'Rahab the prostitute [was] considered righteous for what she did' (James 2:25). The author of the book of Hebrews likewise emphasises that the role of Rahab in the escape of the 'spies' from Jericho was inspired by her faith. That is why her name is also listed in the gallery of faith heroes in Hebrews 11 (vs. 31).

The story does not tell us why the 'spies' chose to lodge with Rahab. However, it seems that somehow Rahab sensed that these men represented something that was very special. She understood that they represented a Power far greater than all the gods of Jericho; and this gave her the certainty that her survival and that of her family depended on that Power.

God gave Rahab an important role. He did not see her merely as a woman who practised the 'world's oldest profession', but first of all as someone who was open to what He wanted to give to people who trust in Him - His saving grace.

My prayer

Lord, teach me not to judge people the moment I see them, but to take time to discover who they really are and to help them find the path to You.

24 October

Rebekah

(band)

Who and when? Daughter of Bethuel, the nephew of Abraham; wife of Isaac and mother of Jacob and Esau.

Want to know more? Read: Genesis 24–27.

Thoughts for today

Isaac had turned forty when he married Rebekah. Abraham had sent his most trusted servant on a mission to the area where he himself had his roots. There this servant was to find a wife for the son of his master. Rebekah was willing to go with Abraham's servant and his entourage to a totally new environment. Immediately upon her arrival at her destination she became Isaac's wife. Apparently, as was the custom of the times, Isaac took her into the tent of his mother Sarah, and this constituted his marriage with Rebekah. 'She became his wife, and he loved her' (Genesis 24:67). Even though it was an 'arranged' marriage, it became a very happy one. That Isaac and Rebekah were close is also clear from a later incident. When they spent some time in Philistine country, the king of the Philistines saw through his window 'Isaac caressing his wife Rebekah' (Genesis 26:8).

Rebekah remained childless for many years, but Isaac pleaded with God that his wife should conceive, and Rebekah also 'went to enquire of the LORD' (Genesis 25:22). God heard their prayers, and Rebekah gave birth to twins. God told her: 'Two nations are in your womb' (vs. 23). We might conclude that Isaac and Rebekah formed an ideal couple – in love with each other and united in their faith in God – yet, at a later stage, Rebekah decided to deceive her husband and schemed with her favourite son Jacob to steal the blessing that was intended for his slightly older brother. How was this possible? Rebekah knew what it was to love someone: but, through her love for Jacob, she sadly became involved in something completely wrong.

My prayer

Loving Father, help us to be totally honest in our love for others, and protect us from the kind of mistake that Rebekah made.

25 October

Rehoboam

(the people have been enlarged)

Who and when? Son of Solomon; the first king of the Southern Kingdom of the ten tribes; ruled from 930 BC to 914 BC.

Want to know more? Read: 1 Kings 12:1-24; 14:21-31.

Thoughts for today

Rehoboam was supposed to succeed his father Solomon. Not everybody, however, liked this idea. Jeroboam was the spokesperson for those who were discontent. He demanded lower taxation, since the taxes had become unbearably high. The inexperienced Rehoboam decided to seek the advice of a number of wise men who had also often served his father Solomon with their counsel. Their opinion was clear: if you want to secure the support of your people, it is advisable to lower the tax to a reasonable level. But that was not the answer Rehoboam had hoped for, for less income in taxes would mean that he would have to revise his ambitions. So, he decided to also ask another group of people for advice: some young men whom he had grown up with. They were keen to profit from their close ties with the king and thought it would also be advantageous for them if the king could further augment his income. They suggested that the king might even increase the tax burden for the people. When the king followed this advice, it soon led to a definite split in the kingdom of his father. Ten of the twelve tribes subsequently chose Jeroboam as their leader.

Asking for advice is a good thing. No one is so wise that he can solve all problems himself. But it is important to choose one's counsellors wisely, and be prepared to follow good advice. Rehoboam only wanted to listen to the kind of advice that confirmed his own wishes. It is a trap far too many people also fall into today.

My prayer

Lord, give me the insight where to find the right people to ask for advice, and then to listen to them.

26 October

Rehum

(the compassionate one)

Who and when? An official of the Persian administration in Samaria who tried to sabotage the rebuilding of Jerusalem after the exile; fifth century BC.

Want to know more? Read: Ezra 4:4-23.

Thoughts for today

Many major building projects are controversial. Whether we speak of the construction of a highway, a tunnel, a mosque or a cultural centre – there is always the likelihood of opposition. At times there are good reasons for this: for example, when the environment is at risk or the interests of a group of people are ignored. But often it is fear of the unknown or the worry that 'strange' elements will disturb the status quo. There may also be some hidden, or not so hidden, discrimination at work; and then there are others who, for some perverse reason, are always 'against' everything.

After the exile, the population of Palestine were far from happy with the large influx of people into 'their' country, even though it was there that these so-called 'newcomers' had their roots. They tried to do everything they could think of to halt the ambitious building projects of the returned exiles, or at least to slow them down. To some extent this seems understandable. But the methods used, at the instigation of, among others, Rehum, were very questionable. In essence it amounted to inciting hate towards these people who had returned from Babylon. Rehum and his associates created a picture (especially in their communications to the Persian king) that was meant to foster a dislike or even hatred for these people. All too often we see something similar today, when groups in our society try to strengthen ethnic prejudice, which easily leads to outright discrimination. It has been a phenomenon of all ages, but that does not make it any less detestable.

My prayer

You are the God of all, and with You there is no discrimination. Help us to be the same.

27 October

Rezon

(high official)

Who and when? A contemporary of King Solomon. He became a fugitive from Hadadezer, organised a band of outlaw troops and then became king over an area around Damascus.

Want to know more? Read: 1 Kings 11:23-25.

Thoughts for today

Things started well when Solomon became king. But as the years went by he no longer served God as faithfully as he had done before. He had an insatiable appetite for women and collected female beauties from far and near. That, in itself, was bad enough, but these women also brought idols with them, and, unfortunately, Solomon also got involved with the worship of their false gods. As a result 'the LORD became angry with Solomon because his heart had turned away from the LORD, the God of Israel' (1 Kings 11:9).

God wanted Solomon to refocus on his earlier ideals. 'The Lord raised up against Solomon an adversary, Hadad the Edomite' (vs. 14). And a few verses on we read: 'God raised up against Solomon another adversary, Rezon son of Eliada' (vs. 23). Does this mean that Rezon was not responsible for his rebellion against Solomon? How are we to interpret these words: 'God raised up'?

It was a thirst for power and his insatiable ambition that propelled Rezon to position himself as Solomon's rival. God allowed this. He could have protected Solomon from this danger, but this time God did not immediately intervene to help Solomon. Solomon had to learn a painful lesson: namely, that turning one's back on God can have fateful consequences. Could it be that God sometimes allows unpleasant things to take place in our lives in an attempt to bring us back on the right track?

My prayer

Lord God, I cannot see what happens behind the scenes. Perhaps You are using other people or difficult circumstances to teach me a lesson. Help me, when this happens, to get back on the right track.

28 October

Rhoda

(rose)

Who and when? Servant of Mary, the mother of John Mark.

Want to know more? Read: Acts 12:1-19.

Thoughts for today

The narrative of Acts 12 transpires about ten years after Jesus' resurrection. A prayer meeting is underway in Jerusalem, in the home of Mary, the mother of John Mark. There is an urgent reason for this gathering. Recently the apostle James has died as a martyr for his faith. Now it seems that Peter will shortly meet the same fate. He is in prison and may soon be executed. No wonder the people have come together for a season of prayer.

All of a sudden there is a knock on the door of Mary's house. Rhoda, her servant, goes to the door to find out who the visitor is. When she hears the voice of Peter, she cannot believe her ears. In her confusion she even forgets to open the door. She rushes inside and exclaims: 'Peter is here! Peter is here!' One would think that everybody would jump up, for their prayer has been answered. But their reaction is totally different. 'You're out of your mind,' they say to Rhoda. But Rhoda insists: 'No, it really is Peter.' The people in the room are still not convinced and respond: 'It must be his angel.' (Acts 12:15.) All the time Peter continues to knock on the door, until at last it is opened.

The incident should make us wonder. The church members are praying for a miracle, but when the miracle happens there is, besides Rhoda, no one who believes that God really has answered their prayers. If we are honest, most of us will recognise this type of reaction. Of course, we pray, but don't we usually have some lingering doubts as to whether God will answer us? And even if there is a Rhoda among us who brings the good news, we may still have difficulty believing that God really has intervened.

My prayer

Help me, Lord, to believe that You do indeed hear and answer our prayers.

29 October

Rizpah

(a baking stone)

Who and when? Concubine of King Saul; ca. 1050 BC.

Want to know more? Read: 2 Samuel 3:7; 21:1-14.

Thoughts for today

In a deal between the Gibeonites and King David it was agreed that the conflict between them would be ended by the execution of seven sons of Saul. Among them were the two sons Saul had with Rizpah, one of his concubines. When Rizpah heard that the bodies of her two sons and of five of their half-brothers had been left exposed on a hillside, she decided to remain close to their bodies to ensure that during the day the scavengers, and during the night the wild animals, would not devour the corpses.

Just try to imagine the terrible scene. A bereaved woman - the victim of what appears to be a callous political power play - has spent weeks on end, living in the open air, guarding the slowly decomposing bodies of her sons. She was not able to prevent their deaths, but this vigil is the final token of her care and love for them.

In the midst of war, violence and the cruellest of events, we sometimes see occasions where people show their love and humanity in remarkable ways. Fortunately, even when rulers who are driven by a thirst for power or revenge are determined to have their way, there are people like Rizpah who show that hatred and destruction do not have the final word.

My prayer

Our loving God, thank You for the wonderful, inspiring example of Rizpah.

30 October

Reuben

(behold, a son)

Who and when? Oldest son of Jacob and Leah.

Want to know more? Read: Genesis 29:32; 35:22; 37.

Thoughts for today

Reuben was the oldest son of Jacob, which gave him certain rights; but he lost these privileges when he misbehaved badly. He committed adultery with one of the concubines of his father (Genesis 35:22). Reuben also played a very dubious role when it was decided to sell Joseph into Egyptian slavery.

Joseph's brothers could not stand his arrogance. When, on a fateful day, Jacob sent his son Joseph on a mission to see how his brothers were doing, they conspired to get rid of him. They threw him into a deep well and were planning to leave him there to die. However, they adapted their plan when a caravan passed by on its way to Egypt, and sold Joseph to the Midianite merchants instead. Reuben was not present when this deal was made. When he returned a little later to the well he wanted to rescue Joseph, but Joseph was no longer there – he was already en route to Egypt.

We get a mixed picture of Reuben. Apparently, he was able to show mercy, but he was not strong enough to tell his brothers that he would have no part in their plan to deceive their father with a fictitious story about some tragic accident that had killed Joseph. Like so many others, Reuben is a sad example of what happens when people fail to apply their principles when they should.

My prayer

Dear God, help me never to silence my conscience and always to choose the way of honesty and truth.

31 October

Rufus

(Latin: red)

Who and when? A member of the church in Rome.

Want to know more? Read: Romans 16:13.

Thoughts for today

I recently read this statement by someone whose name I have forgotten: *All of us have once in a while the need to be embraced.* That is very true. Even those people who seldom show any emotions have moments when they want to feel that someone cares for them.

Many Bible readers have a rather negative view of Paul's personality. They see the apostle as a somewhat distant person who was prone to develop complicated theories about theological issues that the 'ordinary' person finds difficult to understand. He sometimes seems to attach little value to inter-human relationships, advising believers not to get married – unless they cannot remain single. This counsel applied especially to widows and widowers (1 Corinthians 7:8, 9).

However, when we take a closer look at Paul, we discover that he was a human being of flesh and blood, who also appreciated closeness with other people. Just read Romans 16 – the chapter with the long list of greetings to dozens of people in Rome. At the time of writing he had not yet visited Rome, but he already knew a sizeable group of people there. Among the names is that of a certain Rufus. Paul describes him as 'chosen in the Lord' (vs. 13), without adding any further particulars. Paul also greets Rufus's mother, who, he says, has been like a mother for him.

Paul also had moments when he wanted to be embraced. Perhaps there are people we know for whom we could also be like a father or mother – people who have a need to be embraced.

My prayer

Loving heavenly Father, You have embraced us and are as a Father and Mother for us. Help us, like You, to embrace the lonely.

1 November

Ruth

(friend, companion)

Who and when? A Moabite woman; she accompanied her mother-in-law Naomi to the area around Bethlehem and married Boaz; end of the eighth century BC.

Want to know more? Read: Ruth.

Thoughts for today

Ruth decided to link her fate to that of her mother-in-law, and to serve the God whom Naomi worshipped. It was a far-reaching decision to cast her lot in with Naomi. It meant going with her to another country with a new set of customs. For a young Moabite widow it would most likely have been much easier to find a new partner in Moab: but she had become so attached to Naomi that she did not want to separate from her.

Choosing the God of Naomi can not have been easy for Ruth. It seemed that this God had not brought much happiness to Naomi and her family; and Naomi herself was the first to admit that her God had deeply disappointed her. Upon her return to Bethlehem she said to the people who welcomed her: 'The Almighty has made my life very bitter. I went away full, but the LORD has brought me back empty. Why call me Naomi? The LORD has afflicted me; the Almighty has brought misfortune upon me' (Ruth 1:20, 21). Ruth, however, felt that all the unpleasant experiences that she herself, together with Naomi and Orpah (Naomi's other daughter-in-law), had gone through, were not good enough reasons to turn her back on the God of Naomi. There was much that she did not understand, but she kept placing her trust in this God. And she was not to be disappointed in her persistence: for the rest of her life she would be glad and grateful that she had not turned away from the only true God.

My prayer

Lord, help me to persist with my trust in You and to stay close to You, even in those periods of my life when things are difficult.

2 November

Samuel

(God has heard)

Who and when? Son of Elkanah and Hannah; dedicated to God as a Nazirite; prophet and judge (ca. 1050 BC).

Want to know more? Read: 1 Samuel 1-3.

Thoughts for today

At long last Hannah and Elkanah had a son! But they would not keep the little Samuel with them for very long. As soon as it was feasible they brought him to the sanctuary in Shiloh and entrusted him to the care of Eli. That in itself was an act of faith, for Eli did not have a good track record as an educator – as the fiasco with his own sons clearly showed. But the home of Elkanah and Hannah did not remain empty for long: for, beside the children Elkanah fathered with his other wife Peninnah (1 Samuel 1:2), Elkanah and Hannah had another five children – three sons and two daughters (2:21).

The young Samuel prospered. His parents visited him at regular intervals, taking new clothing, among other things, with them. And, notwithstanding the bad example of Eli's sons, 'the boy Samuel continued to grow in stature and in favour with the LORD and with men' (2:26): and when he grew older the people 'recognised that Samuel was attested as a prophet of the LORD' (3:20).

'Being in favour with God and with men' is the best thing that can be said of anyone. Of course, what God thinks about us takes first place, but to live in such a way that we are also 'in favour' with the people around us – as were Samuel and Jesus – is often important too!

My prayer

Almighty and loving God, I want to be 'in favour' with You and with the people around me. Please help me to live in such a way that this becomes a reality.

3 November

Samson

(man of the sun)

Who and when? A 'judge' who fought against the Philistines; from his birth he was called to be a Nazirite.

Want to know more? Read: Judges 13–16.

Thoughts for today

The story has always caused me to wonder. It happened when Samson had a conflict with his father-in-law. Samson's wife, apparently, remained for the time being in her parental home. When Samson returned to visit his spouse in the home of his in-laws, he discovered that in his absence his father-in-law had married his wife off to someone else. 'This time I have a right to get even with the Philistines; I will really harm them,' Samson exclaimed (Judges 15:3). As his revenge 'he went out and caught three hundred foxes and tied them tail to tail in pairs. He then fastened a torch to every pair of tails' (vs. 4, 5). Samson then lit the torches and set the foxes loose in the 'standing corn' in the fields of the Philistines, with a rather predictable result.

I would not be able to catch even one fox, let alone two or three foxes – or three hundred! And how in the world do you tie the tails together of that many foxes? And I can think of a few more questions that are not so easy to answer. The story, however, underlines the fact that Samson was able to perform some astounding feats, because God had provided him with a very special, extraordinary power. Sadly enough, he often used his unusual strength for things that did not agree with God's ideas.

Did you also receive special qualities and opportunities from God? Are you sure that you always use these in a way that has God's approval? Or are you perhaps not so sure . . . ?

My prayer

Almighty God, I really want to use my talents in a way You can approve of. Please help me to make that happen.

4 November

Sanballat

(Assyrian: the moon-god Sin has given life)

Who and when? Governor of Samaria; fierce opponent of Nehemiah.

Want to know more? Read: Nehemiah 2:10, 19, 20; 4:1-3; 6.

Thoughts for today

It stands to reason that Sanballat and other local authorities in Palestine were not enthusiastic about the return of large numbers of Jews from their Babylonian exile. The situation may be somewhat compared to what happened when the Zionists settled in 'their own country' and established the State of Israel. Middle Eastern history of the last half-century shows how immensely difficult it has been to solve the ensuing problems by peaceful negotiations.

Unfortunately, in Sanballat's case, he completely avoided the approach of dialogue as a means to solving the problem. Instead, he did whatever he could think of to thwart the activities of Nehemiah and his people. First he tried to ridicule the project that Nehemiah had started and to insult him. Listen to what Sanballat said: 'What are those feeble Jews doing? Will they restore their wall? Will they offer sacrifices? Will they finish in a day? Can they bring the stones back to life from those heaps of rubble - burned as they are?' (Nehemiah 4:2.) The anger of Sanballat and other opponents of Nehemiah only increased when they saw that, in spite of all the challenges, the work was steadily progressing. They could not torpedo Nehemiah's project, not just because Nehemiah was resolute that he would not be discouraged in any way, but because it was God's project.

My prayer

We realise, heavenly Father, that we may face stiff opposition as we work on Your projects in this world. Give us the faith and the persistence to handle all the insults and opposition that may come our way.

5 November

Sapphira

(Aramaic: beautiful)

Who and when? Wife of Ananias; died together with her husband when they were shown to have been dishonest about the proceeds of the land they had sold.

Want to know more? Read: Acts 5:1-11.

Thoughts for today

Earlier in this book we met Ananias and saw that he was first of all concerned about his own reputation. His principal motive was not to bring a personal sacrifice for the advancement of the Gospel, but that he should look good. His wife, apparently, shared that same thought. As a result both were punished in the severest possible way. It was the first time that something like this had occurred in the early church, and from the outset God wanted to make very clear how displeased He was.

The core of the issue becomes clear in the accusations from the apostle Peter. He confronts Ananias and Sapphira with the words: 'You have not lied to men but to God' (Acts 5:4).

It is always important to realise that it first of all hurts God when we do something that brings pain to people around us. Sin is not in the first place an act that may adversely affect other people - even though this is often the result. In essence, sin is an act of contempt for God, of pure rebellion against Him. This is what the story of Sapphira teaches us. It was a hard lesson, but it was also a razor-sharp demonstration of what sin actually is.

My prayer

Lord, I so often do wrong things without realising that these are first of all hurtful to You. Help me always to be mindful of this.

6 November

Sarah

(princess)

Who and when? The wife of Abraham; mother of Isaac.

Want to know more? Read: Genesis 12:10-20; 16; 17:15-22; 20; 21.

Thoughts for today

Soon after a famine forced Abraham and Sarah (then still called Sarai) to flee to Egypt, a serious problem arose. Sarah was a very attractive woman, and Abraham had reason to fear that such a pretty woman would not escape the attention of the pharaoh, and that this would be a major risk for himself and his wife (Genesis 12:10-20). Therefore, Abraham thought of a ruse. He agreed with Sarah that they would pretend she was his sister and not his wife. That was not an outright lie, for, though Abraham and Sarah did not have the same mother, they had the same father. What Abraham had feared did indeed happen. The scouts of the king saw Sarah's beauty and reported this to the pharaoh, who commanded that she should be added to his harem.

How could Abraham do this? Did he not know what would happen to Sarah once she had disappeared into the royal harem? Later, this same scenario was repeated when Abraham sought protection in the land of Abimelech, the king of Gerar (Genesis 20).

What Abraham did was, of course, totally wrong; but due to divine intervention there was a happy ending in both cases. We may well ask: what role did Sarah play in all of this? Did she try to resist the deceit of her husband? Or did she simply have no choice but to comply with her husband's plan? The Lord could certainly also have rescued them from their awkward situation if they had decided not to lie. Unfortunately, however, in these crucial moments they did not have sufficient trust in God.

My prayer

Help me, Lord, not to try to get out of troublesome situations by lying, but rather to trust in You.

7 November

Saul

(asked of God)

Who and when? The first king of Israel; anointed by Samuel (ca. 1050 BC).

Want to know more? Read: 1 Samuel 3-31.

Thoughts for today

The absolute nadir in the royal career of Saul was his secret visit to a spirit medium in Endor (1 Samuel 28:3-25). Saul was desperate to know what God wanted from him, but the Lord no longer communicated with him. Saul had managed to become estranged from all the people who were significant to him, and the communication channel between him and God was no longer functional. In his desperation he turned to the occult and searched out a medium. It was not easy to find one, because earlier in his rule he had done what he could to get rid of all clairvoyants and diviners.

Saul went in disguise to a woman who was apparently still in business and asked her to make contact with the prophet Samuel, who had passed away some time before this incident took place. She claimed to have made contact with the 'spirit' of Samuel, who then gave Saul this alarming message: 'The LORD will hand over both Israel and you to the Philistines, and tomorrow you and your sons will be with me [dead].'

Consulting the dead is by definition a matter of deceit. If anyone should have known this, it was Saul. He had, however, concluded that God no longer wanted to speak with him, and he was desperate. He was wrong, for God would certainly have been willing to listen to him again, if he had shown remorse and would once again have put his trust in the Lord. The sad reality was that Saul had drifted away from God, and it had become more and more difficult to find the way back to Him. This is what happens when people turn their backs on God.

My prayer

Lord, I trust that You are listening to me. Help me never to turn my back on You.

8 November

Saul

(asked of God)

Who and when? A young Pharisee who persecuted Christians; later his name was changed to Paul.

Want to know more? Read: Acts 7:54-60; 9:1-31; Galatians 1:6-2:14.

Thoughts for today

The stoning of Stephen inspired Saul to become more active in the persecution of the Jesus-followers. We read in Acts 9:1, 2: Saul 'went to the high priest and asked him for letters to the synagogues in Damascus, so that if he found any there who belonged to the Way, whether men or women, he might take them as prisoners to Jerusalem'. God, however, made sure that Saul had to revise his plans. On the road to Damascus Saul met the One he was really persecuting, and was instantly blinded. Having arrived, after this dramatic event, in Damascus, he was visited by a Jesus-believer, Ananias, who had received divine instructions to go and see Saul. This Ananias placed his hands on Saul and 'immediately, something like scales fell from Saul's eyes, and he could see again. He got up and was baptised, and, after taking some food, he regained his strength. Saul spent several days with the disciples in Damascus. At once he began to preach in the synagogues that Jesus is the Son of God' (vss. 18-20): and this was just a short while after he had been totally determined that all people who believed in Jesus should be incarcerated or worse!

The Gospel can completely turn a person's life around. That is what happened to Saul. When he met Jesus Christ, everything in his life was turned upside down. Thank God that, ever since, this miracle has been repeated in the lives of millions of men and women everywhere!

My prayer

Lord, please also give the people around me a Damascus experience and make me, just like Ananias, ready to guide them towards You.

9 November

Sceva

(Greek: *skeuas*; possible meaning: left-handed)

Who and when? A Jew whose seven sons were exorcists; Paul encountered them in Ephesus.

Want to know more? Read: Acts 19:13-20.

Thoughts for today

It is not fully clear who and what Sceva was. He is referred to as 'a Jewish chief priest' (Acts 19:14): but his name was Greek and we encounter his sons in Ephesus. Whatever is the case, he had seven sons, who had some success in their exorcist activities; but they became envious when they saw the miracles Paul was able to perform, and decided to copy the methods of the apostles by addressing the 'evil spirits' 'in the name of Jesus, whom Paul preaches' (19:13). If you do not know the story, you would do well to read chapter 19 of Acts. You will discover that the sons of Sceva came to a rude awakening (19:13-16).

As with so many other Bible stories, this story about the sons of Sceva underlines the dangers of meddling with the occult. The magicians of antiquity, as well as the astrologists and the people who claim to have paranormal gifts today, have all been involved in very deceitful things. One thing, however, is sure: the Light will conquer in every confrontation with the powers of darkness, as is demonstrated by the events that transpired in Ephesus, and this still applies today. The safest route is to avoid everything associated with occultism and to walk only in the way of the Light.

My prayer

I know, dear God, that there is much more between heaven and earth than I can see. Guide me, so that I may avoid all wrong influences and will fully trust in You.

10 November

Segub

(exalted)

Who and when? Youngest son of the Benjamite Hiel, who rebuilt Jericho; was sacrificed by his father (mid-ninth century BC).

Want to know more? Read: 1 Kings 16:34.

Thoughts for today

Jericho was rebuilt at the time when the evil king Ahab ruled over the Northern Kingdom of the ten tribes. When the Israelites took possession of the promised land, after their sojourn in the wilderness, Jericho was the first city to be conquered and destroyed. On this occasion the city was being rebuilt under the leadership of Hiel from Bethel. Towards the end of 1 Kings 16 we read this rather cryptic statement: 'He laid its foundations at the cost of his firstborn son Abiram, and he set up its gates at the cost of his youngest son Segub' (vs. 34). Most Bible commentators are of the opinion that we are here dealing with human sacrifices: of Abiram at the start of the building activities, and of Segub when the work was finished.

For us it is hard to imagine that it was common practice in the ancient world to kill and sacrifice human beings as part of religious rituals. It was one of the things Israel was to resist. God had already made clear to Abraham that He did not want any human sacrifices, and had stated that He Himself would provide the ultimate sacrifice. God's Son would be the only human sacrifice acceptable to Him.

Most modern readers find it hard to swallow the Old Testament stories in which Israel had to annihilate entire nations. Perhaps this practice of the large-scale offering of human sacrifices makes it a little easier to accept: for, if religious abuses such as the ritual killing of Abiram and Segub were also to have become common in Israel, faith in the God of Abraham would have had no chance of survival.

My prayer

Lord, I find many things in the Bible that I cannot understand. But help me to realise that at times draconian measures may have been needed to halt the evils of pandemic idolatry.

11 November

Sennacherib

(may the god Sin increase my brothers)

Who and when? King of Assyria (705-681 BC); enemy of King Hezekiah of Judah.

Want to know more? Read: 2 Kings 18:13-19:37; Isaiah 36; 37.

Thoughts for today

King Hezekiah was at the end of his tether. At an earlier date Assyria had already dealt decisively with the Northern Kingdom of the ten tribes and it now seemed unavoidable that Judah would share in the same fate. Hezekiah had hoped that perhaps the Egyptians could come to his rescue, but this did not offer a realistic chance of success. He received various missives from the Assyrians, urging him to unconditionally subject himself to king Sennacherib. Where was he to go? At long last he found the right address.

When Hezekiah had read the letter that the Assyrian messengers had delivered to him, he went to the temple and 'he spread it out before the LORD' (2 Kings 19:14), and prayed: 'O LORD, God of Israel, enthroned between the cherubim, you alone are God over all the kingdoms of the earth. . . . Listen to the words Sennacherib has sent to insult the living God. It is true, O LORD, that the Assyrian kings have laid waste these nations and their lands. They have thrown their gods into the fire and destroyed them, for they were not gods but only wood and stone, fashioned by men's hands. Now, O LORD our God, deliver us from his hand, so that all kingdoms on earth may know that you alone, O LORD, are God' (2 Kings 19:15-19).

The lesson Hezekiah had to learn is essential for all of us. When we are in a perplexing situation and see no solution, the only possible way out is that of prayer.

My prayer

Almighty God, I know I should come to You when I am surrounded by difficulties. Please remind me constantly that only You can help me out.

12 November

Sergius Paulus

(Sergius, the small one)

Who and when? Proconsul in Cyprus in the time of Paul.

Want to know more? Read: Acts 13:1-12.

Thoughts for today

It was at the beginning of Paul's first missionary journey. Paul and Barnabas had travelled by ship from Antioch, via the neighbouring coastal town of Seleucia, to Cyprus. There they visited the synagogues and 'proclaimed the word of God' (Acts 13:5). Soon they were opposed by a certain Elymas, who is referred to as a 'sorcerer' and a 'false prophet' (vs. 6). This Elymas proved to be a great nuisance, especially once the two apostles had established contact with the proconsul Sergius Paulus, the Roman governor of Cyprus. This official was 'an intelligent man' who sent for the two missionaries, since he wanted to hear what they were saying. Elymas 'tried to turn the proconsul from the faith', but God took care of the situation and made sure that the sorcerer was temporarily removed from the scene: for some time he would not 'see the light of the sun' (vs. 11). When the proconsul saw this he accepted the faith, for 'he was amazed at the teaching about the Lord' (vs. 12).

When we try to tell others about our faith it often happens that people want to obstruct our witness. They may try to convince the person with whom we are sharing our faith not to listen to us. Today the internet often poses a stumbling block too, especially when people start 'surfing' and find a lot of biased or inaccurate information about the Christian faith and our church in particular. On the other hand, we frequently see how God counters such interference so that the Gospel message may be heard loud and clear.

My prayer

Give me, O God, the courage to be a witness of my faith in You, even when there are people who try to block Your message. I firmly believe that You still have the power to deal with them.

13 November

Seth

(substitute)

Who and when? Third son of Adam and Eve; he was born after Abel had been killed by Cain.

Want to know more? Read: Genesis 4:25, 26.

Thoughts for today

Adam and Eve were blessed with another son after Cain had murdered his brother Abel. Eve 'named him Seth, saying, "God has granted me another child in place of Abel" ' (Genesis 4:25). These words may sound a bit strange in our ears. How can a 'new' child replace a child that has died? But it seems that even today some people feel this is possible. When a child dies, some parents may give a child that is subsequently born the same name as the boy or girl they lost. Usually, however, parents recognise that each child is unique. A 'new' child cannot take the place of a dead one. Even identical twins are not fully identical!

Seth could not replace Abel, who had been a unique person in his own right. Abel was Abel and Seth was Seth. There was, however, another dimension to consider. Cain had chosen to go down the path that led away from God, while Abel took the path that led closer to God. It was important that Abel's example be kept alive, and indeed it was; for we read in verse 26: 'Seth also had a son, and he called him Enosh. At that time men began to call on the name of the LORD.'

People in the lineage that began with Seth and continued with Enosh wanted to have God as an essential part of their lives. Adam and Eve had hoped that this would happen and their deepest wish was fulfilled.

My prayer

Lord, today I also want to call on Your name. I want You to play an important role in everything I say and do.

14 November

Shabbethai

(born on a Sabbath)

Who and when? A Levite in Ezra's time who opposed one of Ezra's measures (fifth century BC).

Want to know more? Read: Ezra 10.

Thoughts for today

The problem that is discussed in Ezra 10 probably raises a lot of questions in the minds of most of us. Ezra decided, upon the advice of a certain Shechaniah, that all who had returned from the Babylonian exile to build a new life in Palestine, and who had married 'foreign' women, were to send these spouses away. Such close contacts, it was argued, of Israelites with pagan people would progressively endanger the identity of God's people. One of those who resisted this decision was the Levite Shabbethai.

Studying the list of those who had returned from Babylon, we may ask whether the problem was as urgent as Ezra seemed to think. According to Ezra 10 the total number of men who had married 'foreign' women was 113. Was Ezra right in trying to deal with the problem before things got out of hand? Or was the opposition of Shabbethai and some others against these measures justified? Remarkably enough, Shabbethai's name does not appear on the list of the offenders (10:18-44): so Shabbethai seems to have come to the defence of others, rather than defending his own marital choice. Moreover, Shabbethai was not disciplined for his opposition.

Perhaps we should have at least some admiration for people like the Levite Shabbethai. Whether or not he was right, he had the courage to speak up on behalf of other people, in spite of the risk that this entailed. It is an example that should inspire us to speak out when our conscience tells us to do so.

My prayer

You are a righteous God and You have given me a sense of what is just. Help me to intervene on behalf of others when I see that they are not treated in the way I would regard as just.

15 November

Shadrach

(Babylonian: decree of the moon-god)

Who and when? One of the three Hebrew friends of Daniel who were deported to Babylon and taken to the royal court (sixth century BC).

Want to know more? Read: Daniel 1; 3.

Thoughts for today

Shadrach is best known to us as one of the three men who decided to remain loyal to their God, and ended up in a Babylonian furnace, but who were miraculously protected from its flames. He was originally named Hananiah (God is gracious) but the Babylonians changed his name to Shadrach. This name pointed to a Babylonian god rather than to the God of Israel. The intention was clear: Shadrach and his companions were to forget about their Jewish culture and religion and were meant to become real Babylonians.

When I began my work in Africa (where I lived for almost seven years) I was amazed to discover how many men and women had biblical names. Often these were not their original names, but were the names they acquired when they converted to Christianity. This was a way to underline that these people had forsaken their old ways and their traditional religion and had assumed a Christian identity.

With that background we can easily understand why God has also promised that those who accept Him will one day get a new name (Revelation 2:17). In other words: we will no longer be sinful, imperfect men and women, but beings with a completely new identity. Then, nothing will be left to reflect the old 'Babylonian' culture and lifestyle that once characterised our existence.

My prayer

Heavenly Father, I long for that day when You will give me a new name to certify that in every respect I belong to You.

16 November

Shalmaneser

(the god Sulman is powerful)

Who and when? Experts think this concerns Shalmaneser V, who at the time of King Hosea was responsible for the conquest of Samaria (722 BC).

Want to know more? Read: 2 Kings 17:2-6; 18:9-12.

Thoughts for today

In 722 BC the Northern Kingdom of ten tribes came to an ignominious end. The Assyrians deported a major part of the population to other regions of their vast empire (2 Kings 17:6) and what ultimately became of the ten tribes has remained an unsolved mystery. Many theories have been put forward – the one even more far-fetched than the other.

We can give a clearer answer to the question of *why* the ten tribes disappeared from the face of the earth. The most obvious answer is that, like so many other relatively small nations, it was destroyed by the Assyrian fighting machine, and that, from a political and military perspective, they simply had no chance of survival as an independent nation. That seems to be a very convincing response; but this is not the reason given in the Bible. It doesn't leave us in any uncertainty about the fact that Israel itself was to blame for its demise: 'All this took place because the Israelites had sinned against the LORD their God. . . . They worshipped other gods and followed the practices of the nations the LORD had driven out before them. . . . They did wicked things that provoked the LORD to anger. They . . . were as stiff-necked as their fathers, who did not trust in the LORD their God' (2 Kings 17:7-14). God's patience with Israel had continued for almost three centuries, but at long last the curtain fell over their national existence. They had been the architects of their own downfall.

My prayer

I thank You, Lord, that You are such a patient God. Help me, however, not to test Your patience endlessly, but to decide to serve You faithfully.

17 November

Shamgar

(probably a Hurrian/Hittite name; meaning is unclear)

Who and when? The third judge, after Othniel and Ehud, and possibly a contemporary of Deborah and Barak. Ca. 1200 BC.

Want to know more? Read: Judges 3:31.

Thoughts for today

Shamgar is only mentioned in passing in the book of Judges. He 'struck down six hundred Philistines with an ox-goad'. An ox goad was a long stick, probably with a metal point, which was used by a person behind the plough to spur on the oxen that pulled it. It may well be that Shamgar had just begun a new day when he was suddenly confronted with a band of Philistines. Somehow he found the courage – and was given the power by God – to deal decisively with the six hundred men who were threatening to kill him.

We do not know whether Shamgar is to be credited with other heroic deeds or whether this was just one isolated incident. But the incident may inspire us, however unusual it may seem to us. Shamgar was a man who had not studied in a military academy; nor did he possess any advanced technology to wipe out his enemy. The only thing he had was his ox goad: and yet with this simple tool he was able to achieve more than he could have done with professional armour and a sharp sword.

When God gives us a challenge, our own knowledge and skills and the technology that we have at our disposal are not the most important things. Trusting faith comes first. But when we do trust Him we may also experience that God can enable us to do great things with our 'ox goad'.

My prayer

Lord, let me also rely today on Your presence and on Your assistance in solving the problems that may arise, and not trust mostly in my own skills.

18 November

Shaphan (badger)

Who and when? Secretary of King Josiah (639 BC to 609 BC); was involved in the rediscovery of the scroll with the law in the temple.

Want to know more? Read: 2 Kings 22:3, 8-13; 2 Chronicles 34:8, 14-21.

Thoughts for today

Judah had lost its way to the extent that, even in the temple, the sacred scrolls were no longer used. When King Josiah decided that the temple was due for serious renovation, suddenly a scroll was found that contained part of the book of Deuteronomy. Fortunately, the high priest Hilkiah understood immediately that this was an important discovery. He went to Shaphan, the 'secretary' of the king, who took the scroll to the king and read the contents to him. Shaphan, as well as Josiah, instantly recognised the significance of this discovery and understood that the words in this book were the ones that God had addressed, through Moses, to His people.

We do not have to worry that the Word of God has been lost in the twenty-first century in any physical sense. The Bible societies regularly provide new translations in most major languages. As soon as a new translation appears it becomes a bestseller. In actual fact, however, the Bible has been 'lost' in many Christian institutions and families. In many homes, where a Bible can still be found on a bookshelf, it gathers dust and is hardly ever opened and read; and many people who happen to hear some Bible verses have no idea that they are actually taken from the Word of God. In our day we need many men and women like Shaphan, who can point the people to the importance of the Bible and vigorously promote its reading. In Josiah's days the rediscovery of the Bible resulted in a reformation. Our society (and our personal and family life) would also change for the better if the Word of God were to be rediscovered on a large scale.

My prayer

We thank You, Lord God, for Your Word. Give us the desire and interest to read it more regularly and to allow it to change our lives.

19 November

Shear-Jashub

(a remnant shall return)

Who and when? Son of the prophet Isaiah (eighth century BC)

Want to know more? Read: Isaiah 7:3; 10:21.

Thoughts for today

Isaiah was married and had two sons, both of whom received a symbolic name. One was named Maher-shalal-hash-baz, meaning 'the booty hastens, the spoil speeds' (Isaiah 8:1-4). This name contained a prediction of the imminent occupation by Assyria. 'Before the boy knows how to say "My father" or "My mother", the wealth of Damascus and the plunder of Samaria will be carried off by the king of Assyria' (8:4). The other son of the prophet and 'the prophetess' (8:3) also received a very special name: Shear-Jashub. The meaning of this name is: 'a remnant shall return'.

Nowadays we would not burden our children with such unusual names: but, when today's parents are considering what name to give to their son or daughter, they still often choose a biblical name or one that is derived from such a name. However, I have yet to hear of a baby called Maher-shalal-hash-baz or Shear-Jashub. But in Bible times names often had a different function. Frequently parents chose a name that either expressed their hopes regarding the future of their child or was a testimony to their trust in God. Shear-Jashub was to be a reminder to everyone he came in contact with that God would ensure a good future for His people. Although there would be all kinds of misery (the name of his brother pointed to this), things would end well: a remnant would be saved and able to make a new start.

Our name may not contain a spiritual message for the people around us, but hopefully we will radiate something of the hope that all Christians may have: *God is not going to forsake us!*

My prayer

I thank You, Lord, that You will never forsake Your people, and that this includes me. Help me to radiate that hope to others.

20 November

Shebna

(shortened form of Shebaniah: the Lord is powerful)

Who and when? Secretary of King Hezekiah (eighth century BC)

Want to know more? Read: 2 Kings 18:13-37; Isaiah 22:15-19.

Thoughts for today

Shebna was a high official at the court of King Hezekiah (726 BC to 696 BC). In Isaiah 22:15 he is described as the person who was 'in charge of the palace', while he is referred to in 2 Kings as the 'secretary'. There it tells how Shebna played a role in the communication process between the Assyrian enemy and Hezekiah. In Isaiah 22 we get a different view of Shebna's activities. Isaiah is sent by the Lord to Shebna to reprimand him about something else. Shebna had made arrangements that a prestigious tomb would be hewn out for him in the rocks to serve as his final resting place. It seems that he wanted to make sure that long after his death he would still be remembered. Interestingly enough, this tomb has probably been found on the slope of the Mount of Olives. With considerable difficulty the inscriptions that were found on it have been deciphered, and in all likelihood this is Shebna's tomb.

While the country was facing extreme difficulties, Shebna was preoccupied with his own name and fame. This is hardly a unique phenomenon. In the midst of all kinds of challenges people often worry first about how to safeguard their own status and secure their own future. Isaiah visited Shebna to tell him how God looks at this: 'Beware, the LORD is about to take firm hold of you and hurl you away, O you mighty man. He will roll you up tightly like a ball and throw you into a large country. There you will die and there your splendid chariots will remain – you disgrace to your master's house!' This rebuke to Shebna stands as a lesson for all in every age.

My prayer

Help me, almighty God, that I will not be constantly preoccupied with my own reputation and status.

21 November

Shem

(name, renown)

Who and when? The second oldest son of Noah; the 'father' of the Semitic peoples.

Want to know more? Read: Genesis 9:20-27.

Thoughts for today

According to the Genesis account the distribution of humankind over the face of the earth started with the three sons of Noah, of whom Shem was one. We usually link his name with the Jewish people, and when we speak of anti-Semitism we refer to hatred against Jews: but Shem was not only the forefather of the Jewish people, but of all the Semitic peoples, which included the Babylonians, the Assyrians, the Arameans and the Arabs. We find more information of this topic in the so-called 'table of nations' in Genesis 10.

Knowing this gives an extra tragic dimension to current events in the Middle East. The nations that constantly quarrel or even wage war with each other are, in fact, close relatives. There is more in their background that they have in common than there are things that separate them.

Shem is a link in the human genealogy of Jesus (Luke 3:36); but he was not the first link in this long chain. It all began with the first human being: Adam. All of us are his descendants. Speaking of this, my mind is drawn to the beautiful piece of music of Arvo Pärt, *Which was the son of . . .*, in which a fabulous choir sings about the genealogy of Luke 3. It ends in an explosion of sounds with the words, '*which was the son of Adam*' – followed by the unforgettable climax: '*which was the son of God*' (Luke 3:38).

All descendants of Shem are also sons of Adam: as are all non-Semitic people too – all of us are children of God.

My prayer

Thank You, heavenly Father, that I am Your child. May I never forget that all people, whatever their background, are also part of Your family.

22 November

Shemaiah

(the Lord has heard)

Who and when? Prophet in the time of Rehoboam (ca. 925 BC).

Want to know more? Read: 1 Kings 12:21-23; 2 Chronicles 11:1-4; 12:5-8.

Thoughts for today

When Solomon died his empire fell apart: the ten tribes in the north chose Jeroboam as their king, while the other two tribes (Judah and Benjamin) united under the rule of Rehoboam. This was not according to God's original plan. It did not mean, however, that God now withdrew and wanted to leave the two parties to their own designs, or that from this moment onward one party would be His favourite. Looking at the period of the divided kingdom – before the ten tribes were deported to Assyria and the two tribes were taken into Babylonian exile – we see how God stayed in contact with both parties through His prophets. Shemaiah was one of these spokespersons for God who served in the Southern Kingdom of the two tribes.

The prophet Shemaiah played an important role in the controversy between Jeroboam (the king of the ten tribes) and Rehoboam (the ruler over the two tribes). This controversy could easily have led to carnage on a large scale. But Shemaiah was commissioned by God to approach Rehoboam with the message that he was not to begin a war against the nation of his brothers. Fortunately, Rehoboam listened to the words of the prophet. And we also read about another occasion when the king listened to a message brought to him by the prophet.

Sadly enough, we see that throughout history God's prophets were often ignored. They continue to speak to us through their words, which we find in our Bibles. But are we always prepared to listen to them?

My prayer

We thank You, Lord, for Your prophetic Word. Help us to be prepared to listen to it.

23 November

Shishak

(meaning is unclear)

Who and when? The Egyptian pharaoh who gave asylum to Jeroboam after his rebellion against Solomon; ruled from ca. 945 BC to 924 BC.

Want to know more? Read: 1 Kings 11:40; 14:25; 2 Chronicles 12:1-9.

Thoughts for today

Shishak was the first Egyptian king whose name was mentioned in the Bible. He gave Jeroboam political asylum when he rebelled against Solomon. Jeroboam remained in Egypt until the death of Solomon. Some time later Shishak was engaged in a war against the kingdom of the ten tribes, a record of which is found on the walls of the temple of Karnak. In the fifth year of Rehoboam, who was now the king of Judah, Shishak pillaged Jerusalem and helped himself to the temple treasures and many exquisite articles from the royal palace; 2 Chronicles 12 paints in more detail what happened.

Shishak could easily have annihilated the entire kingdom of Judah. He came with 'twelve hundred chariots and sixty thousand horsemen and . . . innumerable troops'! (Vs. 3.) But the damage done remained relatively small. This was because of a divine intervention. God sent the prophet Shemaiah, who appealed to Rehoboam and his people to return to the Lord. When they did, the judgement was suspended and the danger subsided. Through His messenger God let His people know that His 'wrath' would 'not be poured out' and that they would not be destroyed, because of their *last-minute* conversion (vs. 7).

As in the past, God's people are still subject to many negative influences and must face formidable powers that want to crush them. But God continues to intervene, and, when the time is right, He delivers His people. His condition is and remains, however, that they make clear that they want to belong to the Lord and will show this in their words and actions.

My prayer

Merciful God, I want to belong to You. Protect me against all influences and powers that want to destroy Your children today.

24 November

Silas

(Greek form of Saul)

Who and when? Associate of Paul during his second missionary journey.

Want to know more? Read: Acts 15:22–18:5.

Thoughts for today

Silas participated in the first church council that was held in Jerusalem. During this meeting the discussions centred on the requirements that were to be imposed on Christians converting 'from the Gentiles'. Silas was appointed as a member of the delegation that was charged to communicate the decision of 'the brethren' at the Jerusalem council to the church in Antioch. This meant a journey on foot of about 500 kilometres. When Silas had completed his mission in Antioch he did not return to Jerusalem, but joined Paul on his second missionary journey.

Speaking about this and the other missionary journeys, our attention is mostly focused on Paul. I would, however, suggest that you read Acts chapter 16 carefully and discover what Silas had to go through. Like Paul, he was attacked and beaten by a mob. He was imprisoned in Philippi, and shortly afterwards became a victim of the troubles that erupted in Thessalonica. It is abundantly clear that those who accompanied Paul were also confronted with a range of difficulties.

Often we are focused on what happens to the most prominent leaders and hardly notice what people who have a less prestigious status must endure. In other words: we pay much more attention to the Pauls than to the Silases, which is not right. The Silases of the past as well as of the present merit our interest, prayers and admiration too.

My prayer

Looking around in the church I see people like Paul, but also like Silas. Help me also to notice the accomplishments of people who are less in the spotlight, but who may be true role models for me.

25 November

Simeon

(He hears)

Who and when? The second son of Jacob and Leah; the 'father' of one of the twelve tribes of Israel.

Want to know more? Read: Genesis 29:33; 34; 35:23; Exodus 6:15.

Thoughts for today

We do not know much about Simeon, but Scripture tells us that his mother Leah was very happy when she gave birth to her second son. She knew that Jacob did not love her with the same passion as he loved her sister Rachel, which made her utter this when her son was born: ' "Because the LORD has heard that I am not loved, he gave me this one too." So she named him Simeon' (Genesis 29:33).

Simeon comes into sharpest focus during the Bible narrative about the tragic events in Shechem, when a man who had the same name as the place where this occurred raped his sister Dinah.

Rape is a terrible crime that deserves severe punishment. In the culture of the ancient Middle East – as in many cultures in today's world – rape would usually result in an honour killing. It should therefore hardly surprise us that the incident in which Dinah was the victim was followed by violent action. Levi and Simeon, in particular, decided to avenge their sister, with the assistance of the other brothers. But their violent response was by any standards disproportionate. They killed not only the perpetrator, but also all other men in the town. They also plundered the town and abducted the women and children. Even in that time this was unheard of. We may be glad to live in a country where we have other ways to react to a rape crime. However, it remains a despicable crime that must be dealt with decisively by the authorities wherever it occurs. At the same time, the victims of rape – male or female – must be supported in every way possible.

My prayer

I pray, Lord, that Your people in this world will do all they can to resist sexual violence against women.

26 November

Simeon

(He hears)

Who and when? Simeon was present when the newborn baby Jesus was 'presented in the temple'.

Want to know more? Read: Luke 2:25-35.

Thoughts for today

We may assume that Simeon was advanced in age when he had the privilege of holding Jesus in his arms. He had felt the Spirit's urge to go to the temple, and he arrived at the very moment when 'the parents brought in the child Jesus to do for him what the custom of the Law required'. Simeon was not only a 'righteous and devout' man, but also had the prophetic gift. 'It had been revealed to him by the Holy Spirit that he would not die before he had seen the Lord's Christ' (Luke 2:25-27).

Holding Jesus in his arms, Simeon praised God: 'For my eyes have seen your salvation, which you have prepared in the sight of all people' (vss. 30, 31). He then blessed Mary and Joseph and, addressing Mary in particular, he said: 'This child is designed to cause the falling and rising of many in Israel, and to be a sign that will be spoken against, so that the thoughts of many hearts will be revealed. And a sword will pierce your own soul too' (vss. 34, 35).

Not until much later did Mary understand the full meaning of these words of Simeon. Indeed, 'many in Israel' - but also among many other nations - would be 'falling' or 'rising' because of Jesus. Mankind was forever split into two groups: those who are for or against Jesus. Mary experienced that being 'for' Jesus would at times be costly. She was prepared to go down that route, regardless of 'the sword' that would 'pierce' her soul. Is that also true for us?

My prayer

I ask You, almighty and loving God, for the strength always to remain with all those who, because of Your Son, will not be 'falling' but will be 'rising'.

27 November

Simon (the sorcerer)

(also known as Simon Magus)

Who and when? A practitioner of the occult in Samaria in the days of the apostles.

Want to know more? Read: Acts 8:9-25.

Thoughts for today

Simon the Sorcerer has given his name to a phenomenon that we know as 'simony'. This term refers to paying money in order to acquire a church office. This was a rather common practice in the medieval church. When this Simon in the city of Samaria saw how all his tricks could not begin to compare with what Peter and John were able to do in the power of God, he was anxious also to acquire the skills so that he could operate with the same spiritual authority. This led to his failed attempt to buy this technique from the two apostles.

We do not often see, in the church of today, that people try to offer money to acquire a church office. But all too often money is used in more subtle ways to exert influence in a church organisation. Big donations frequently come with certain strings attached. It happens all too often that generous givers want to determine the agenda of the church. They stipulate that their money may only be used for purposes that support their theological or church-political convictions!

Churches and other religious organisations need money for the pursuit of their goals, but monetary contributions should be given without any manipulative motives. There are situations in which the money should be refused as resolutely as Peter and John responded when Simon approached them with his financial proposal.

My prayer

I ask You, who are the Giver of all that I possess, always to protect me in my giving pattern against unworthy motives.

28 November

Simon from Cyrene

(He hears)

Who and when? Diaspora-Jew from North Africa; visited Jerusalem at the time of the Passover feast; was forced to carry Jesus' cross.

Want to know more? Read: Matthew 27:32.

Thoughts for today

You may sometimes become involved in an incident simply because you were somewhere at a certain time. This happened to Simon when he was in Jerusalem to participate in the festivities of the Passover season. Perhaps he had become curious to find out what a nearby commotion was all about, or perhaps he was just passing by when a Man, bent under the cross on His shoulders, was pushed along through a narrow street by a group of soldiers and other people. Suddenly Simon was recruited by a Roman soldier to take the wooden cross from the Man who could no longer bear the weight.

We do not know how far Simon had to go before they arrived at the execution place where the cross was taken from his shoulders. From that moment it was, in a very real sense, the cross of Jesus. But note the enormous difference between Simon's cross-bearing and that of Jesus. Simon may have carried the cross for fifteen minutes or half an hour. It was heavy, but his burden was temporary. Jesus not only bore a heavy piece of wood, but he carried the excruciating load of the sins and the guilt of all humanity.

When we get close to Christ, we cease to be just spectators. Like Simon, we may have to bear a cross. The duration of our cross bearing may vary; but, however heavy that cross may be, it is like a feather when compared to the burden that Jesus took upon Himself – for you and me.

My prayer

Father in heaven, I ask You for the strength I need to bear my cross – in the realisation that Jesus' cross was infinitely heavier.

29 November

Sisera (meaning is unclear)

Who and when? Commander of a Canaanite army that had subdued the northern part of Israel. Was killed by Jael (ca. 1200 BC).

Want to know more? Read: Judges 4; 5:24-30; 1 Samuel 12:9; Psalm 83:9, 10.

Thoughts for today

Those who know a bit of Dutch history will have heard of a woman called Kenau. She showed extraordinary courage and assisted in carrying buckets with piping hot oil that was poured on the Spanish enemies who in 1573 tried to scale the walls of the city of Haarlem. When I think of Jael I think of her as an Old Testament 'Kenau'.

Sisera was the commander of the enemy in the war that Barak and Deborah fought with the Canaanites. It was essential that Sisera be eliminated. If that were to happen it would surely undermine the morale of his troops! However, this did not occur on the battlefield, but in a tent where Sisera was taking a nap. He assumed that he was in a safe place, but that proved to be a serious miscalculation. Jael managed to slip into the tent and drove a peg through the skull of the sleeping Sisera (Judges 4:21).

There is one detail, however, that is not mentioned until we reach chapter 5. Deborah, who accompanied Barak in the battle against the enemy, sings in this chapter her praises for Jael. But she also describes the mother of Sisera, peering 'through the window and crying out, "Why is his chariot so long in coming?" ' (Vs. 28.) All in Israel were delighted that the cruel Sisera was no more, but his mother was mourning the death of her son. It is something we easily forget: that most people have family and friends, even those that society sheds no tears for. Let's remember that even those who have died after committing serious crimes are missed and mourned by friends and family, who deserve our sympathy and our comfort.

My prayer

Lord, give us empathy for those who suffer, even when it concerns people we see as our enemies.

30 November

Solomon

(man of peace)

Who and when? The son of David and Bathsheba; succeeded David as king; ruled from ca. 971 BC to ca. 931 BC.

Want to know more? Read: 1 Kings 2-11.

Thoughts for today

Solomon asked for wisdom when God told him he could choose whatever he wanted (1 Kings 3:5-14). It would not be long before he badly needed this wisdom. Two women came to see the king (vss. 16-28). They were involved in an acrimonious quarrel and the king had to decide who was right. The two women had each given birth to a child around the same time and in the same house. However, shortly after this, something tragic happened. During the night one of the women lay on her child and suffocated it. Now both women claimed that the living baby was their child.

How was Solomon to solve this dilemma? When talking had no success, he called a servant with a sword and commanded the man to cut the living child in two. One of the women agreed to this, saying: 'He shall be neither mine nor yours; divide him!' But the other woman reacted differently: 'Oh, my lord, give her the living child, and by no means kill him' (NASB). That made things clear to Solomon. He recognised that the real mother was the woman who was willing to give the child to the other woman, if that would spare its life.

Although he certainly wanted justice for this woman, Solomon also wanted the child to have the best possible chances for a good future. He was not primarily interested in how the problem had originated, but looked towards making the best decision for the future. That is true wisdom.

My prayer

All-wise God, give me the kind of wisdom that Solomon had, and help me not so much to be interested in how things began, but in how things can end well.

1 December

Sostheness

(of unbroken strength)

Who and when? The supervisor of the synagogue in Corinth; became a Christian.

Want to know more? Read: Acts 18:17; 1 Corinthians 1:1.

Thoughts for today

Every so often the Bible surprises us, and the story of Sosthenes is one of its many examples. He was the 'ruler' of the synagogue in Corinth. Like so many of his fellow Jews he belonged to the diaspora – the large group of Jews who had become dispersed over the ancient world. This explains why there were so many synagogues in the Near East in the days of the New Testament. Sosthenes was in charge of just such a Jewish house of worship in Corinth. When Paul arrived in this major city to proclaim the good news of Jesus Christ, a conflict with the leaders of the synagogue erupted. The Jews succeeded in bringing Paul before the local tribunal. Somehow Sosthenes became involved in the fight that followed and got a severe beating.

A few years later Paul wrote a letter to the church in Corinth, of which he was one of the founders. By now Sosthenes is no longer the leader of the synagogue, but is 'our brother Sosthenes', who is with Paul in Ephesus where 1 Corinthians was written. He has accepted the Gospel message and is now an associate of Paul.

It is always a miracle when men and women come to faith and turn their lives around, whether they are convinced by strong arguments, or by some remarkable event that made them think. Often they themselves do not know what has been the deciding factor; but at a given moment they know that Jesus is their Lord and that they want to follow Him. That miracle occurred in the life of Sosthenes, and we may rejoice in the fact that it continues to occur in many lives today.

My prayer

Heavenly Father, help me to persist in my efforts to share my faith with others, knowing that the miracle through which people come to believe in You still frequently happens.

2 December

Susanna

(lily)

Who and when? One of the female disciples of Jesus.

Want to know more? Read: Luke 8:1-3.

Thoughts for today

Those who believe that certain positions in the church should only be for men often point out that the twelve disciples Jesus chose – later to be called the twelve apostles – were all men! That is true and it fits with the customs that were common in Bible times. However, it is remarkable to see how often Jesus was surrounded by women, and how often He talked with women, without worrying about the prejudices of the men around Him. And the most remarkable thing is that women were the first to meet Jesus after His resurrection.

A few women are mentioned by name in Luke 8. Some of them had been healed from their physical or mental illnesses, which had inspired them to become grateful and loyal followers of Jesus. Among them at least some enjoyed a prestigious status. We read about Joanna, 'the wife of Chuza, the manager of Herod's household', and also about a 'Susanna' (Luke 8:3). Together with some others they 'were helping to support them [Jesus and His disciples] out of their own means'. They had not followed Jesus out of mere curiosity and because of the sensation that He created. They were actively involved in Jesus' mission and were willing to commit their financial resources to that end.

The picture that the New Testament provides is that Jesus called men and women, and was supported by both men and women! The society of Jesus' days knew a lot of discrimination against women, but in the eyes of the Lord men and women were fully equal.

My prayer

Loving and righteous Lord, You are always there for both men and women, and we thank You that men and women may always be there for You!

3 December

Tamar

(date palm)

Who and when? The daughter-in-law of Judah, who became pregnant with his child.

Want to know more? Read: Genesis 38.

Thoughts for today

Tamar's name is found in Jesus' genealogy, as reported by Matthew 1:3. That has surprised many, because we know her from the Old Testament in the role of a prostitute. Reading the story of Genesis 38, we discover that her customer was none other than Judah, one of the sons of Jacob. And this Judah was, in fact, her father-in-law. If we do not try to learn a little more of the customs of her times, we might come to the wrong conclusion.

Tamar was childless when she became a widow. According to the rules of the so-called levirate marriage, her father-in-law Judah should have made arrangements that one of his other sons (that is, one of Tamar's brothers-in-law) would help Tamar conceive a child. Onan was the first in line for this duty, but from selfish and material motives he made sure that his relationship with Tamar would remain childless. When Onan died, the levirate duty fell upon Shelah, the third son of Judah. However, Judah was unwilling to give his third son to Tamar. This is the reason why Tamar hatched a plan to ensure that, through Judah, she would in the end have posterity.

The story raises all kinds of questions in our mind – certainly also with regard to Judah's conduct. But, as so often, some knowledge of the historical background is helpful in understanding why Tamar decided to do something that we find utterly objectionable. And it remains true that we must often delay our judgement because we do not know enough of the background of a particular event.

My prayer

I confess, Lord, that I often stand ready to judge others without knowing enough of their background and their culture.

4 December

Terah

(meaning is unclear)

Who and when? Descendant of Shem; father of Abraham.

Want to know more? Read: Genesis 11:24-32.

Thoughts for today

Abraham was not alone when he left Ur on a journey to a place that God would yet reveal to him. Terah, Abraham's father, was one of a group that departed with him on this adventure into the unknown. Lot and his family also joined them. The Bible story tells us that Lot would eventually settle near Sodom, with all its dire consequences. But Terah did not stay with the group all the way, and for some reason stopped halfway to the land of Canaan. He remained in Haran, where he would also die. We do not know why he did not want to go any further. It is rather surprising, considering that he was earlier described as the leader of the expedition (Genesis 11:31).

So, Terah started his journey to Canaan, but halted in Haran? Was the trip too tiresome for him? Did he have second thoughts about the purpose of this collective move? Or did Haran seem so attractive that he preferred to settle there? All of these are possibilities.

Terah was not the only person who did not want to go further along the route to the destiny God had in mind for him. We see all the time how, even today, people start on their pilgrimage with God, but then seem to lose the strength to go on, deciding rather to stop along the way. It may be that the journey is too rough. It may be that they have lost their initial enthusiasm and do not have the courage and the persistence to continue and, therefore, they settle in their 'Haran'. It is a tragedy when that happens! Let us all make sure that we do not give up halfway during our journey towards our God-given destiny.

My prayer

God of Abraham, help me to persist and to arrive at the destination You have in mind for me.

5 December

Tertius

(Latin: the third [son])

Who and when? The scribe who wrote Paul's letter to the Romans.

Want to know more? Read: Romans 16:22.

Thoughts for today

We meet Tertius at the very end of Paul's epistle to the Romans. He joins Paul in greeting the Christians in Rome; but, in passing, he mentions that he is the one 'who wrote down this letter' (Romans 16:22). Paul may not have been an expert scribe. At the end of his letter to the Galatians (6:11) we read: 'See what large letters I use as I write to you with my own hand!' It has been suggested that Paul had a problem with his vision as a result of his Damascus experience, and that this may well have been the reason why he wrote with 'large letters'. In any case, in the first century writing long letters required more skills than we need in our time of *laptops* and *iPads*.

However, the remark that Paul was assisted by someone else in the writing of his epistle to the Romans, and possibly in other writing projects, is quite significant. It confirms that the Bible did not originate in a process whereby a number of persons sat down and just recorded the divine message dictated by a supernatural voice. God was the source of their inspiration, but a lot of hard work was also required by the authors and their assistants. And it is important to remember that, when it concerns the letters of the apostles, only one copy was sent to the church to which it was addressed, and it was read to the congregation. It was then copied by hand and forwarded to other churches. The ensuing centuries saw a process of constant copying - a work that in later times was mostly done by monks. All things considered, it truly is a miracle that today we can still read the letter which Tertius committed to parchment on behalf of Paul.

My prayer

We thank You, Lord, for Your Word, which has survived the centuries and still speaks to us today.

6 December

Theophilus

(friend of God)

Who and when? The person to whom Luke dedicated both his gospel and the book of Acts.

Want to know more? Read: Luke 1:3; Acts 1:1.

Thoughts for today

Who was this Theophilus for whom Luke wrote his gospel and also his second book (Acts)? One theory is that we are dealing with Theophilus ben Ananus, who was the high priest from 37 AD to 41 AD. This Theophilus, who was both a priest and a Sadducee, was the son of Annas and a brother-in-law of Caiaphas. Proponents of this theory point to the fact that, by comparison with the other gospels, Luke's is rather mild in its comments about the Sadducees. They also refer to the interesting fact that the Gospel of Luke does not mention Caiaphas by name. The theory sounds plausible, but there is no definitive proof.

The name Theophilus means: *Friend of God*. But, apparently, he was also a friend of Luke. It seems that he held an important position, for Luke addressed him as the 'most excellent Theophilus'. Luke was determined to provide a trustworthy record about Jesus and His ministry, and of the first phase of the movement that developed after Jesus' death and resurrection. We do not know whether it convinced Theophilus, but, fortunately, these two documents did not remain in his private possession. They also became available to us as a source from which we can learn about Jesus and the history of the early church. In fact, like this Theophilus, we are also 'friends of God', and this part of the Word of God is, therefore, also addressed to us, with the purpose that we may also 'know the certainty of the things [we] have been taught' (Luke 1:4).

My prayer

I thank You, O God, that even today we may be inspired by Luke's work and be convinced of the truth of the Christian message.

7 December

Theudas

(Shortened Greek form of Theodorus: gift from God)

Who and when? A rebel leader in Palestine at the beginning of the first century.

Want to know more? Read: Acts 5:33-42.

Thoughts for today

Theudas owes it to the wisdom of Gamaliel that he is mentioned in the Bible. When the Sanhedrin – the Jewish Council – was deeply concerned about the success of the apostles in the proclamation of their message in Jerusalem, Gamaliel reminded the other council members how important it is to see things in historical perspective. Events that seem extremely important at a particular moment in time are later often viewed as a storm in a teacup. Gamaliel pointed the council to the problem a certain Theudas had caused some years earlier. In those days he had some four hundred dedicated followers, but his movement was by then no more than a footnote in the annals of Palestine's history. And the same, he said, was true of Judas the Galilean, who a little later tried to start a revolution, but who also quickly disappeared from the scene.

Gamaliel's speech contains a valuable lesson for us to place the things we experience in historical perspective. There are moments in the history of every religious movement when people promote ideas that cause consternation. For a while it may seem that they will inflict much damage on the movement/denomination/faith community. But, usually, just a decade or so later they will have faded from the scene and few people will even remember their names or know what all the fuss was about. Being able to put things in such historical perspective helps to prevent panic when the next troublemaker calls for attention.

My prayer

You, O God, are the Lord of history. Help me, when needed, to put the things I hear, see and experience in a historical perspective.

8 December

Thomas

(Aramaic: twin)

Who and when? One of Jesus' twelve disciples; well known for his period of doubt; also referred to as Didymus.

Want to know more? Read: Matthew 10:2-4; John 14:1-7; 20:24-29.

Thoughts for today

Some people are renowned for their great faith. We find an extensive gallery of such heroes of faith in Hebrews 11. We look in vain, however, for Thomas in that famous chapter. He became known as a doubter. When Jesus appeared to His disciples after His resurrection, Thomas happened to be absent. It is, therefore, perhaps not so strange that he showed some doubt when he heard the report of the apostles, and that he was anxious also to see and feel for himself that Jesus had indeed risen from the tomb.

We can be sure that Thomas left this episode of doubt behind him. When, one week later, Thomas met the Lord, he confessed his faith in words full of meaning: 'My Lord and my God' (John 20:28). Reliable traditions tell us that in AD 52 Thomas travelled to the South of India, where he preached the Gospel message to the Jews who had settled in that region. Even today there is a group of Christians in India who call themselves 'Thomas Christians'. Since most of them live along the Malabar coast, they are also referred to as 'Malabar Christians'. There is good reason to believe that Thomas gave his life for the Lord during his service in India. Maybe he should, after all, have been included in Hebrews 11!

It is not sinful to have doubts: but we do not have to succumb to our doubts. Jesus had patience with the doubting Thomas. That gives us the confidence that He is also patient with us if we go through periods of doubt.

My prayer

Help me, Lord, in periods of doubt to always return to the point where I can confess from the bottom of my heart: 'My Lord and my God!'

9 December

Timothy

(one who reverences God)

Who and when? Came from Lystra; son of a Greek father and a Jewish mother; became a Christian and was coached by Paul; accompanied Paul in various missionary activities.

Want to know more? Read: Acts 16:1–20:4; 1 Timothy; 2 Timothy.

Thoughts for today

Many people who have reached middle age, or passed that point some time ago, tend to be hesitant when it comes to appointing young persons in responsible positions. This applies to society as a whole as well as to the church. They stress the importance of experience and of having a good track record. But it happens all too often that they forget how they themselves were put in responsible positions when they were still quite young, and that people can only get experience by getting the opportunity to be involved with tasks in which they can hone their skills.

This was Timothy's problem. When still young, he was 'discovered' by Paul and coached into a leadership role. But Timothy was afraid that many people would not appreciate his youthful age, and he feared the future. Paul, however, insisted that Timothy should not be afraid of the negative remarks of those who felt that he was too young, and wrote this to him: 'Don't let anyone look down on you because you are young, but set an example for the believers in speech, in life, in love, in faith and in purity' (1 Timothy 4:12).

Young people should receive the opportunity to gain experience. However, this carries some definite responsibilities with it. They must be an example for their peers and also for those who are older, in what they do and say. That is the only way in which they will win the confidence of the people around them.

My prayer

Lord, make us ready to give one another challenging opportunities, regardless of age and previous experience.

10 December

Titus

(Latin: title of honour)

Who and when? Titus was a Christian with a pagan background; friend, travel companion and assistant of Paul.

Want to know more? Read: 2 Corinthians 2:12, 13; Galatians 2:1, 3; 2 Timothy 4:10; Titus.

Thoughts for today

The name of Titus is not found in the book of Acts. He may have been included in the delegation that was sent to Jerusalem for consultation with the church leaders (Acts 15:2). But in Paul's letters we repeatedly encounter Titus, and in the New Testament we find a brief letter from the apostle Paul to him.

There clearly was a close tie between Paul and Titus. Paul may well have been the one who led Titus to faith in Christ. However, the path of faith that connected these two men may be characterised as one of two-way traffic. We read in 2 Corinthians 7:6 that Paul was encouraged by the arrival of Titus. Titus accompanied Paul during some of his missionary journeys, but was also sent by Paul on specific missions to particular churches. Upon his return to Paul after such missions, he reported what he had heard and seen. Paul did not just appreciate getting this information, but the renewed contact with Titus gave him a spiritual boost – something that Titus must have felt too (2 Corinthians 7:13).

At times we may feel that we live and work in isolation. For this reason, we must seize every opportunity to seek the company and co-operation of others who cherish the same ideals. It is a blessing to have friends and colleagues who can encourage us and whom we may, in turn, inspire – as was the case with Paul and Titus.

My prayer

I thank You, heavenly Father, for friends who can encourage me. Show me the opportunities for me to encourage and inspire others.

11 December

Trophimus

(nourishing)

Who and when? Companion of Paul during his third missionary journey.

Want to know more? Read: Acts 20:4; 21:27-36; 2 Timothy 4:20.

Thoughts for today

Trophimus had come from Ephesus. He was a 'Greek' who had converted to Christianity. Paul's first visit to Ephesus was of short duration, but when he returned he stayed for about three years. When Paul left this time, Trophimus was part of the group that accompanied the apostle (Acts 20:4). Upon their arrival in Jerusalem the presence of Trophimus led to an incident which began a long legal battle that would eventually bring Paul to Rome. Paul was (falsely) accused by the Roman leaders of having brought Trophimus, a non-Jew, into the temple, which was regarded as a serious offence.

We read in 2 Timothy 4:20 that Paul had to leave Trophimus behind in Miletus because of illness. It is not clear when this occurred, as we also read that Trophimus accompanied Paul to Jerusalem at the end of his third missionary journey. Was there a moment when Paul and Trophimus were both in Miletus and when Trophimus was not able to continue his journey with Paul? We can only imagine what kind of experience that must have been for Trophimus. He had witnessed with his own eyes how Paul had healed some of the sick people they had encountered. He was with Paul in Troas when Eutychus fell out of a window and Paul raised him from the dead. Why then did Trophimus have to remain behind because of ill health?

Trophimus experienced what many others have lived through. The fact that you are an active believer in the cause of God does not mean that you will always be protected against unpleasant circumstances. That does not, however, mean that God has forsaken you.

My prayer

Almighty God, help me to accept that, although I am a believer, I may have to go through difficult experiences. Help me never to lose my trust in You.

12 December

Uriah (my light is the Lord)

Who and when? A Hittite soldier in David's army; husband of Bathsheba; ca. 1000 BC.

Want to know more? Read: 2 Samuel 11:1–12:25; 1 Kings 15:5; 1 Chronicles 11:41.

Thoughts for today

Bathsheba, the wife of Uriah, became pregnant after sleeping with King David. This presented David with a serious problem. When he heard from Bathsheba that she was expecting a child, he came up with a plan that was to ensure that Uriah, who was a soldier in his army, would be home for a few days. That would, of course, mean that he would have a few nights together with his wife, and when her pregnancy became clearly visible everybody would think that Uriah was the father. However, this plan did not work out. When Uriah was in Jerusalem and reported to the king on the state of the war he did not want to use this opportunity to spend a few days with his wife, while his comrades were out on the battlefield. This pushed David to come up with an even more detestable plan, which would result in Uriah's death in the next battle.

David belonged to God's special people. He had been chosen to lead his nation. Uriah was a Hittite, a foreigner. He was a hireling who did not fight for a lofty ideal, but as a means to earn a living. But notice the difference. The man who was chosen by God failed miserably. Besides the fact that he should not have gotten involved with Bathsheba, he should have been loyal to someone who on a daily basis risked his life for him. It would have been quite normal for Uriah to gratefully enjoy a brief, unexpected holiday with his wife. But Uriah had clear principles and put those into practice, contrary to the man God had chosen. Let us take this lesson to heart.

My prayer

Lord, help me to practise my principles and to be loyal to You every day.

13 December

Uzzah

(strength)

Who and when? Accompanied the ark when David had it transported to Jerusalem; died because he touched the ark when it was in danger of sliding from the cart.

Want to know more? Read: 2 Samuel 6:1-11.

Thoughts for today

At first sight the story of Uzzah does not make much sense. For a considerable time after it had been retrieved from the Philistines who had captured it, the ark of the covenant had been in a private home. It was now being transported to Jerusalem, but things did not go as expected. The ark was in danger of sliding from the new cart on which the holy object had been placed. Uzzah was one of the men who were in charge of the logistics of this project. When he saw what was happening he stuck out his hand to protect the sliding ark. God became very angry and punished Uzzah instantaneously because of 'his irreverent act' (2 Samuel 6:7).

God's reaction may seem disproportionate or even unjust; but more was at stake than we might perhaps think. God had given very detailed instructions as to how the ark was to be transported (see Exodus 25:10-22 and Numbers 4:4-6). These rules were now being completely ignored. David had turned the return of the ark into a military circus, with thirty thousand men participating. The ark was not reverently covered and carried by the priests, but instead this most holy object was put on a cart drawn by some oxen. Uzzah should have known better; but, apparently, he gladly co-operated in a venture that was completely at odds with the divine instructions. It remains difficult for us to accept that God punished him in the way He did. However, it does make it very clear that God is utterly serious when He asks us to ensure that holy things are, indeed, kept holy.

My prayer

Merciful God, I fail to understand why Uzzah was given the death penalty. But help me always to follow Your instructions in dealing with holy things.

14 December

Uzziah

(the Lord is my strength)

Who and when? King of Judah (reigned from 788 BC to 735 BC); also referred to as Azariah.

Want to know more? Read: 2 Kings 15:1-7; 2 Chronicles 26:3-23.

Thoughts for today

During much of his reign King Uzziah was rather successful. 'His fame spread far and wide, for he was greatly helped until he became powerful' (2 Chronicles 26:15). Initially he was also given credit for his trust in the Lord: 'He did what was right in the eyes of the LORD' (vs. 4). But some words are added to this remark: 'As long as he sought the LORD, God gave him success' (vs. 5).

Sadly, once Uzziah had become powerful 'his pride led to his downfall' (vs. 16). The king was, of course, well aware that he was not allowed to enter the holy apartment of the temple and burn incense on the altar. But, as a successful king, he thought that he was above the law of God and he became extremely upset when the priests tried to convince him that what he did was unacceptable. At that moment God intervened and he was struck with a terrible disease: 'Leprosy broke out on his forehead.' This probably was not the kind of leprosy that we know today, but it could be fatal nonetheless, and it required that he be placed in quarantine. The result was that until his death his son Jotham had to take care of all government business.

The moral of the story of Uzziah is crystal clear. No one can put himself above the law – and ignore the instructions that God has given.

My prayer

Keep us, almighty Father, from the kind of pride that will convince us that we can safely ignore Your laws.

15 December

Vashti

(Persian: the desired one)

Who and when? The wife of the Persian king Ahasuerus (reigned from 486 to 465 BC); was dethroned by the king and succeeded by Esther.

Want to know more? Read: Esther 1.

Thoughts for today

The heroine of the book of Esther is, of course, the woman who has given her name to this short section of the Bible. Her courage and trust in God were more than remarkable. But Vashti must also get considerable credit. She was an attractive woman, as her name indicated, and her husband liked to show her off. When the king organised an extravagant party in the garden of his palace for all high officials in his empire - which went on for days on end - he decided on the seventh day of the feast to call for Queen Vashti. She was commanded to 'display' her beauty to all 'the people and nobles'. Then, what nobody could have believed happened. The queen refused to come. 'Then the king became furious and burned with anger' (Esther 1:12). Such a wayward attitude could not be tolerated. His advisors agreed, fearing that this behaviour might tempt other women to do the same. What if their own wives began to ignore the orders of their husbands! All this resulted in the decision of the king to deprive Vashti of her royal status.

Vashti had the courage to stick to her principles. She did not want to demean herself and serve as a sex object for a group of intoxicated men. She felt this would be worth the sacrifice she would have to make, and she was aware of the risks of her action. But she was prepared to accept those risks, for in the future she wanted to be able to look at herself without shame.

My prayer

Lord, I realise that as a follower of Christ I should live according to the norms that Your Son modelled for us. Help me not to compromise my principles, even when that would be risky.

16 December

X

Who and when? This X represents the large number of men and women who are not mentioned by name in the Bible.

Want to know more? Throughout the Old and in the New Testament you find men and women who have remained anonymous.

Thoughts for today

Having come to the letter X, this seems the most suitable place to pay attention to the many hundreds of persons who play a role in the annals of the Bible, but have remained nameless. Think, for instance, of Job's wife, and of the daughter of Jairus, or of the poor widow who put her last few coins in the offertory box in the temple. Other examples could include the 'man of God' from Judah who came to speak to King Jeroboam, the rich young ruler who approached Jesus with his questions, and the prison guard in Philippi. And so on! Why are we left in the dark concerning their names? It may well be that many names were not known to the authors of the stories in which they play a role. The Bible writers were inspired by God, but this does not mean that God informed them about every small detail. And perhaps the authors of the Bible felt that certain men and women were not important enough to be mentioned by name. Looking at ordinary secular history, we also often find that the kings, famous generals and important politicians are the ones mentioned by name. The countless persons who stay in the background, facilitating the work of the 'important' people, usually remain anonymous.

It may be that our names will soon be forgotten, that no street will be named after us and no stamps will ever be issued with our portrait on them; but our 'importance' is not to be measured by such standards, and - what is far more crucial - it is not measured by God in such superficial ways. For Him all men and women are equally important, and all those we can only refer to with the letter X are well known to Him.

My prayer

I thank You, dear Lord, that I am important in Your sight!

17 December

YHWH

(I am)

Who and when? The name by which God identified Himself to Moses.

Want to know more? Read: Exodus 3:13, 14.

Thoughts for today

When Moses was called to deliver Israel from its slavery, he wanted to know the precise mandate that God would give him. The Lord told him not to worry about this, since he was sent by God Himself. But Moses objected: 'What am I to say when the people ask me about Your name? What is Your name? The gods of the nations around us have names. What is Yours?'

God then identified Himself as YHWH – four consonants which seem to be a form of the Hebrew verb *to be* – following the revelation of Himself as *The One Who Is* in verse 14. Most Bible translations translate verse 14 as: 'I am', or: 'I am who I am'. Some translations prefer the future form: 'I will be who I will be'. In this name the very essence of the God of Israel (and thus of our God) is revealed in a magnificent way. *God is there for us, and that will always be so.*

We begin most statements that explain something of what we are with the words: 'I am . . .', but what follows is always subject to qualifications. When we say: 'I am a husband,' or: 'I am a wife,' or: 'I am a mother,' or: 'I am a father,' it raises some immediate questions. What kind of husband or wife am I? How good a father or mother am I? This is true of everything we say about ourselves. Only God *is what He is* in an absolute sense and in the perfect meaning of the word. What He is never needs further qualification. He is who He is. We will never be disappointed, for we will never discover that, after all, God is not what He pretends to be. He is the *I am* and the *I will be there.* What else needs to be said?

My prayer

God, You are always who You are and who You will forever be. Help me, also in this respect, to better reflect Your image.

18 December

Zacchaeus

(Greek form of *zakkai*, pure)

Who and when? The chief tax collector who turned to Jesus and tried to compensate as much as possible for his dishonest actions.

Want to know more? Read: Luke 19:1-10.

Thoughts for today

Here we meet, close to Jericho, a man who wants to see Jesus. He was, however, 'a short man' (Luke 19:3). This prompted him to climb a tree, so that he would have a better view of the road. Was he just curious? No, it was more than that. 'He wanted to see who Jesus was' (vs. 3). But the fact that *Jesus* saw Zacchaeus was far more important than that *Zacchaeus* could get a glimpse of Jesus.

This 'seeing' by Jesus was more than a physical observance of a male person in a tree. Jesus saw who Zacchaeus was. He was a tax collector working for the Roman authorities, who had occupied his country. And his job gave him plenty of opportunities to extort money from his own people in the process.

But Jesus saw more than just the ugly outside. He recognised in Zacchaeus a candidate for His kingdom. He knew that Zacchaeus was 'a son of Abraham' (vs. 9) whom He wanted to save. This was the reason why Jesus took the time to accompany Zacchaeus to his home, where Zacchaeus made Him feel very welcome (vs. 6).

What may have begun as mere curiosity soon became an urgent desire to follow Jesus and to make a radical change in his life. Are we just as alert as Jesus was, and do we look around us to see whether there are people who may want to meet Jesus Christ and start a new life?

My prayer

I thank You, Lord, that You saw me and called me to come to You. Help me to see whether there are some people whom I might bring to You as I go through this day.

19 December

Zadok

(righteous)

Who and when? Zadok was one of the chief priests during David's reign (ca. 1000 BC).

Want to know more? Read: 2 Samuel 8:15-17; 15:23-29; 1 Kings 1:8; Ezekiel 40:46.

Thoughts for today

The Bible has a few references to Zadok, in particular dealing with his pedigree. He was a son of a priest and the father of a priest. The prophet Ezekiel repeatedly referred to the descendants of Zadok as the legitimate priests in the future temple that he describes.

The most important aspect in the record of Zadok's activities was his loyalty to David. When David was confronted with the rebellion of his son Absalom a number of important leaders deserted him, but Zadok stayed with him. And when, towards the end of David's life, Adonijah was plotting a coup, Zadok refused to give him any support. He knew that David had been chosen by God to sit on the throne of Israel and Zadok remained loyal to the king - even when others thought it was to their advantage to align themselves with David's rivals.

Loyalty is an important quality. Most important is, of course, loyalty to God: that is, staying close to Him even when doubts and questions may arise, and continuing without God may seem easier. But it also has to do with loyalty towards other people: family, friends, colleagues and others who are part of our social network - even at moments when self-interest may tempt us to switch our loyalty to others.

My prayer

You, O God, are loyal to me. I want to remain loyal to You. Give me the inner strength that I need, and help me also to be loyal to the people around me.

20 December

Zaphenath-Paneah

(meaning uncertain; perhaps a title)

Who and when? Zaphenath-Paneah was the Egyptian name given to Joseph when he became the second most important person in Egypt.

Want to know more? Read: Genesis 41:45.

Thoughts for today

The story of Joseph is a kind of roller coaster. Being raised as the favourite son of a patriarch in Palestine, he ended up as a slave in Egypt, but eventually became the highest official under the pharaoh of Egypt. In many ways the story resembles that of Daniel: a believer in the Hebrew God, who was deported to another country, became immersed in a totally different culture, had a successful career and was put in a high position – and through it all remained loyal to his God.

In both cases – that of Daniel and of Joseph – a new name was given to seal the expected loyalty to their new country. After Joseph had explained the meaning of the pharaoh's dream, and had given the king some solid advice, he was entrusted with the task of implementing his own plan. He became the second most powerful man in the Egyptian empire and was renamed as Zaphenath-Paneah.

Remaining firm in one's faith as a Christian believer, while upholding values that differ from those of many of the people around us, is a challenge that requires support from on high. That challenge becomes more pressing the further a person moves up in the world. Many men and women who have decided to be true to their principles have experienced this, like Zaphenath-Paneah (alias Joseph) did. It may require a lot of courage to say 'no', and careful consideration of how to proceed in some difficult situations. But, above all, it requires faith – trusting that God will show the way, if we give Him the chance to do so.

My prayer

Lord, give me the same trusting faith that men like Joseph and Daniel had, to stay faithful to You and to follow my conscience, even when I am in difficult situations.

21 December

Zebedee

(given)

Who and when? Fisherman; father of the disciples James and John.

Want to know more? Read: Mark 1:16-20; Matthew 20:20-28.

Thoughts for today

Zebedee had two sons, James and John – two quick-tempered young men, who, apparently with reason, were called 'sons of thunder' (Mark 3:17). Zebedee was a fisherman who employed his sons along with some 'hired men' (Mark 1:20). He was, therefore, probably not without some means.

It has often been suggested that Zebedee was married to Salome, one of the women who went to Jesus' tomb on the resurrection morning with the purpose of caring for Jesus' body. We cannot be totally certain about this. But the fact that Zebedee's wife came to Jesus to ask for a special status for her sons in His coming kingdom does suggest that she belonged to Jesus' inner circle. In Matthew 20:20 she is referred to as 'the mother of Zebedee's sons'. That a woman was simply known as 'the wife of . . .' or 'the mother of . . .' has long remained a custom in many cultures and is all too frequently the case in 'the West' as well.

We know nothing else about Zebedee. We are not given any indication that he tried to prevent his sons from leaving his business and following Jesus; and we may conclude that he also permitted his wife to be with Jesus. That would make him an example for many husbands and fathers. Fathers are often inclined to steer their children, when it concerns their future, in a certain direction (for instance, to work in the family business), and may also be less than supportive when their wives operate too independently!

My prayer

Thank You, Lord, for people who give space to each other (also within families) to make their own choices.

22 December

Zebulun

(habitation)

Who and when? The sixth son of Jacob and Leah; the forefather of the tribe of Zebulun.

Want to know more? Read: Genesis 30:19, 20; 49:13.

Thoughts for today

At the end of his life Jacob gave his prophetic blessings to his sons (see Genesis 49:1-27), including Zebulun. This is what Jacob said: 'Zebulun will live by the seashore and become a haven for ships; his border will extend towards Sidon' (vs. 13). When we look at Joshua 19:10-16 to discover what area was allotted to the tribe of Zebulun after Canaan had been conquered, we notice that their land did not extend to the sea. However, in later years it did reach the sea. In any case, Zebulun had the potential to develop into a sizeable clan with important commercial interests, as a number of caravan routes ran through their area.

Often Naphtali and Zebulun are mentioned in the same context. We find this, for instance, in Isaiah 9:1, where the prophet predicts that one day the area that was allotted to these two tribes will be hugely advantaged, saying that amid 'those who were in distress' 'there will be no more gloom'. Many centuries later a major part of this land of Zebulun would be the area where Jesus - the Living Light - would conduct much of His ministry!

The geographical location of a particular population segment may have advantages or disadvantages. But the main thing to remember is that, whatever the 'gloomy' side might be, there is always the prospect that Jesus can change the situation in a dramatic way. This also applies to us as individuals. Wherever life has brought us, the crucial thing is that we do not 'walk in darkness', but in the light that God is willing to let shine on all of us.

My prayer

Let me, Lord, always 'walk' in Your light.

23 December

Zechariah

(the Lord has remembered)

Who and when? A prophet in the time of the rebuilding of Jerusalem after the Babylonian captivity; a record of Zechariah's visions are found in the Old Testament book that bears his name.

Want to know more? Read: Ezra 5:1; 6:14; Zechariah.

Thoughts for today

In the book of Zechariah we mainly find messages addressed to Joshua and Zerubbabel, the two important leaders during the rebuilding of the city of Jerusalem and of the temple, after groups of Judeans had returned from Babylon. That it was a turbulent time is very clear from the content of this prophetic section of the Bible. It is advisable to read all fourteen short chapters of the book in one session for maximum impact. Those who have studied the book of Revelation will know that John the Seer has borrowed many images from the visionary messages of Zechariah. While reading the book of Zechariah we will also detect many details that hint at a future Messiah – whom we recognise in Jesus Christ.

In reading and rereading the record of Zechariah's visions, I am particularly impressed by the absolute difference between God's opinion about those who want to serve Him, and of all those who make the other choice. The prophet could not have used more striking language than the words that we find in Zechariah 1:14, 15: 'This is what the LORD Almighty says: . . . "I am very angry with the nations that feel secure. I was only a little angry, but they added to the calamity." ' But by way of contrast He also states: 'I am very jealous for Jerusalem and Zion!' The people of Israel have disappointed God many times, but God does not give up. The prophet assures his contemporaries, and us, centuries later: 'This is what the LORD Almighty says: "My towns will again overflow with prosperity, and the LORD will again comfort Zion and choose Jerusalem" ' (vs. 17).

My prayer

Thank You, almighty God, that You are 'jealous' for us. It is good to know this.

24 December

Zechariah

(the Lord has remembered)

Who and when? Priest; father of John the Baptist.

Want to know more? Read: Luke 1:5-25 and 57-80; 3:2.

Thoughts for today

Both Zechariah and his wife Elisabeth were 'upright in the sight of God' (Luke 1:6). Both came from priestly families. Luke tells us how Zechariah had travelled to Jerusalem because he was on duty to serve in the temple. 'He was chosen by lot, according to the custom of the priesthood, to go into the temple of the Lord and burn incense' (vs. 9). The altar for the burning of the incense stood in 'the holy' - the one-but-holiest apartment of the temple.

While Zechariah was doing his work, and 'all the assembled worshippers were praying outside' (vs. 10), an angel appeared to Zechariah, and this was his reaction: 'He was startled and was gripped with fear' (vs. 12). We might say: 'Well, we can understand this reaction. We would also be "startled" if something like this were to happen to us.'

But wait a minute. Zechariah was a priest. He was exempt from all 'normal' work and was available full-time for the service of the Lord. He had the privilege of entering into the Holy Place. He knew that the incense symbolised man's connection with God. But when God established contact with him in this very direct way he was frightened, and even worse. When an angel gave him a message from God he was not ready to believe what he heard. A temporary punishment followed.

Could this also happen to us? Could we be involved, either professionally or as volunteers, in church work - busy with 'holy' things - and not expect that God may actually speak to us?

My prayer

Help us, dear God, to expect that You may want to speak to us, and not to be 'startled' when something extraordinary happens in our lives.

25 December

Zedekiah

(the Lord is righteousness)

Who and when? The last king of Judah; was a vassal of Babylon, but sought help from Egypt; Babylon intervened and Zedekiah was tortured and imprisoned; he ruled from 597 BC to 586 BC.

Want to know more? Read: 2 Kings 24:17–25:12; Jeremiah 52:1-11.

Thoughts for today

Things did not look very bright for the small kingdom of Judah when Zedekiah began his reign at the age of twenty-one. Judah had become completely dependent on Babylon, the new superpower in the ancient Middle East. Against the advice of the prophet Jeremiah, Judah decided to seek help from Egypt, the other superpower of that time. With Egyptian support Zedekiah thought he could turn against Babylon. But things went terribly wrong – just as the prophet had predicted. The Babylonians came with a large army to Jerusalem and that was the end of Judah as a state. A significant part of the population was deported to Babylon. Zedekiah briefly succeeded in escaping, but was soon caught. He had to witness how his sons and closest advisors were brutally killed, before the Babylonians 'put out' his eyes (Jeremiah 52:11). He was bound 'with bronze shackles' (after all, he had been a king!) and they 'took him to Babylon', where he was put in prison 'till the day of his death'.

Did Zedekiah have any chance to reign successfully after he had ascended the throne? From a political perspective things looked very bleak. But, if he had placed his full trust in the Lord, God would, no doubt, have positively surprised him. Unfortunately, he did 'evil in the eyes of the LORD' (Jeremiah 52:2). That was the reason why God drew a line. Eventually there comes a moment when even God runs out of patience.

My prayer

I realise, Lord, that I have all too often seriously tested Your patience. Give me the strength not to do this for so long that You run out of patience with me.

26 December

Zephaniah

(the Lord has protected)

Who and when? Prophet during the reign of Josiah (639-609 BC); contemporary of Jeremiah.

Want to know more? Read: Zephaniah.

Thoughts for today

The prophet Zephaniah was the great-great-grandson of someone named Hezekiah. Was he related to King Hezekiah? It is possible, but we can only guess. Zephaniah prophesied during the reign of King Josiah. This was most likely during the early part of King Josiah's reign, and Zephaniah may well have played a role in the religious reforms that were realised by Josiah.

Zephaniah's name is linked to a document that we now find in our Bibles as the ninth book of the 'minor prophets'. It is structured in the same way as various other prophetic writings: words of judgement against Israel, followed by words of judgement addressed to other nations, and a promise of salvation for a 'remnant' of Israel (Zephaniah 3:13). This seems to make the content of the book of Zephaniah rather predictable, for by now we know this pattern. But we cannot hear it often enough. After all, God's people are far from perfect, even today. And things are even worse when we look at the world at large, with all its evil and atrocities. However, God's message is never only negative and pessimistic. There is always a divine promise that those who will remain (or will become) loyal to God will be saved. This was Zephaniah's message, and that message must still be given to the world by all possible means.

My prayer

Loving Father, I know that one day You will judge the world. But I thank You that You are a God of justice and of love, and that You do Your utmost to save as many people as possible. This gives me the confidence that I may be among those who will be saved!

27 December

Zerubbabel

(Akkadian: offspring of Babylon)

Who and when? Leader who returned from Babylon (538 BC); helped to rebuild the temple in Jerusalem.

Want to know more? Read: Ezra 2:1, 2; 3; Nehemiah 7:6, 7; 12:47; Zechariah 4:1-10.

Thoughts for today

After the Babylonian captivity the rebuilding of the Jerusalem temple has the support of some prophets, among whom is Zechariah. He praises the role of the high priest Joshua (see Zechariah 3), but especially that of Zerubbabel. The prophet does not primarily focus on Zerubbabel's technical and administrative expertise, but rather on his solid trust in the Lord. The marvellous words of Zechariah are worth quoting: 'This is the word of the LORD to Zerubbabel: Not by might, nor by power, but by my spirit, says the LORD of hosts. What are you, O great mountain? Before Zerubbabel you shall become a plain; and he shall bring out the top stone amid shouts of "Grace, grace to it!" Moreover the word of the LORD came to me, saying, "The hands of Zerubbabel have laid the foundation of this house; his hands shall also complete it. Then you will know that the LORD of hosts has sent me to you" ' (Zechariah 4:6-9, NRSV).

When reading the context of these verses we see that these words are embedded in a prophecy that would later inspire John the Revelator. What we must understand from this passage most of all is that Zerubbabel was so successful in his work – even more than he had ever thought possible – because he saw his work as a *spiritual* task, in which trust in God was of the essence. This remains true for all of us: we can only accomplish things for God if we do not build on our own strength or skills, but rely on the assistance and guidance of the Spirit of God.

My prayer

Dear God, remind me today that my success in life does not depend on my own capabilities, but on the guidance of Your Spirit.

28 December

Zeruiah

(perfumed with mastic)

Who and when? Sister of David and mother of Joab.

Want to know more? Read: 2 Samuel 17:25; 1 Chronicles 2:16.

Thoughts for today

Jesse had eight sons, but only two daughters: Zeruiah and Abigail. It seems likely that Jesse and his wife were delighted when at last they were also blessed with two girls. Does the name of Zeruiah perhaps express some of that delight?

Zeruiah plays no role of any significance in the biblical narrative. Nevertheless, her name occurs some twenty-five times. In all these cases the name is linked to her sons. She is, for instance, referred to several times as the mother of Joab. This is rather remarkable, as usually men are referred to as the son of their father, who is then mentioned by name, and not as the son of a particular mother. What was so special about Zeruiah that her name had replaced that of her husband? Was Zeruiah perhaps the centre of the family?

It is often said that there is a strong wife behind every successful man. This is more than just a saying, as there is a lot of truth in it. But it is equally true that the influence of the parents – and especially of the mother – is of decisive importance for the later success of the children. Joab was an important and successful man, as was his brother Abishai – another son of Zeruiah – who excelled in courage (see 1 Samuel 26). We do not know whether they were supported by strong wives, but, in any case, they had a strong mother. And this is likely the reason why Zeruiah was not forgotten.

My prayer

We thank You, almighty God, for spouses and parents – and especially for mothers – who had such an important role in making us into who we are.

29 December

Ziba

(plantation of strength)

Who and when? Was a servant of Mephibosheth; tried to obtain his master's property by accusing his master of treachery, and ended up with half of it.

Want to know more? Read: 2 Samuel 9:2-12; 16:1-4; 19:24-30.

Thoughts for today

The story is somewhat complicated. King David put Ziba in charge of the former properties of King Saul that were given to Saul's son Mephibosheth. Ziba had fifteen sons and twenty servants of his own, and with them he administered the estate. But at a given moment he went to David with some gifts, while claiming that Mephibosheth was disloyal to David and had plans to usurp the throne. In his anger the king now made Ziba the legal owner of the properties that were given to Mephibosheth.

A little later Mephibosheth met with David and protested his innocence. Apparently Mephibosheth was not able to completely convince David, who was now faced with a dilemma. Could he believe Ziba, or was Mephibosheth's version of the events perhaps true? Not knowing what exactly had happened, the king went for a compromise: Ziba was not punished and was allowed to retain half of the property, while half of it was to be returned to Mephibosheth. It appears that the two men accepted this compromise.

Similar situations as the one in which Ziba played a key role still occur. When we are faced with such dilemmas the best we can do is, like David, look for a compromise that – for lack of evidence – is the best solution under the circumstances. But, of course, we must always be willing to reconsider the matter, should new evidence emerge.

My prayer

Lord, give me the wisdom to reach the best possible solution when I am unable to ascertain the exact course of events.

30 December

Zipporah

(female bird)

Who and when? Daughter of the priest Jethro and wife of Moses.

Want to know more? Read: Exodus 2:16-22; 4:18-26; 18:1-7.

Thoughts for today

The marriage between Moses and the Midianite Zipporah was not always plain sailing. For a lengthy period Zipporah and her children were not living with Moses but stayed in the home of Moses' father-in-law Jethro. Cultural and religious differences were not always easily overcome. This is what we conclude from a few remarkable texts in Exodus 4. We read that, when Moses returned with his family to Egypt (where God had commanded Moses to go to the pharaoh with a divine message), the Lord 'met Moses and was about to kill him' (vs. 24). Was this an experience similar to what Jacob had gone through near the brook Jabbok? Or had Moses been struck by an acute and very serious illness?

Zipporah concluded that the Lord was angry, and she thought she knew why. Their oldest son had been circumcised, but thus far their youngest son had not. Had Zipporah perhaps felt that circumcision was not important? And did she now take the initiative to have their youngest son (belatedly) circumcised, seeing that the lives of her and of her husband and children were in jeopardy? It is clear that she showed very little enthusiasm for the ritual, but she hoped that this would help defuse the crisis. And, indeed, the crisis passed: 'So the LORD let him [Moses] alone' (vs. 26). In His mercy God accepted what Zipporah did, even though it was done much later than He had instructed. It was important to Him that His people be constantly reminded of their special calling.

My prayer

Lord, You want us never to forget that we belong to Your people. Help us to show this in the way in which we live.

31 December

Zophar

(chirper)

Who and when? One of Job's 'friends'.

Want to know more? Read: Job 2:11-13; 11; 20; 42:7-10

Thoughts for today

Zophar came from Naama, thought by some to be a village in Judah, but others suggest that it was a region in Arabia. Whatever be the case, Zophar was one of the people who, upon hearing about Job's troubles, came to visit him with two other 'friends'.

Reading what Zophar has to say gives me an uneasy feeling. He is a man who claims to know everything. He hardly listens to what others have to say. When he starts his speech he calls Job 'this talker', whose barrage of words demands a clear response (11:2). When somewhat later it is his turn to speak again, he is adamant that he can no longer remain silent, having heard all Job's arguments. 'I hear a rebuke that dishonours me, and my understanding inspires me to reply' (20:3). Zophar thought that Job owed all his difficulties to himself. If he would only show true remorse, his fate could be reversed! Dr C. I. Scofield, an American theologian (1843-1921), described Zophar as a 'religious dogmatic, who knows exactly why God does the things that may happen to us'. Such men are dangerous, for they not only confuse us, but may hurt us too. Zophar believed that Job had a lot to learn from him, but the opposite was true. Zophar had to learn to be more modest and realise that there are many things that God has revealed to us, but also that there are many things that God, for one reason or another, has kept hidden from us (Deuteronomy 29:29).

Do you sometimes detect in yourself some inclination to be like Zophar? If so, then realise that you may often have to say: 'I do not understand, but I trust that God knows what He is doing.'

My prayer

Teach me, O God, to recognise my own limitations and to realise that there are many answers I do not know.